# A Particle of Faith

JASON A. DENSLEY

# DEDICATION

This book is dedicated to my four children: Chandler, Logan, Madison and Noah. A father could not love his children more than I love them, or be more proud of whom they have become.

# PREFACE

*But behold, if ye will awake and arouse your faculties, even to an experiment upon my words, and exercise a particle of faith, yea, even if ye can no more than desire to believe, let this desire work in you, even until ye believe...*

*—Alma 32:27*

*For verily I say unto you, That whosoever shall say unto this mountain, Be thou removed, and be thou cast into the sea; and shall not doubt in his heart, but shall believe that those things which he saith shall come to pass; he shall have whatsoever he saith.*

*Therefore I say unto you, What things soever ye desire, when ye pray, believe that ye receive them, and ye shall have them*

*—Mark 11:23 & 24*

# CHAPTER 1

*And in the fourth watch of the night Jesus went unto them, walking on the sea. And when the disciples saw him walking on the sea, they were troubled, saying, it is a spirit; and they cried out for fear. But straightway Jesus spake unto them, saying, Be of good cheer; it is I; be not afraid. And Peter answered him and said, Lord, if it be thou, bid me come unto thee on the water. And he said, Come. And when Peter was come down out of the ship, he walked on the water, to go to Jesus. But when he saw the wind boisterous, he was afraid; and beginning to sink, he cried, saying, Lord, save me. And immediately Jesus stretched forth his hand, and caught him, and said unto him, O thou of little faith, wherefore didst thou doubt?*
*—Matthew 14:25–31*

Elder Aaron Daniels no longer noticed the scorching heat and choking humidity permeating the air throughout the Philippines. It wasn't that the rainy season brought any reprieve—any decrease in temperature was countered by the increase in humidity. The reason Elder Daniels wiped unconsciously at the sweat running down his face was that, after two and a half months, he'd finally acclimatized. He could now work in the noonday sun without his mind trying to convince him he was suffocating.

One thing he could not ignore was the black, asphyxiating exhaust rising from the congested streets of Rosales, a city in Northern Luzon heavily traveled by commercial trucks and passenger busses. He was extremely conscious of the heavy pollution that made him want to hold his breath every time a bus or jeepney passed. Along the busy thoroughfare on which he walked, people held handkerchiefs over their faces in a futile attempt to filter out the harmful emissions they inhaled.

More miserable than he was his companion, Elder Flores. A native Filipino, he stood more than a foot shorter than Elder Daniels which put him even closer to the dense pollution that appeared visibly thicker closer to the ground. Elder Flores turned his head from a wall of black smoke floating lazily toward them from the rear of a sputtering diesel bus. His coughing began mildly at first but soon erupted into a spastic asthma attack causing his chest to heave violently as he struggled for air.

"We're almost there, Comp," Elder Daniels said sympathetically. In the three weeks they had been assigned together, Elder Daniels had witnessed the ravaging effects of asthma on his companion and how it nearly dropped him to his knees gasping for air.

To an observer, the bouts of asthma appeared to hurt the healthy American more than the feeble Filipino. Elder Daniels cringed with every breath, clenching his teeth in agony over the battle that raged within his companion. To see his much smaller companion suffer so greatly tore at Elder Daniels' heart. In the short time they'd been together, Elder Daniels had developed a great love for his companion—one so great he wished he could somehow bare the other's affliction.

On more than one occasion, he'd raised the question of how God could allow such a meek and humble servant as Elder Flores to be plagued with his condition. But in each instance his companion was quick to reply, "God has His own purpose. It's not my place to question Him."

Although that explanation may have appeased Elder Flores, it did very little for Elder Daniels. He needed a more tangible answer—an answer he never seemed to receive.

Taking the next side street away from the town plaza, the two missionaries found some relief from the pollution and Elder Flores' coughing subsided with the assistance of an inhaler. Walking in silence, Elder Daniels kept an eye on his smaller companion. So intent was he with his thoughts that he walked right past the green, metal gate leading to their apartment.

"Aren't we going to eat lunch?" Elder Flores asked jokingly, knowing his American companion never missed a meal.

"Oh, yeah," Elder Daniels remarked, immediately forgetting his previous thought.

Twenty minutes later the two Mormon missionaries were sitting down to a healthy portion of rice, fried chicken, and bananas. It had been a long morning and Elder Daniels was more than ready for lunch. At six-foot, two-inches and weighing 175 pounds, Elder Daniels filled out his athletic frame proportionately well. Nevertheless, his tall, fit appearance belied his voracious appetite.

Just as he was about to bury the serving spoon into the pot of rice and dish up his plate, his companion asked, "Elder, don't you think we should ask a blessing first?"

"Probably." Elder Daniels sarcastically admitted, as he set the spoon back on the table.

Elder Daniels shut his eyes and began to pray without even folding his arms or bowing his head. "Father in Heaven. Thank you for this day. And for this food. Please bless it. In the name of Jesus Christ, amen."

But before he could get his hand back to the spoon, Elder Flores, who had not even raised his head, halted his companion by continuing the prayer where the younger missionary had left off.

"And Father, we thank thee for the wonderful discussion we had this morning with the Baribal Family. We know that this family has been prepared by thy hand to receive us into their home and we pray that we may be instruments in thy hand in bringing to them the gospel truths."

Intently he continued, "We ask thee to testify unto them of the truthfulness of the things we shared with them this morning—that they may know for themselves that these things are true."

"Father, we know that we receive all blessings from thee. The food set upon this table is plentiful—more than many of our brothers and sisters will see in a week's time. Please bless it that our bodies may be strong and healthy, that we might consecrate our energy to thy work. This is our prayer, in the name of our Lord and Savior, Jesus Christ, Amen."

As his companion's voice trailed off, Elder Daniels' chin fell to his chest. Humbled by his companion's gentle rebuke, he chastised himself.

*I'm nothing like him. What am I doing here?*

Never in his life had Elder Daniels met anyone like Elder Flores. From the moment he laid eyes on him he knew there was something special about his companion. It wasn't just that he spoke perfect English, as well as his native languages of Tagalog and Cebuano, there was something more—something different, almost magical—something that Elder Daniels knew he didn't have. Never had that been more obvious than during the discussion they'd taught earlier that morning.

\* \* \* \* \*

Elder Daniels ignored the yawns and lifeless stares of the family seated before him. For the last five minutes he'd plodded on, word after word, reading most of the discussion out of his makeshift discussion booklet his companion had given him with the lessons written in Tagalog. He'd taught about prophets and God's continued call to righteous men to testify of Him in these latter days, just as He had done in times past. But his audience was bored and thinking about other things.

Looking to his companion for help, all he received was a wink and a nod—a simple gesture telling him he was doing fine. He'd already stumbled over many of the difficult words, sounding them out syllable-by-syllable, much like a little child would do with a first-grade reader. Once he'd even used the word 'tae' for 'people,' instead of the correct word 'tao,' saying, "Most bowel movements believe in a Supreme Being." The smaller children in the room had burst out into hysterical laugher, draining the rest of the young missionary's self-confidence. Needless to say, he was grateful when it came time to share his testimony and then let his companion teach.

A master teacher, Elder Flores picked up right where his companion left off. His enthusiasm surprised the seven investigators who had nearly fallen asleep. He captured his audience's attention within his first few words.

"My friends, if God loved his children enough to call a Prophet to guide them in Bible times, why wouldn't He call a Prophet to help us in these latter days?"

As they looked at him inquisitively, Elder Flores began teaching about a young 14-year old boy, named Joseph Smith, who lived in the early 1800s and wanted to know which church he should join.

His teaching was magnificent. He spoke softly, but clearly—boldly, but with humility. He captivated the small family sitting on the dirt floor of their modest, one-room nipa hut. When he told them the story about young Joseph kneeling in prayer in the quiet grove, the peacefulness in the room surprised even Elder Daniels.

"In his own words, Joseph Smith said, 'I saw a pillar of light...exactly over my head...above the brightness of the sun, which descended gradually until it fell upon me.'"

Elder Flores paused, letting each person digest the words in their hearts and in their minds. When he spoke again, his voice was even softer—so soft that each of the investigators leaned forward, hanging on every word.

"When the light rested upon me...I saw two personages standing above me in the air. One of them spake unto me...calling me by name...saying, 'Joseph, this is my Beloved Son. Hear Him.'"

As he finished the account of the Prophet's testimony, he said, "In answer to his prayer, God the Father and his Son, Jesus Christ, appeared to him and told him not to join any of the churches of that day. The Lord told him that he had a very important work for him to do and that He would restore the fullness of His gospel through Joseph Smith.

Elder Daniels leaned back in his chair, realizing how intently his companion's teaching style had entranced him.

"I want you to know," Elder Flores testified, "that what Elder Daniels and I have shared with you today is true. Joseph Smith was indeed a prophet of God. He spoke to God, face to face, just like Moses and Abraham, and the Lord, Jesus Christ called him as a Prophet to guide us in these latter days."

Looking directly at the patriarch of the family, he asked, "Brother Baribal, how do you feel right now?"

"I . . . I . . . I don't know," he stuttered, astonished at his own emotions. "I guess...peaceful."

"And, Jocelyn, how do you feel?"

Amused at the irony of what she was about to say, the eldest daughter wiped tears from her eyes and said, "I feel...happy."

Turning back to the father, Elder Flores asked, "Where do you think these feelings of peace and happiness come from?"

Brother Baribal sat with his head bowed, staring at the floor. After a long pause he looked at his children, trying to hold back emotions that were not foreign to him.

"The Holy Ghost."

"That's right, brother," Elder Flores confirmed. "They come from the Holy Ghost. What do you think the Holy Ghost is telling you?"

Brother Baribal looked in Elder Flores' eyes, unable to deny his feelings. "He is telling me that what you said is true."

\* \* \* \* \*

Picking at a large piece of chicken with his fingers, Elder Daniels sat at the kitchen table quietly. He was often accused of being pensive. When something was on his mind, he was silent, almost withdrawn. Like so many times in the last few months, serious questions raced through his mind.

*Am I ever going to learn Tagalog?*

*Will I ever teach like Elder Flores?*

*Should I even be here at all?*

Elder Daniels sat in silence. There was a black hole of doubt in his stomach draining his self-confidence and faith. Although he'd seldom expressed his emotions outwardly, he knew where things were heading. The downward spiral of self-pity and doubt often led to depression.

With a deep breath he pushed the negative thoughts aside, trying his best to think positively.

*I have faith, right?*

*I'm here on a mission, aren't I? That takes faith.*

*Maybe when I can teach better I won't feel this way.*

The chicken he was eating faded from sight as tears filled his eyes.

\* \* \* \* \*

It had taken over 28 hours to travel from Salt Lake City, Utah, to Manila, the capital city of the Philippines. In the process, Elder Daniels had lost a day crossing the International Date Line and experienced a full range of emotions.

He'd had his choice of seats on the last four-hour flight from Tokyo to Manila. Re-energized by the excitement of international travel, he'd selected a window seat, trying to remember everything he saw so he could tell his family about it in a letter.

Never in his life had he been out of the Northwest United States and now he was about to live in a foreign country for the next twenty-two months. The thought kept him from sleeping most of the way.

Twice he'd tried giving out copies of The Book of Mormon as he was instructed to do in the Missionary Training Center (MTC). Twice he'd been denied. The middle-aged man he'd sat next to from Salt Lake City to Seattle had been LDS. That was obvious by the Church magazine he was reading and the warm smile he'd greeted Elder Daniels with as he sat down. For the first few minutes the man had watched him intently as he positioned his carry-on under his seat and wiped at the tears he'd not let his mother see in the airport terminal. Perhaps the man was reliving a missionary experience of his own, or the thoughts of a son setting out on his own mission.

His second effort had been met with a kind, but firm "no thank you" as he sat next to a young mother refereeing between her two small children, neither of which was impressed with flying. Every time he tried to start a conversation, she'd had to reprimand her son or daughter for kicking the seat in front of them or fighting with the other child.

The rest of the trip gave him the opportunity to experience the full range of human emotions. From excitement to anxiety, anticipation to boredom, he'd truly felt like he was on an emotional roller-coaster. The feeling that gave him the most trouble was the growing fear he felt in the pit of his stomach.

He'd passed the time with his companions between flights talking about things they were going to miss on their missions: music, movies, family members and girlfriends. It wasn't exactly an "appropriate" missionary conversation when they had been instructed to keep their thoughts on missionary work, but they were still learning how to be missionaries.

In his seat, with his closest neighbor snoring heavily, Elder Daniels had time to ponder what he had gotten himself into. As the weight of his eyelids overcame his emotions, he drifted to sleep, where his hopes became dreams and his fears became nightmares. He dreamt he was in a dark and ominous cave. The flashlight in his hand went out, leaving him in the pitch-black darkness.

With a jump he awoke two hours later, feeling the plane start its descent from thirty-three thousand feet. Outside his window he saw nothing but darkness. When he had fallen asleep it was still early afternoon. Now, all sunlight had faded—and so too had some of his excitement.

Thousands of miles from home, the distant lights below told him just how far that was. Unlike the organized streetlights of Orem, Utah, the dim lights below were sparse and sporadic. There was no rhythm to the way they flowed, no structure to their organization, it was simply here a light, there a light—like scattered embers of a dying fire. It was at that moment that he first questioned his ability, his preparation, and his desire to be a missionary.

Elder Daniels felt alone for the first time in his life. Gone were his friends and family. Gone were his instructors at the MTC. Gone, also, was the assurance he'd left home with concerning his mission call.

\* \* \* \* \*

After a day in the US Embassy waiting to get temporary visas, the group of 16 missionaries, 12 Americans and 4 Filipinos, were herded into a small bus and taken to the Manila Temple. It was a majestic and beautiful sight, sitting on a small rise in the middle of the most congested, polluted city Elder Daniels had ever seen. But even the peace within did little to make the temple session enjoyable. Elder Daniels couldn't wait for the session to be over. The jet lag of two 9-hour flights and a 7-hour layover was excruciating.

The following morning the missionaries woke to a heavy-handed knock on the door at 5:00 A.M. They were instructed to shower and eat a small breakfast before the bus arrived that would take them north to Baguio. Even the plate of eggs looked unappealing when his body's clock was completely out of sync. Elder Daniels gulped down a banana and a glass of juice just in time to get on the bus.

Though he tried to sleep, the constant weaving through heavy traffic made him feel uneasy. The American missionaries passed the time by gazing out the window, amazed at the diverse landscapes that passed along the way. From Manila to Baguio they caught glimpses of rice fields, fishing villages, naked children playing in the dirt, old men on huge animals plowing the fields and alleyways filled with trash and debris.

The bus was air conditioned but each time it stopped a wave of heat belted Elder Daniels in the face. He felt sticky and dirty and his white missionary shirt looked exactly like he felt.

By the time they reached the base of the mountains in the Benguet Province of Northern Luzon, Elder Daniels was exhausted. He'd eaten nothing more than a banana and a couple of dinner rolls over the past twenty-four hours.

As the winding road began to level, houses came into view and Elder Daniels realized they'd arrived in Baguio—the summer capital of the Philippines and the headquarters of the mission for 168 full-time missionaries.

\* \* \* \* \*

At their first meeting, shortly after getting off the bus and being shown to their temporary quarters, President Hart, looked at him across a large desk with a solemn expression.

"Elder Daniels, you'll be assigned to Binalonan, a small town in the southern part of the mission."

*Great,* Elder Daniels thought, *then why did I have to come all the way up here?*

"You'll be companions with Elder Juarez. He's been in the mission 21 months and will be your trainer"

Exhausted and hungry Elder Daniels just nodded.

"Do you have any questions?"

Looking around the room impatiently, he asked, "What's for dinner?"

\* \* \* \* \*

Studying him across the expansive dinner table gave Elder Daniels an opportunity to form an impression of his mission president. President Hart was a serious man, maybe even stern. He was not at all what Elder Daniels had expected.

As he and his companions finished eating, President Hart pushed back his chair and stood at the head of the large dining room table.

"Sisters and Elders, welcome to the Philippines Baguio Mission. You have been called of God to take the Gospel of Jesus Christ and our Heavenly Father's plan of salvation to our Filipino brothers and sisters. You will invite them to the Lord's table, much as we are gathered around this table."

Elder Daniels looked around at the other missionaries. He could tell that some of the Filipinos were having a hard time understanding the large American mission president.

"You are expected to give your heart, might, mind, and strength to this work. You will experience joy and grief—happiness and sadness. Some of you will experience a culture shock, making it necessary to adjust to living with a companion twenty-four hours a day, food you have never seen before and maybe even homesickness." With a slight pause, President Hart continued. "But the rewards will far surpass anything you can now imagine."

"The Philippines Baguio Mission has a history of being one of the top baptizing missions in the world. There will be few weeks in your mission that you will not have baptisms. With hard work and personal sacrifice, you and your families will be blessed for your diligent service."

"But let me make sure you understand one very important thing. Although you may baptize many, none of you will convert a soul."

"President?" A young missionary with a furled brow asked. "If we're not going to convert anybody, how are we going to baptize them?"

"Exactly!" President Hart answered. "You *will not* baptize anyone who is not converted to the Gospel of Jesus Christ…but it will not be *you* that converts them. Only the Holy Ghost can truly convert an individual to the Gospel of Jesus Christ. You are here to carry the message of which the Holy Ghost will testify."

"But don't think for a second it will be easy," the mission president continued. "Your every thought, action and word will determine whether or not your investigators hear the whisperings of the Holy Ghost and feel his assurance. Whether or not the Holy Spirit is able to convert your brothers and sisters to His holy word depends largely upon you. Be of great faith, my young missionaries. Be of great faith!"

# CHAPTER 2

*But if ye neglect the tree, and take no thought for its nourishment, behold it will not get any root; and when the heat of the sun cometh and scorcheth it, because it hath no root it withers away, and ye pluck it up and cast it out.*

*Now, this is not because the seed was not good, neither is it because the fruit thereof would not be desirable; but it is because your ground is barren, and ye will not nourish the tree, therefore ye cannot have the fruit thereof.*

*—Alma 32: 38 & 39*

Elder Daniels had spent two months with Elder Juarez and those two months were difficult, at best. When President Hart had told him his trainer would return home in a few months, Elder Daniels hadn't suspected that Elder Juarez's bags were already packed. "Trunky" is a term that missionaries use for those who quit working before their mission is over. Their "trunks" are packed, ready to go home.

Elder Juarez was definitely "trunky." He slept in, skipped companionship study, flirted with girls at church and watched television at members' houses. He retired to the missionary apartment early every evening, confining himself to the bedroom to write letters back home, even on days not designated as Preparation-Days, or "P-Days" for short. While these behaviors were expressly forbidden in the mission rules, Elder Daniels went along with it, justifying his own part as only being the "trainee" and junior companion.

Upon first arriving in Binalonan, a small provincial town nondescript of any distinguishing landmarks, he'd immediately taken a liking to his new companion. Elder Juarez was very laid back. After the blistering pace of the MTC, Elder Daniels was happy to slow things down a bit.

A missionary at the MTC learns quickly that missionary work is just that—work! Many missionary journals begin with exasperated descriptions of that first day. From the first sounds of the alarm clock, to the moment the lights are turned out at night, a missionary is completely engrossed in adjusting to missionary life. With nine hours of class, split into three-hour segments, an hour of gym time, personal study, and three meals, there is a military-like urgency and structure to each day.

For eight weeks Elder Daniels awoke each morning at 6:30 A.M., an unusual and cruel hour for a nineteen-year-old. Each night it was "lights out" at 10:30 P.M. There was no "snooze button," no TV, no cell phone, no X-Box— nothing that resembled his former life.

The most difficult adjustment was no Alicia Decker.

He and Alicia had dated for the past two years. They'd met in high school and she'd followed him to Brigham Young University. Alicia was also a big reason he was serving a mission.

On a date six months earlier, she had told him that she would only marry a returned missionary. The statement had shocked him and he'd wondered why she'd never mentioned it before. Perhaps it was their activity in a student ward attended by many returned missionaries and newly married couples.

Adept at the obvious, but surely externally motivated, Elder Daniels had submitted his missionary application within two weeks. If serving a mission was what it took to marry Alicia Decker, he would do it, even if he had no idea what he was getting himself into.

\* \* \* \* \*

Elder Juarez was happy to let Elder Daniels ease his way into mission life. For the senior companion who had already served twenty-two months, he believed they both deserved a break from the work.

The two took it slowly from the start, sleeping in the first few mornings to let Elder Daniels recover from jet lag. Then there was relaxing at members' houses for hours at a time. As for actual proselyting, they taught one discussion a day, perhaps two, if they didn't have to knock on too many doors to get it.

While Elder Daniels welcomed it at first, he was quick to realize this wasn't normal behavior in the mission field. What was it President Hart had said? *'You will be expected to give your heart, might, mind, and strength to the work.'*

The president's expectations crept into his mind between conversations with pretty girls. It wasn't that he was concerned that their behavior would get back to President Hart, it just seemed odd that this was what missionary work entailed. He'd seen missionaries back in his home ward and they didn't flirt with pretty girls or hang out at members' houses like this. Over time, his conscience began to bother him.

By his fourth Sunday in Binalonan Elder Daniels could no longer kid himself about their work ethic. They'd only taught six discussions that week and two were to new members, which really didn't count as investigator discussions. On top of that, only one of their five investigators had accompanied them to church that Sunday.

To make matters worse, their one investigator that did attend church was a nine-year-old boy from an inactive family. They'd found him in the ward roster and asked the father if they could teach him. The boy's father agreed to let the boy take the lessons as long as he didn't have to be bothered by the missionaries. The other four lessons they'd taught that week were to the little boy, who'd agreed to hear the lessons and go to church with the missionaries when Elder Juarez promised to bring him a bag of candy. By the looks of things, this nine-year-old would be their only baptism for the month.

President Hart's words echoed in his mind again. "The Philippines Baguio Mission has a history of being one of the top baptizing missions in the world. There will be few weeks in your mission that you will not have baptisms." Elder Daniels knew this wasn't the vision the mission president had given them.

It was all Elder Daniels could do to get out of bed each morning knowing that he would sit through countless more hours of boredom. He woke up, ate breakfast, half-consciously read in the Book of Mormon and flipped through a few pages in *Preach My Gospel: A Guide to Missionary Service*. The monotony of each day began to override the novelty of being a new missionary.

Listening to people speak a language he didn't understand drove him crazy. Left out of most conversations completely, it didn't take long for his thoughts to focus on things back home. From there, it was an easy transition to question why he was on a mission in the first place. His experience in the mission field also made him question why returned missionaries had described their missions as 'the best two years of their lives.'

\* \* \* \* \*

The sun was already blazing hot at 6:30 A.M. on an otherwise unordinary Tuesday morning. Just like any other day, the heat would soon be scorching and the humidity completely ruthless. Elder Daniels usually enjoyed the brightness coming through the window helping him stir the cobwebs from his head. Today, however, not even the tropic sun could part the fog of depression that clouded his mind.

Rolling over on his back, he let out a deep sigh. There was no reason to rush out of bed because his companion had already beaten him to the bathroom. This meant that he would have to go out to the hand pump at the rear of the house and carry buckets of water in to fill the 30-gallon water container. It wasn't really much of a shower anyway—just a round, black, plastic tub like they used back home to put trash in or grass clippings from the yard. In the Philippines, the same was used in the bathroom from which the Elders scooped water with a gallon jug and then poured it over their heads. The term the Filipinos used was "bucket shower."

Elder Daniels wasn't in the mood to hurry anyway. What did he have to look forward to? He was not at all excited to set in motion the plan he'd devised the night before.

The letter lay on the hardwood desk by his bed addressed, stamped, and sealed. It was right next to the five-by-seven glossy of Alicia Decker.

Elder Juarez had gone to sleep early the night before while Elder Daniels lay on his bed contemplating his options. Since there were no computers with internet access in the missionary apartments, and the fact that President Hart didn't allow email correspondence, he had no choice but to write a letter—and this letter was long overdue.

It had taken him an hour to put his thoughts on paper. But as difficult as it was to write, there were two things he *was* sure of—he was miserable and he was going home.

He'd hoped for a transfer but before he could even bring the matter up in his interview with President Hart the mission president had informed him he would spend another two months with Elder Juarez. That simply wasn't possible.

Maybe it was good he couldn't notify his family by email—at least they wouldn't be able to try to talk him out of leaving. Sure, he'd probably have to call home at some point and tell them the news, but writing the letter had given him an opportunity to seal his decision—at least he'd told himself that when he sealed the envelope.

Leaving his mission early would be difficult for many to accept. Alicia would not understand and would surely blame herself. His ward back home would want to know why but few would understand. Anticipating the talk he would have with President Hart was not something he looked forward to doing either. But *nothing* compared to the anxiety he had of telling his parents.

His father would be embarrassed—probably even upset. His mother would be crushed! He hated disappointing them. He'd done that too many times in his life already.

Like many teenagers, he'd tested the limits of his parent's patience. He'd given them moments of grief and pain, yet a special bond had developed between he and his mother very early in his life—a bond that ran deeper than most mother-son relationships.

Ann Daniels' father died when she was just an infant but she saw him every time she looked at her son. She'd often pointed out the common features in their faces, hairstyles, hands and personalities. He could have been her father's twin if he'd lived forty years earlier. Though she'd grown up hearing stories about her father, she'd come to know him through her son.

\* \* \* \* \*

As he carried the fourth and last bucket of water from the hand pump to the bathroom, Elder Daniels nearly tripped on the large plastic tub in which their house-help washed clothes. Chastising the tub for being in his path, he added another item to his list of things he wouldn't miss about the Philippines.

As he poured the bucket of water into the larger container the overflowing water splashed off the bathroom tile and onto his bare legs and the shorts.

With a start, he jumped back, the chill of the cold water jerking him from his thoughts. That was another thing he hated. Cold bucket showers! He'd never figured out how a country as hot as the Philippines could have such cold water in the morning.

Now, fully alert, he took the water scoop and poured it directly over his head. He hadn't even bothered to take off the shorts and t-shirt he was wearing. The broken window in the bathroom provided no privacy—at least, not enough for mission standards. A large mosquito landed on his forearm only to be carried away with the next scoop of water.

Yes, Elder Daniels would be perfectly happy leaving the Philippines. The heat, the insects, the language, the poverty, the dust and countless other inconveniences, added up to nothing more than misery.

After drying himself with a damp towel still damp from the previous night's shower, he walked back into the bedroom where his companion was tying his shoes. Elder Juarez would normally still be sound asleep, but he wasn't on this particular morning. Elder Juarez had a pan of rice on the stove by the time Elder Daniels put on his pants. As he reached for a clean shirt from a clothesline strung across the living room, his companion entered the room.

"Zone leaders come in morning," he said in broken English.

"Wait. What? When're they coming?"

"Ten minutes."

Now Elder Daniels understood why his companion didn't need any nudging to get out of bed. The zone leaders would be there in a matter of minutes and see Elder Juarez put on his best act of being an obedient missionary.

A few minutes later Elder Daniels was also dressed and sitting in front of a plate of rice. There was no time for anything else this morning. Reaching for the sugar, he picked out a couple of ants and sprinkled two heaping tablespoons onto the steaming rice.

"How do you know the zone leaders are coming this morning?" he asked over his shoulder, spitting a couple grains of rice onto the floor as he spoke.

Elder Juarez sat on the only chair in the living room pretending to read his scriptures. His sigh was indicative of the contempt he had for the English language he was forced to speak around his companion.

"Yesterday is zone leader seminar in Baguio. They bring message today. . . and mails."

Elder Daniels just shook his head. Elder Juarez was manipulative. He had the mission figured out and knew exactly when the district leader and zone leaders would visit them. This convenient awareness enabled him to plan his "good" days. It was no wonder only companions assigned with him knew he was not an obedient missionary—no one else ever caught him disobeying.

Just as Elder Daniels opened his scriptures, a knock on the door broke the strained silence in the missionaries' apartment.

"Good morning!" Elder Jones said as he stuck out a huge hand to greet the two missionaries.

Elder Daniels shook hands with him timidly. At twenty years old, Elder Jones was a mountain of a man. As he stood in the doorway, his massive frame allowed very little sunlight into the apartment. His broad smile brightened the room just the same.

Unbeknownst to Elder Daniels, Elder Jones was the gentlest missionary he would ever meet. It wasn't hard imagining this linebacker-sized man tackling running backs on the football field at BYU a year earlier.

Taking a seat on the couch he wasted no time getting down to business. "What do you Elders have planned this morning?"

"Well, we haven't talked about that yet," Elder Daniels said with a sneer, eyeing Elder Juarez out of the corner of his eye. The convenient way his companion had forgotten to warn him of the zone leaders' visit hadn't sat well with him and he wasn't afraid to let the fact be known.

"We have discussion in afternoon with projection for baptism. Visiting members this morning to find referrals," Elder Juarez interjected, trying to cover up their lack of planning.

Elder Jones clapped his hands together. "All right! Then you don't mind if we join you." It was a statement, not a question.

*Crap!* Elder Daniels sighed wearily, though not loud enough for anyone else to hear. He hated splits! Even the worst day with Elder Juarez was better than the best day with Elder Tolentino.

Elder Tolentino just stood next to his large American companion with a smile on his face. He hadn't said a word, other than "Hello," which surprised none of them. Both times the zone leaders had come to work with them on splits, Elder Daniels and Elder Tolentino had worked together leaving the other two missionaries to work together in another part of the area.

The four hours they'd worked together were long and grueling. Since Elder Tolentino didn't know the area, it was up to Elder Daniels to get them to their appointments. The difficulty wasn't getting to the appointments—it was the conversations with investigators that followed.

Elder Tolentino said very little, favoring the opportunity to see how the new missionary was getting along. Both times they'd worked together left Elder Daniels more frustrated with his language skills than ever before.

Elder Jones must have seen the concern on Elder Daniels' face. "I think perhaps this would be a good day for me to work with our newest Elder in the zone. I'll go with Elder Daniels."

For the first time all morning Elder Daniels smiled. His spirit soared for the first time in weeks as he realized he would be able to talk to an American for a few hours.

"Cool!" he said. "Just let me grab a letter I need to mail before we go."

"That reminds me," Elder Jones said while Elder Daniels was back in the room, "We have something for you."

Reaching into his backpack he took out a handful of letters.

"I don't know another missionary who gets as much mail as you Elder Juarez. You must spend your entire P-Day writing letters."

14

Elder Juarez simply shrugged his shoulders and reached for the letters, tucking them into his backpack just before Elder Daniels returned with the letter he'd written the night before.

"All right, let's go."

Elder Juarez was out the door and halfway to the gate when Elder Jones yelled out the open doorway, "Elder Juarez, aren't you forgetting something?"

The headstrong Filipino stopped walking but he didn't turn around. Although he knew the zone leaders were coming by, all he'd expected them to do was leave "mails" and move on to the next apartment. This did not at all figure into his plan.

Rarely did they work with missionaries after a day in Baguio. The way he figured it, there were five other companionships in the zone they needed to visit as well—not to mention working in their own area.

"Shouldn't we say a prayer before we go?"

Elder Juarez turned and walked back to the apartment—his eyes never meeting those of Elder Jones. There was too much anger at that moment—anger he knew he couldn't hide. Nothing upset him more than being put in his place by an American.

Shutting the door behind him, Elder Juarez joined the other three missionaries standing in a circle. Content that they were all there, Elder Jones looked at his companion, who nodded, bowed his head, and offered a prayer in Tagalog.

If Elder Daniels had listened to the prayer he may have understood a little of what Elder Tolentino said, but he didn't listen to a word. In his mind, he was already thinking of what he'd say to Elder Jones about going home. This was the perfect opportunity to get word to the mission president of his intentions. He knew Elder Jones would try to talk him out of it. Elder Jones was just going to have to get the message to President Hart.

Before Elder Tolentino said "Amen," Elder Juarez had turned back toward the door.

Grabbing the backpack he'd dropped at his feet, Elder Daniels took a step toward the door as well. A very large hand on his shoulder stopped him in his tracks. "Elder Daniels, let's talk for a minute before we go."

Elder Juarez and Elder Tolentino were already out the door before he could say, "Okay." To Elder Daniels' surprise, Elder Tolentino had even shut the door behind him.

*Wait. Was this planned?*

Elder Jones eased himself into a chair across the room carefully. It was no secret that on more than one occasion Elder Jones had sat down on a bamboo chair at a member's or investigator's home only to have it collapse under his weight.

"How are you doing?" he asked.

"Okay, I guess."

"You know, it's not a coincidence that Elder Tolentino and I are here this morning."

"What do you mean?" Elder Daniels asked.

"Well, we'd planned to deliver the mail to the other missionaries in the zone this morning and stop by here tomorrow."

Elder Daniels cocked his head to the side, "But Elder Juarez knew you would be here this morning. He said you always come by the day after the zone leaders' seminar."

Rolling his eyes, Elder Jones chuckled. "Elder Juarez is a little too smart for his own good. I've known him awhile. We do get into a routine sometimes but this month we'd decided to change things up a bit."

When Elder Jones received nothing more than a blank stare, he continued.

"When I was a zone leader in San Fernando, my companion and I had a distinct impression one month that we needed to change our routine for visiting companionships in our zone."

"You mean, like a prompting from the Holy Ghost?"

"That's exactly what it was! You see, we'd always leave our apartment as early as possible and head out on a bus to the north end of our zone. We'd usually get there about the time the elders were getting out of bed. After that, we'd work our way south, stopping in each area as companionships were getting ready, eating breakfast or in their study time."

"Zone leaders all over the mission pretty much do it the same way because we can deliver the mail before the companionships leave in the morning and get back to our own areas in time for our own appointments. Larger zones may have to break it up into two days. It also gives us a chance to check in with everybody and relay any messages from President Hart, like upcoming transfers."

"Anyway, the thought struck me as I was sitting there on the bus one morning of how predictable we'd become. I got this uneasy feeling that if we were predictable to missionaries, like Elder Juarez, who knew our system, then just about anybody could figure out our travel routine."

"So?"

"So, I got the feeling we needed to change our routine for our own protection"

"You mean by altering your route?"

"Exactly. It's not that we carry a lot of money on us or anything, but missionaries have been held up before."

"But you're like what? Six-foot-six? 250 pounds? Who'd be crazy enough to mess with you?"

"I don't know," Elder Jones admitted. "But I do know what a prompting of the Spirit feels like. And that's not something for me to question."

"So what does that have to do with you being here this morning?" Elder Daniels asked.

"That's just it!" Elder Jones said. "Elder Tolentino and I decided to leave the apartment when it was light out and reverse the order, meaning we would get to the Elders in Tayug last instead of first. But that would work out great because we could work with them for the rest of the morning."

With a puzzled look on his face Elder Daniels remarked, "But you're not with them. You're here working with us."

"Right again. You see, this morning my comp and I had planned to visit the Manaoag Elders as our first stop but, as we said our prayer, something didn't feel right to me. I asked Elder Tolentino and he said he felt the same . . . you know . . . like something was wrong with our plan. We talked it over and prayed about it and knew we needed to end up here to work with the two of you this morning."

"But, why?" Elder Daniels asked.

Elder Jones sat forward in his chair. "I don't know Elder Daniels...you tell me."

\* \* \* \* \*

Elder Daniels mind went completely blank. As Elder Jones sat a meter in front of him waiting for an answer, he could not think of a single thing to say. Just moments before he had been ready to tell his new zone leader he was going home and there was nothing anyone could do about it. But for some reason he couldn't find the words to explain his situation.

Elder Jones was the kind of missionary Elder Daniels wanted to be—a missionary who listened to and followed the Spirit. He respected Elder Jones and looked up to him. He knew exactly what he would say to President Hart when he called him to his office, but when it came to telling Elder Jones, he froze.

As the silence continued, the awkwardness overwhelmed him. Elder Daniel's confidence in his decision faltered and he blurted out the first thought that came to his mind.

"I have no idea. Everything's fine."

It was Elder Jones' turn to be surprised. "Are you sure?" he asked, his eyebrows narrowing slightly.

Elder Daniels lied. "We haven't been able to find many good contacts lately, but, yeah, everything's great."

"And your companionship is good?" Elder Jones asked.

"Yup."

"Well, how about homesickness? Anything bothering you?"

"Nope, it's all good. I'm still adjusting to the food and stuff, but it's getting easier."

If Elder Jones knew the younger missionary was lying, he didn't show it. The only time Elder Daniels thought the zone leader was on to him was when he looked deep into his eyes. It felt like Elder Jones was looking straight into his soul.

There was another long pause that made Elder Daniels even more nervous. At that moment he realized talking to Elder Jones about his decision was just like what it would feel like talking to his parents when he returned home.

Taking Elder Daniels by surprise, Elder Jones jumped to his feet. With one giant step, he came at Elder Daniels with surprising quickness.

"Congratulations Elder Daniels!" he said loudly. "It only gets better from here!"

Cautiously, but relieved, Elder Daniels returned the handshake.

Elder Jones continued, "I just wish you had more time to work this area and get to know the members better."

Elder Daniels head snapped around. "Wait. What?"

You're being transferred tomorrow, Elder Daniels." The shock on his face made Elder Jones burst into laughter.

"Transferred? But President Hart said he was leaving me here for two more months!"

"That's what he told us too, but in our interview with him yesterday at the zone leaders' seminar, he said the Lord wants you in Rosales."

"Who's my companion going to be?"

"Elder Flores!" he announced, beaming with delight. "The best companion I ever had."

Elder Daniels' mind was reeling. *Transferred? What the heck just happened?*

When President Hart had told him that he wouldn't be transferred, he'd lost all faith in the mission president. Surely he couldn't be an inspired man if he was going to leave him in this area another two months with Elder Juarez.

"Oh, by the way, you were in the other room when I handed out the mail. Sorry I don't have more to give you but it looks like this one may be a letter from home."

Elder Daniels reached for the single letter Elder Jones was examining. He'd received only a few letters from home since arriving in the Philippines. Each letter had taken almost three weeks to get to him from the central office at mission headquarters. As he took the letter he looked at the postmark. This letter had only taken four days to get from his parents' hands in Orem, Utah, to his own, half a world away.

Elder Jones put down his backpack and headed toward the bathroom in the back of the apartment. "Let me make a quick stop at the CR then we'll be on our way." Turning around halfway there, he mused, "You know, I've never understood why they call bathrooms here 'Comfort Rooms'— none of the tin-roofed outhouses I've visited provide much comfort. Especially the ones with nothing more than a hole and a bucket of water."

Catching none of what Elder Jones had just said, Elder Daniels tore open the envelope and removed the one-page letter inside. A frown appeared on his face when he realized it only contained a single page inside. That frown instantaneously morphed into a smile when he realized it was a letter from his father. It was the first letter he'd received from his father since he'd left the MTC, and typed, in his father's meticulous style.

Dear Aaron,

Never has a father been more proud of his son than I am of you. In the past few months I have spent many moments contemplating the impact your mission is having, not only on you, but your family at home, as well. I can only imagine the things you are doing and learning while serving the Lord. I often reflect on my own mission and the experiences I enjoyed as a full-time missionary. I can only tell you from experience that your mission will change your life in ways you cannot yet comprehend.

I hope you will write often. Your mother reads them through many times. The rest of us are equally thrilled to receive them and many dinner conversations center around what you might be doing at that very moment.

These past couple of days I have had the impression that things may not be all that you had expected as you set out on your mission. I can only imagine how difficult it must be living in a foreign country, learning a foreign language, and the cultural differences of being assigned with a foreign companion. Please know that my heart is with you and that the Lord will bless you.

Son, there may be times you get discouraged. Don't let the adversary do that to you! Discouragement is one of his most cunning tools. You may not understand why you have to pass through some of the difficulties you will encounter but, as you encounter those trials, remember the council the Lord gave to the Prophet Joseph while he was in the Liberty Jail. "All these things shall give thee experience and shall be for thy good."

The last advice I will give you is the same advice given by a wise father to his own son, Gordon B. Hinckley. When Elder Hinckley began his mission in Preston, England, he found himself in conditions more difficult than he thought he could bear. When his father learned of his feelings by letter, he responded with a brief and direct reply. "Dear Gordon, I have your recent letter. I have only one suggestion: forget yourself and go to work."

Son, I love you. Go to work. You will have the rest of your life to thank yourself for it, not to mention the generations you will influence as you diligently serve the Lord.

All my love,
Dad

Elder Daniels stood perfectly still. He felt a lump in his throat, making it difficult to swallow. The selfishness and shame he felt at that moment made his stomach hurt. With his head bowed in humility, he walked to the wastebasket next to the refrigerator and pulled his own letter from his shirt pocket. With one slow motion, he made an even tear through the middle of the envelope and dropped it in the garbage can.

Just as the two halves settled in the bottom of the trash, Elder Jones appeared from the hallway where he'd disappeared moments earlier. "Ready to go?"

Elder Daniels looked up with tearstained eyes. "I am," he replied. "As ready as I've ever been!"

# CHAPTER 3

*But if ye will nourish the word, yea, nourish the tree as it beginneth to grow, by your faith with great diligence, and with patience, looking forward to the fruit thereof, it shall take root; and behold it shall be a tree springing up unto everlasting life.*

*—Alma 32: 41*

The sharp, clattering sound of a rock skipping across concrete brought Elder Daniels to a quick halt. For a moment he didn't move, holding his breath as he searched the darkness around him. It wasn't just the noise that made the hair on the back of his neck stand, but also the knowledge that they were not in the safest part of town. To make matters worse, it was long after dark and few strayed this far off the main road but drunkards and stray animals.

"Sorry, Comp. I didn't mean to scare you," Elder Flores apologized. "I kicked a rock."

Elder Daniels breathed out a long, slow breath, trying to relax himself as he got back in step with his companion. Having the longer stride, Elder Daniels normally set the pace as they walked back to their apartment each night.

On this particular night, however, the American missionary was content to let his companion lead out. Just thinking of the thirty-minute walk back home made his bamboo pack feel twenty pounds heavier.

For the most part the night was still. Other than two frogs chirping at one another in the distance, everything was quiet. The jeepneys and trikes had shut down shortly after dark.

Not more than five minutes passed and Elder Daniels was again fighting the sleep that pulled at his eyelids. This time, instead of resisting, he simply let them close.

Elder Daniels couldn't remember ever feeling so tired. Though he'd never really enjoyed riding in trikes, he'd have willingly paid three times the normal fare if they could find a driver that would take them home.

While most Americans loved the novelty of the motorcycle-style taxi service, complete with sidecar, Elder Daniels felt claustrophobic in the small confined spaces. The tiny sidecars were not built for people over 5-feet, 4 inches. For an American over 6-feet tall, one either had to be a toothpick or a gymnast to fit inside. Add to that a companion and two backpacks and his discomfort was multiplied by a factor of ten.

Elder Flores walked a step ahead of Elder Daniels, his gait more determined than the wayward meander of his companion. The Filipino Elder did not like this part of town any more than his companion and had vocalized his concern as they had left their last appointment. He'd have felt more comfortable walking through town, where there were more lights and less shadows, but his companion had begged him to take the shortcut home.

Elder Flores was also weary but understood his new companion was still acclimating to the heat and humidity, which drained his energy from head to toe. Noticing Elder Daniels eyes were closed, Elder Flores dropped back a step and looped his arm through his companion's arm. Elder Daniels opened his eyes briefly and smiled.

As he closed his eyes again he wondered how he'd gotten so lucky—not just to have such a wonderful companion—but also a friend. Though his eyes were closed the smile remained, and Elder Daniels was content just putting one foot in front of the other.

* * * * *

Rubbing his knees, Elder Daniels slipped his foot into the cheap flip-flops he'd been kneeling on during his morning prayers. Even the 'tsenilas,' as his companion called them, with their three quarter-inch foam soles, did little to cushion the hard linoleum floor next to his bed.

"How do you feel this morning, Comp?"

"Not bad, for only five hours of sleep." Elder Daniels replied cheerfully.

"Me too." Elder Flores agreed, "I'm convinced the Lord really does renew our bodies in this work. But then, if he didn't, we'd all go home looking twenty years older. And none of us would get married."

"Look," Elder Daniels explained. "If you think any girl in her right mind is going to marry you, Elder Flores? You've got more faith than I thought!"

A smile broke out on Elder Flores's face. "Yeah, but at least I'll still have some hair on my head when I get home."

Both missionaries laughed at that one.

The bond that had developed between these two missionaries over the past two weeks was the kind that few companionships ever achieved. Elder Daniels felt as comfortable with his new companion as anyone he'd ever known. They talked for hours each day, joked with each other like brothers and developed a genuine love for one another. Miraculously, Elder Daniels smile had returned and he began to actually enjoy being a missionary.

Elder Daniels looked at himself in the hazy mirror hanging on their apartment wall. He really did look pathetic. Not a hair on his head stood over a quarter of a half-inch high. And though his companion teased him about his hair, he knew that without him he would have even less.

A week into their companionship, he'd sat down in a barber's chair thinking he would get a little trim before the upcoming zone conference. Elder Flores had been in the chair just before him and come away with a beautifully tapered haircut that accented his straight black hair. Elder Daniels assumed he'd get a similar haircut, but apparently the barber did not understand very much English.

Perfectly at ease watching his companion introduce himself to an elderly man in the waiting area, Elder Daniels didn't realize how efficiently the well-oiled scissors danced in the barber's hands behind him. After about five minutes, Elder Flores just happened to look up from his conversation with the man and saw what was happening to his companion. With clumps of dark brown hair lying about his shoulders, Elder Daniels looked more like an Army recruit than a missionary.

Rushing to his side, Elder Flores asked the barber what he was doing. The barber had simply shrugged his shoulders and said, "American GI's like short hair,"

A few minutes later, he'd walked outside rubbing his prickly head. He was still in shock at what had just happened. It would be a long time before he'd trust a Filipino barber again. Needless to say, it would also be a long time before he'd need a haircut.

"Don't worry, Comp, at least it doesn't take you an hour to fix your hair anymore."

Elder Daniels tried to laugh. He wasn't yet accustomed to his reflection in the mirror—even though two weeks had passed.

"Oh, Comp! You're not still worried about what President Hart said, are you?"

"No, . . . well, . . . a little," Elder Daniels admitted. "Doesn't he realize I didn't do it on purpose?"

Mimicking President Hart's Texan drawl, Elder Daniels stood tall and stern, exaggerating the slowness with which his mission president spoke. "Elder, not even a *mission president* should have hair that short."

Elder Flores came to his companion's side, looking into his eyes through the mirror. "I need to let you in on a little secret."

"What's that?"

"Well, you think President Hart is hard on you. Don't you?"

"Yeah. I do! But he's not that way with everyone. Why would he be that way with me?"

"President Hart has high expectations of you because he sees something different in you."

"What do you mean?"

"Well, do you remember in The Book of Mormon when Nephi broke his bow?"

"Sure, his brothers got mad at him because they all had to go hungry,"

"Right. But who besides his brothers murmured?"

"I don't know," Elder Daniels shrugged. "Probably the sons of Ishmael."

"You're right. But Lehi murmured too."

"He *did?*" Elder Daniels inquired.

"Yes. The Book of Mormon tells us that Laman, Lemuel and the sons of Ishmael murmured 'exceedingly,' because of their afflictions in the wilderness. But Lehi was also so sorrowful that even he, the great prophet, began to murmur."

"Think about it," he continued, "Laman, Lemuel, and the sons of Ishmael are complaining because they're hungry. But they're not about to do anything to help themselves, like make another bow, or set traps, or anything."

"So Nephi makes a bow and an arrow out of wood and goes to his father. He says something like, 'All right, Dad, I've made a bow and an arrow. Now, because you're the patriarch of this family, tell me where I should go to get food.'"

Elder Flores stepped between Elder Daniels and the mirror. "Why do you think Nephi asked his father instead of just asking The Lord himself?"

Elder Daniels shrugged his shoulders.

"Can you imagine how Lehi must have felt at that moment? "Elder Flores continued. "Here he is, the prophet, being reminded by his son that if anyone needs to trust the Lord, it's *him*. I'll bet that one question from his faithful son, Nephi, was enough to humble Lehi."

"I mean, think about it. Your faith is wavering and your son says, 'Hey, Dad! Don't forget it was the Lord who gave *you* the vision about Jerusalem being destroyed. And it was *you* he told to lead us into the wilderness. Oh, and he told *you* to send my brothers and I back to get the brass plates from Laban, right Dad? He's guided us this far—don't lose faith in Him now.'"

"That must have been pretty humbling for Lehi, wouldn't you say?"

Elder Daniels nodded. "So what does that have to do with me and President Hart?"

"Well, Lehi finally asks the Lord where Nephi should go to find food. But the Lord chastens him. The scriptures tell us the Lord chastens him so harshly that Lehi 'was brought down into the depths of sorrow.' And to make things worse, when he looks into the Liahona, the things he sees written there cause him to 'fear and tremble exceedingly.'"

"Well, what did the Lord do with Laman and Lemuel?" Elder Daniels asked.

"Nothing, that's the interesting thing," Elder Flores remarked. "The Lord doesn't chasten Laman and Lemuel, or the sons of Ishmael, or anyone else. He chastens Lehi. And, remember, Lehi had only *begun* to murmur."

"That's not really fair!" Elder Daniels exclaimed.

Smiling, Elder Flores explained, "Well, think about the scripture in the Doctrine and Covenants (D&C), Section 82. 'For of him unto whom much is given much is required; and he who sins against the greater light shall receive the greater condemnation.'"

Putting his hand on his companion's shoulder, Elder Flores explained, "President Hart is very hard on you because he expects more from you than he does other missionaries. He knows you have the potential to be a great leader. You see, just as the Lord held Lehi to a higher standard than his rebellious sons, President Hart is going to hold you to a higher standard as well."

"So you're saying he's harder on me because I'm a better missionary than someone else?"

"No, Elder Daniels, not because you're a better missionary. But because the Lord has given you talents He hasn't given to other missionaries."

Elder Daniels took a seat on the edge of his bed. "This doesn't really have anything to do with my hair, does it?"

The small Filipino laughed, "Well, not directly. But take for example who he assigned you with in your first area."

"Elder Juarez? That doesn't make any sense! You just said that President Hart sees potential in me to be a great missionary. Why would he assign me with the worst possible trainer in the mission?"

Elder Flores' response came quickly. "Because of what you *learned*."

"Sure. How to be lazy. How to disobey mission rules. How to hit on girls..."

"Because you learned firsthand what other missionaries would experience in their missions. Homesickness. Disappointment. Frustration. Maybe even temptation."

Elder Daniels was quiet.

"You see, President Hart saw qualities of leadership in you in your first interview with him but he knew you also needed to experience those things in Binalonan with Elder Juarez so you can help other missionaries through similar trials in their missions."

"Hold on!" Elder Daniels interjected. "You're saying President Hart didn't know where I was to be assigned until I met with him the night before we left the mission home?"

"That's right."

"I only talked to him for like five minutes! He asked me about my family and if anything had happened since leaving the MTC that he needed to be aware of. How could he have determined the kind of missionary I'd be from that?"

"By listening to the promptings of the Holy Ghost."

"You're saying the Lord told him where I needed to be assigned seconds before he told me?"

"President Hart fasts for 24 hours before a batch of new missionaries arrive. He spends most the day in prayer, preparing himself to receive revelation about where to assign them. He makes that decision when he meets with them and the Lord reveals that information to him."

Elder Daniels sat down on his bed, carefully pondering his companion's explanation.

"The Spirit helped him discern in that short interview what kind of missionary you can be and what type of experiences you needed in your first area to help you on that journey. The Lord told him you needed to be assigned to Binalonan, with Elder Juarez, to learn obedience. Just think back to some of those experiences you've shared with me and what you gained from them. The Lord knew all that and how those experiences would help you grow. Rest assured, both President Hart and the Lord know what you need."

Looking directly into his companion's eyes, he continued. "So, you, Elder Daniels, have the potential to be a great leader in this mission, but in order to achieve that, you can expect more trials and challenges than the average missionary. You can expect more stubborn companions, more difficult areas, and more experiences requiring greater faith. Not because the Lord knows who you *are*—but who you can *become*."

Elder Flores could tell his companion was still processing the information.

"That's why President Hart gave us the challenge that he did," Elder Flores continued.

"You mean to baptize six people this month or else he'll have to close the area?"

"That's right," Elder Flores nodded. "Think about it for a minute. Would President Hart close an area that was really baptizing well?"

"No."

"So he challenges us to prove this is a productive area."

"But it's not a productive area!" Elder Daniels objected. "There haven't been more than six or seven baptisms here in the last six months!"

"Do you believe that Elder Daniels?"

"Do I believe what?"

"Do you believe this is not a productive area?"

"Well, you know what the other missionaries say."

"And what's that, Elder Daniels?"

"They say you can't baptize in Rosales. The members aren't helpful and the bishop doesn't set a good example, . . ."

"I know what the other missionaries believe. What I want to know is what *you* believe!"

Elder Daniels was silent again. This time Elder Flores waited, knowing how crucial it was that his companion discovered the next truth on his own.

When Elder Daniels looked in his companion's eyes, his eyes revealed his weariness. The late-night-early-morning routine; the hours of tracting; the agonizing frustration with Elder Juarez—all had taken their toll on the young missionary.

"What difference does it make what I believe?" he finally asked.

Elder Flores smiled. The time had come for him to begin the training President Hart had entrusted him to do.

"That's the whole key Elder Daniels. What *you* believe makes *all* the difference."

Elder Flores grabbed a chair, placing it in front of his companion who was still seated on his bed. Sitting back in the chair, Elder Flores continued to teach.

"One day, early in the Lord's ministry, a man brought his son to the Savior. The Bible tells us the boy had a 'dumb spirit,' a demon, which made him tear at himself and bite himself and other strange things. The man told Jesus that he'd asked his disciples to cast the demon out but reported that not one of them had been able to do it."

"Jesus asked how long his son had been tormented with the evil spirit. The man said since birth and that the demon had so much power over him that he'd thrown himself in the fire and even tried to drown himself."

"And as any loving parent would do, the man pleaded with Jesus, saying, 'If thou canst do anything, have compassion on us and help us.' Do you know what the Lord said to the man, Elder Daniels?"

"No."

"He said, 'If thou canst believe, all things are possible to him that believeth.'"

"If who believes?" Elder Daniels inquired.

"Good question," Elder Flores replied. "You see, it didn't matter what the Lord believed. He knew what he could do. It didn't even matter what the boy believed. He wasn't the one asking for the miracle. It all depended on what the boy's *father* believed.

"And that's what the man finally began to understand. He realized that, ultimately, whether or not his son was healed, depended on his faith, not the Savior's faith, not his disciples' faith. It all depended on what the one asking for the miracle believed.

"At that moment," Elder Flores explained, "the man cried out, 'Lord, I believe; help thou mine unbelief.'"

For a few moments, neither missionary said a word. Elder Flores could see his companion was deep in thought. Alas, Elder Daniels hadn't quite put all the pieces together. "But it sounds like the man said he *didn't* believe. How could the Lord help him?"

Elder Flores smiled, "Comp, you're wiser than you know. When the man came to Jesus he'd said, '*If* thou canst do anything.' In other words he wasn't sure if the Savior could heal his son. To this the Lord basically said to him, 'you must have faith in me in order for me to do what you're asking.'"

"And that was the point that the man finally understood what Jesus was talking about. Up until then, he assumed it all depended on Jesus, but then he realized that his son being healed depended on his own faith, not Jesus' faith. Sure, the man trusted Jesus, and he truly hoped that something could be done for his son, but it's doubtful that he really knew what 'real faith' meant.

"So now that the man understood what was required of him," Elder Flores continued, "and with the encouragement given him in the words 'all things are possible to him that believeth,' he shouted, 'Lord, I believe.' But understanding that his faith was small, he cried unto the Lord, "help thou mine unbelief.' Or, basically, 'I believe you can heal my son. But I don't have perfect faith. Please help me *know* it.' So the Lord healed his son."

Once again the room was still. Quietly, Elder Flores pulled his chair still closer to his companion, the silence in the room barely broken when he spoke. "Comp, now do you see how the success of this area depends on what *you* believe?"

"But do you really think we can baptize six people this month? I mean, we're already into the third week and don't have one solid contact."

Elder Flores smiled, his confidence beaming through his eyes. "There's no doubt in my mind, Elder Daniels. You see, all we have to do is let the Lord guide us to a family that he's prepared for us."

Elder Daniels slowly slid off the edge of the bed onto his knees. His voice saturated with humility. "Comp, then let's ask the Lord to help *my* unbelief."

# CHAPTER 4

*And now, I, Moroni, would speak somewhat concerning these things; I would show
unto the world that faith is things which are hoped for and not seen; wherefore,
dispute not because ye see not, for ye receive no witness until after the trial of your
faith.*

*—Ether 12:6*

Elder Daniels swatted at the large mosquito circling above his ear. The
buzzing sound reminded him of a small airplane motor, humming steadily as it
rose above his head and flew away. Amazed at how long he could see the
mosquito against the billowy background of clouds, he remembered how much
larger this variety of mosquitoes was compared to those back home. The
Philippines, with its tropic heat and above average rainfall, was the perfect
breeding ground for the pesky insects.

In his first area, Elder Daniels had swatted at every mosquito that came
within a one-meter radius of him. He'd found that even while teaching
discussions he had to be on constant guard or else end up a free meal. After his
second full day of proselyting, he counted forty-six mosquito bites on his arms
alone. He didn't even bother to count what he couldn't see on his legs, back
and neck. There was nothing he could do about it anyways.

His Filipino companions sympathized with him but had little empathy.
Mosquitos simply were not attracted to them. Elder Juarez attributed it to the
fact that Americans ate more sweets and, in correlation, had more sugar in their
bloodstream. Elder Daniels now wondered if that was true. Two-and-a-half
months later, the mosquitoes rarely bothered him, and sure enough, he hadn't
eaten any candy since his last care package at the MTC.

The dirt path on which the two missionaries walked was worn and uneven.
Alongside the path the vegetation grew in thick bands, spanning from tree to
tree like ivy on a garden pergola. Occasionally, where the banana trees and

vines thinned out, Elder Daniels could see the outline of a nipa hut or a rice field in the distance.

Although the missionaries were walking through a well-established barangay, or small village, neither of them had seen anyone except a young girl washing clothes and an old man atop a caribou plowing a rice field. Neither the old man nor the young girl noticed the two young men as they passed by. The stillness around them made the road feel even more secluded. It felt strange not having people point and whisper while they passed but, then, Elder Daniels didn't blame them. Even to him traipsing through the sultry jungle in white shirts and ties seemed ridiculous.

The two Elders had been working in this barangay the entire morning, looking for new contacts to add to their teaching pool. Knocking on doors was rarely an effective tool for finding investigators so Elder Flores had suggested they visit members whose names and addresses were listed in the ward directory. Perhaps they would have friends or relatives they could refer to the missionaries.

The only problem with finding members in an area like this was that, more often than not, the nipa huts didn't have addresses. The only reference given in the ward directory was the members' names, birthdays, and name of the barangay in which they lived.

The missionaries stopped at the first nipa hut they came to and knocked on the thin strips of bamboo fastened together to form a door. They waited for someone to answer but moved on when no one came to the door. Impatient as ever, Elder Daniels didn't even want to knock since he could see through the strips of bamboo that the nipa hut was empty.

The second and third nipa huts were also unoccupied. At the fourth, they found a girl squatting next to a water pump, washing clothes by hand. It turned out that the girl had never heard of the people they asked about but was able to explain why very few people were around that particular morning.

She spoke to Elder Flores in Tagalog but Elder Daniels was able to understand a few words: 'Wednesday' and 'market day.'

Elder Flores turned to his companion explaining that in the smaller villages the traveling market came only one day a week. It was necessary to buy supplies, such as vegetables, dried fish, candles, spices, and so forth, on this day or have to travel much further into Rosales for the items. If they didn't make the trip to the market, many families ate nothing but the rice they harvested.

Thanking the young girl for her time and promising they would stop by again when her parents were home, the two Elders continued on their way. So far, it was beginning to feel like an unproductive day. Elder Daniels thought back to the conversation they'd had about whether or not he believed they could baptize in Rosales.

Elder Daniels reached into his back pocket and pulled out a handkerchief to mop the perspiration from his brow. Realizing it was saturated after countless earlier attempts, he returned it to the pocket, resorting to the back of his hand instead. It was a little past noon and the sun was already high in the summer sky, pumping out scorching ultraviolet rays that not even the dense canopy shade from the tall banana trees could parry.

The morning's efforts had brought little more success than the previous two weeks. Not only had they not found the members they were looking for, they'd not been able to set any return appointments with the few people they did meet either. Each time they introduced themselves and asked to share a message with the family, they heard the same complaint—it was harvest time and every waking moment was spent preparing rice they would sell at the market.

The biggest disappointment of all had come two days earlier when the Baribal family asked them not to return. Elder Daniels had nearly broken down as Brother Baribal described the persecution his family had received from their neighbors.

The next morning, after kneeling in prayer, Elder Daniels and his companion had decided that in order to meet President Hart's challenge, a special fast was in order. It began immediately after lunch and the twenty-four hours were nearly up.

The hot sun drained what energy Elder Daniels had left and he knew from the pounding headache that he was severely dehydrated.

"Comp, it's almost lunch time, let's just go home."

Elder Flores stopped and turned around, looking nearly as weak as his companion. The smile that seemed a permanent feature on his face was gone and fatigue was dulling his own senses.

Stopping momentarily, Elder Flores admitted, "It has been a long morning."

Elder Daniels let his backpack slide down his arm and fall to the ground at his feet. Succumbing to the weariness that made his body ache, he dropped to one knee to escape the harsh sun that peaked over the tallest trees. In frustration he looked up at his companion.

"Why can't we find people to teach? We've been praying for days now and even fasted for help."

Shaking off his own exhaustion, Elder Flores recognized his own mistake. Instantaneously, he pulled his shoulders back and lifted his head. From somewhere deep inside, his smile returned to its rightful place. With every bit of strength he had, the small Filipino repositioned his own backpack and stood to his full 5 foot 1 inch height.

His companion relied on him for strength and for a brief moment, he had shown signs of discouragement and frustration. He'd shown weakness. He'd shown doubt.

Like a cat, he was at his companion's side, lifting him by his arm. He hefted the fallen backpack onto his own overburdened shoulders, and said, "Yeah, but you know what the scriptures say about moments like this, right?"

Elder Daniels, surprised at his companion's sudden change, nearly fell backwards as he was gently but firmly pulled to his feet.

"What are you talking about?"

Elder Flores had him by the hand and before he knew it, the diminutive Filipino was dragging him back down the trail in the direction they'd come.

Without looking at him, Elder Flores continued, "You know! The one in Ether about receiving no witness until after the trial of your faith!"

Elder Daniels pulled his hand away and stopped, swinging his companion around as he did so. "What in the world are you talking about, Elder Flores?"

Realizing that he wasn't going to get the big American to move until he had fully explained himself, Elder Flores stopped and took a step toward his companion. "Remember the devotional Elder Bradley gave at our last district meeting?"

The heat and hunger were wearing at his patience. "Yeah, so what?"

"Remember how he talked about the baptism they had for that old man who slammed the door in his face on their first visit?"

"Yeah," Elder Daniels answered, void of any enthusiasm whatsoever.

"Well, he testified that when things aren't going our way we have to push ourselves harder. That's when the blessings come."

"I remember what he said, but what does that have to do with you jumping up and dragging me through this freaking jungle? Although I don't mind heading in that direction," he added.

"Elder Bradley was talking about 'the pure blessing zone.'"

Elder Daniels could see another teaching moment coming on and was not in the mood for it. Throwing his arms up in frustration he said, "Forget it. I'm sorry I asked. Let's just go home and eat!"

Elder Flores ignored his companion's emotional appeal. Searching for a way to help him understand, he said, "Look at it this way. Let's say the Lord gives us one blessing each time we do something right."

Elder Daniels could see there was no getting out of this one. Crossing his arms, and hoping for a swift explanation, he said, "Fine."

"Then let's just say one act of faith gets one blessing, okay?"

Shrugging his shoulders, Elder Daniels replied, "Sure."

"So for most people that's enough. We obey a commandment and we receive a blessing. But for a missionary who understands the principle of faith, it's not enough."

Elder Flores broke a twig off a tree and dropped to his knees on the dirt path. "You see, Comp, it's like this . . ."

With the twig Elder Flores drew a vertical line in the dirt. He then drew a horizontal line intersecting it near the bottom. Elder Daniels, a tiny bit curious, examined the drawing as it took shape. He recognized an X-Y diagram taking shape. Halfway up the vertical scale his companion drew another horizontal line parallel to the baseline below.

"Just for the sake of argument, we'll say that each act of obedience earns us a blessing of equal value. In reality," he explained, "the Lord blesses us in ways far greater than we deserve." With that he then drew a bar about three-quarters of the way up to the second horizontal line. "This bar represents our obedience." Next to it he drew another of equal height, but this one he drew hash marks in for shading. "This one represents the blessings we receive. You see? One for one."

Elder Daniels had forgotten his hunger and peered closer at the drawing. A bit farther down the diagram, Elder Flores drew a third bar, this one entering the space barely above the second horizontal line. "This space represents the pure blessing zone," he explained, pointing to the area above the line before shading it in. "Anytime our obedience reaches this point, we qualify for extra blessings." With the stick, Elder Flores drew a "blessing bar" that extended much higher than the "obedience bar" and well into the pure blessing zone.

Elder Flores put down the stick. On eye level with his companion he continued, "Comp, if you had to determine where our obedience level is on this chart, where would you put it?"

This was a new concept for Elder Daniels and not easy to understand. Sure, he understood that if he did what was right that the Lord blessed him for it. But what were these extra blessings his companion was talking about? Elder Daniels continued to study the drawing, comparing the bars representing obedience and blessings. Shrugging his shoulders he asked, "What kind of obedience are you talking about?"

Anticipating that question Elder Flores clarified, "Well, like our fasting today—we weren't expected to fast today. I mean, it's not fast Sunday, right?"

"Right."

"And how about getting up a half-hour earlier each day and taking shorter lunches like we've been doing?"

Cocking his head to the side, Elder Daniels asked, "So you're saying these little sacrifices we've been making qualify us for extra blessings?"

The corners of Elder Flores mouth twisted upward into a smile as he said, "No, I'm saying they qualify us for a *multiplicity* of blessings!"

Ignoring the fact that English was Elder Flores' second language and spoke it better than he, Elder Daniels asked, "What's a 'multiplicity of blessings?'"

"Remember the scripture in Malachi about tithing?"

Elder Daniels nodded, "You mean about the windows of heaven?"

"Exactly! The Lord said, 'Prove me now herewith, saith the Lord of Hosts, if I will not open you the windows of heaven, and pour you out a blessing, that there shall not be room enough to receive it.' He wants to bless us so much that we won't know what to do with all the blessings." Pointing back to the dirt drawing, he continued, "That's a multiplicity of blessings and that's what we receive when our obedience level extends into the pure blessing zone!"

Elder Flores studied his companion as his companion studied the drawing. After a brief moment, Elder Flores put his hand on his companion's arm. "Comp, I don't know about you, but I think the Lord *owes* us a couple blessings."

Elder Daniels turned to his companion, thinking the statement sounded a touch heretical. "*Owes* us blessings?"

"That's right, He owes us blessings," Elder Flores remarked, nonchalantly.

"What does Doctrine and Covenants 82:10 say?"

Reciting the only scripture he memorized from seminary, Elder Daniels replied, "I, the Lord am bound when ye do what I say; but when ye do not what I say ye have no promise."

"That's right! The Lord says he's bound when we do what he says. Do you know what it means to be bound, Elder Daniels?"

"Of course! It means you can't get out of it!" he remarked a bit sharply.

"So we can bind the Lord when we are obedient. He is bound to bless us when we do what he commands. And," pointing back to the drawing in the road, "when our faith and righteousness extend into the pure blessing zone, he is required to bless us even more!"

Elder Daniels let out a deep breath. Remembering the hollowness in his stomach, the long, hot morning of little success, and the many nights he'd collapsed face first on his bed after an exhausting day of proselyting, Elder Daniels slowly nodded. "I think you're right. I think the Lord owes us a *multiplicity* of blessings."

* * * * *

They were lucky to catch the first minibus that came along. The next wouldn't be along for another half hour. Elder Flores sat by a Plexiglas window lowered as far as it would go. The windows provided the only ventilation in the bus, which allowed exhaust fumes to fill the cabin.

Next to him sat Elder Daniels, preferring the aisle seat where he could sit diagonally and extend his legs. Although troublesome when other passengers had to get by him, it was better than having his knees crammed in his chest in the space between seats. Many times in the past, Elder Daniels had stepped off a minibus limping on a leg that had fallen asleep.

It was only about twelve kilometers from the barangay to their apartment but Elder Daniels was fighting sleep the whole way. Twice, he'd closed his eyes only to stiffen and awaken because of the irregular weaving of the bus. The second time he'd nearly fallen out of his seat when the bus lurched right and stopped, waved down at the last possible moment by an elderly woman with a sack of rice over her shoulder. After that, Elder Daniels placed his arm across the seat in front of him and rested his head on his forearm. Light-headed from heat, hunger, and noxious fumes, he longed for his own bed.

Leaning against the Plexiglas window, Elder Flores was also nearly lulled to sleep by the hum of the diesel engines, but was also eager to get off the bus and scanned the landmarks to keep from passing their stop. He knew Elder Daniels was sleeping but did nothing to disturb him. Out of habit, he thought about prompting his junior companion to start up a conversation with the elderly woman in the seat next to them. There was never a bad time to find a new contact.

*Not today,* he told himself, and let his companion catch a few minutes of rest.

Outside the window the scenery changed from dense jungle to a residential setting with houses made of concrete instead of bamboo. The dust of the rural countryside was also replaced with the toxic exhaust from the tailpipes of passing automobiles, trucks, jeepneys, buses and trikes.

Elder Daniels heard the sound of someone tapping the roof of the bus. So exhausted, he didn't even realize it was his companion who was signaling the driver to stop.

"We've got to get off here, Comp."

Still dazed, Elder Daniels nearly stumbled in the aisle as he made his way to the front of the bus, stepping over bags of rice, grocery sacks, and a small goat tied to one of the seat posts. The fact that the bus was still slowing made it even harder to walk down the crowded aisle.

"Why are we getting off here?" he asked, realizing they were nowhere close to their apartment.

"Look over there," Elder Flores said, pointing to an old weather-beaten sign.

"Barangay Villasis? This is where the Baribal family lives."

"Exactly," Elder Flores replied as he turned and started walking down the street.

Elder Daniels didn't move, watching his companion walk into the little village. Realizing what his companion had in mind, he finally adjusted the backpack on his shoulders and ran to catch up.

"Why are we going back there after they told us not to come back?"

Smiling from ear to ear, Elder Flores replied, "To commit them to baptism!"

\* \* \* \* \*

José Baribal was a welder and owned his own vulcanizing shop. He'd worked alone for years and supported his family the best he could. The only time he hired any help was when he accepted orders he couldn't complete by himself.

In recent years his sons—Eddie, who was fourteen, and Lawrence, barely ten—had become partners, working side by side with their father. Since that time, rarely did José ever lift a hammer without his two apprentices scrambling around for the best view of their father's work. The two boys had already mastered much of the technical knowledge required to run the shop and were given additional responsibilities with each passing year.

Nothing could have crushed José Baribal more than the death of his wife. His faithful childhood love had been taken by tuberculosis four years earlier, leaving behind a mortified husband and six devastated children. The next year was the most difficult of his life. Having no one else to help him with his grief, José turned to alcohol, often spending weeks at a time in a drunken stupor.

His oldest daughter, Jocelyn, was thirteen at the time and took on the role of guardian for her five younger siblings. With her father incapacitated by grief and drink, she became the breadwinner for the family taking in laundry to wash and earning a mere fifty-three pesos per day—the equivalent of a dollar and twenty cents.

Because of his drunkenness, the business José Baribal had slaved eleven years to build was disappearing before his eyes. No longer able to depend on him, customers turned to other welders for their work. It wasn't until his youngest son Alex was caught stealing a loaf of bread from the local bakery that he realized what he was doing to his family.

José Baribal swore off alcohol forever and rebuilt his business one customer at a time. It took three full years. Not once in those three years did José Baribal put a drop of alcohol in his body.

Elder Daniels knew the Baribal's story well. Not only had he recorded the story in his missionary journal, he'd also written about them to his family, his girlfriend, and his mission president. This was a very special family to him, and the only thing that hurt him more than the pain they'd lived through was being told to forget them and to never return.

* * * * *

When a young man or woman receives a mission call in The Church of Jesus Christ of Latter-Day Saints a near ritualistic ceremony takes place. Family members and friends gather from near and far to watch the prospective missionary open and read the letter. Not only is the letter special because it comes from a prophet of God, but also because the missionary learns where he or she will serve.

Unlike many churches throughout the world, a prospective missionary does not select where in the world he or she will serve. There is no lobbying or requesting a particular country. There is no negotiating for a specific locale. Members of the Church believe the call is a call from God, given by revelation through a living prophet. Elder Daniels' mission call was no different.

THE CHURCH OF JESUS CHRIST OF LATTER-DAY SAINTS
OFFICE OF THE FIRST PRESIDENCY
47 East South Temple Street, Salt Lake City, Utah 84160-1203

*October 11, 2011*

*Elder Aaron Steven Daniels*
*1102 E. Golden Street*
*Orem, UT 84059*

*Dear Elder Daniels:*

*You are hereby called to serve as a missionary for The Church of Jesus Christ of Latter-day Saints. You are assigned to labor in the Philippines, Baguio Mission. It is anticipated that you will serve for a period of 24 months.*

*You should report to the Provo Missionary Training Center on Wednesday, December 21, 2011. You will prepare to preach the gospel in the Tagalog language. Your assignment may be modified according to the needs of the Mission President.*

*You have been recommended as one worthy to represent the Lord as a minister of the restored gospel. You will be an official representative of the Church. As such, you will be expected to maintain the highest standards of conduct and appearance by keeping the commandments, living the mission rules, and following the counsel of your mission president. As you devote your time and attention to serving the Lord, leaving behind all other personal affairs, the Lord will bless you with increased knowledge and testimony of the Restoration and of the truths of the gospel of Jesus Christ.*

*Your purpose will be to invite others to come unto Christ by helping them receive the restored gospel through faith in Jesus Christ and His atonement, repentance, baptism, receiving the gift of the Holy Ghost, and enduring to the end. As you serve with all your heart, might, and strength, the Lord will lead you to those who are prepared to be baptized.*

*The Lord will reward the goodness of your life. Greater blessings and more happiness than you have yet experienced await you as you humbly and prayerfully serve the Lord in this labor of love among His children. We place in you our confidence and pray that the Lord will help you become an effective missionary.*

*You will be set apart as a missionary by your stake president. Please send your written acceptance promptly, endorsed by your bishop.*

*Sincerely,*

*Thomas S. Monson*
*President*

At some point in the service of every missionary, an experience or acquaintance further attests that it was the Lord who assigned them to a particular mission. The same can be said for a particular area. Feelings alone can testify that a covenant was made between a missionary and a particular investigator in a pre-mortal life—a covenant to bring that investigator the gospel, and a promise to accept it when it is heard. Such was the case for Elder Daniels and this special family he became reacquainted with in Barangay Villasis.

\* \* \* \* \*

There was nothing unusual about the member referral the Elders received two weeks into their companionship in Rosales—other than the fact it was the only referral they received. Having both been transferred into the area together, there was not much of a "teaching pool" coming from the two previous missionaries. It was uncommon for one of them to not have a month overlap with one of the out-going missionaries. But, in this case, both had returned to their homes—one completed with his mission, the other not prepared to serve. After many home teaching visits, the bishop's eldest daughter referred a friend whom she believed might be interested in the missionary discussions. Her name was Jocelyn Baribal.

On the walk from the branch president's home that first evening, Elder Flores and Elder Daniels heard the story of José and his family. Intrigued by Brother Baribal's dauntless efforts to raise six children by himself, and hearing what sort of work he did, the Elders were somewhat surprised at the man's small stature.

Standing just under five-feet tall and not much over ninety pounds, José Baribal could've easily been mistaken for his own son—except, of course, for his silver hair and toothless smile. If his diminutive size belied his age, his receding hairline and thinning flattop corrected the misperception. Adding to that four missing front teeth lost to a ricocheting hammer blow years earlier, and you had José Baribal.

Although small, José was big-hearted. He graciously welcomed the two Elders into his home and introduced them to his six children. To Elder Daniels' disappointment, Brother Baribal spoke little English, requiring his companion to translate most of his words.

With a gentle command from his father, Dante, the youngest son, ran out the front door only to return moments later with three bottles of soda for their guests. Brother Baribal took a seat on a small crate next to his daughter Marisa, offering his guests the three battered folding chairs that decorated the living area.

A quick survey of the house told Elder Daniels all he needed to know about the family's financial state. The one-room dwelling was no bigger than ten square-meters, or a little larger than his own bedroom back home. The room was dimly lit and overcrowded with ten people now occupying it.

In one corner was the kitchen area, with cooking pots, bowls, and utensils stacked next to a gas stove. Similar to a camping stove Elder Daniels had used with his father and brother, their living conditions appeared to him as rudimentary.

In the adjacent corner was a four-drawer dresser. The dresser was shared by all seven people and contained every piece of clothing the family owned. In another corner stood a small table with, a picture of each of the children in their school uniforms and a black-and-white photo of his late wife.

In the last corner, stacked neatly on top of each other, lay six bedrolls. When Elder Daniels saw them he knew this room in which the family sat, cooked, and dined, also served as their sleeping quarters. They had no beds— only a mat for each child with a light blanket for cooler nights.

The only furnishing providing any measure of comfort was a squeaky fan atop the dresser. Although the house had electricity, the low current output was visible in the dim light bulb that hung from the ceiling and the fan blades that turned at an inconsistent rate.

Elder Daniels turned his attention to the family, no longer feeling the level of heartache he'd felt before for families in such circumstances. His first few weeks in the Philippines had proven quite a culture shock. Now he was more accustomed to the poverty of this third-world country. It was actually good that he was becoming desensitized to the conditions in which these good people lived. It allowed him to focus on the family rather than their economic circumstances.

As taught in the MTC and *Preach My Gospel*, Elder Flores was already building relationships of trust. From the little Elder Daniels understood, his companion was explaining how they knew Jocelyn's friend, Rachel, and how her father was the ecclesiastical leader in the area.

Elder Daniels surveyed the children, who stared at him and snickered to one another about his hairy arms. Seeing his own opportunity to build trust with the family, he pulled out a peso from his pocket and performed a magic trick. In his hand one second and gone the next, the children clapped when the peso reappeared behind little Dante's ear. That simple gesture won the children's attention and the respect of their father for taking an interest in his family.

José Baribal liked his visitors right away. Their gentle nature impressed him and he sensed their interest was genuine. Many missionaries from other churches had knocked on his door with the sole intention of 'bible-bashing' him into baptism. José felt that was not the intent of these two young men. There was something different about them and he basked in the peace and solace that filled his humble home. By the time the Elders and Rachel were finished with their refreshments, he was very curious about what these two young men wanted to share with his family.

Sitting his youngest on his lap he said, "All right, children, I'm sure these missionaries didn't come here just to perform magic tricks. Let's listen to what they have to say."

Turning to the Elders, he said, "In the past few years we've opened the door of our home to many missionaries. We've talked with Jehovah's Witnesses, the Church of Christ, and many others but none of them could answer a question my children and I have asked over and over again."

"What question is that? Elder Flores asked.

"What happens to us when we die?"

The discussion that evening couldn't have gone any better. The Spirit testified of gospel truths and the Elders committed the family to begin reading The Book of Mormon.

After teaching about Joseph Smith and the First Vision, Elder Flores asked, "Brother Baribal, would you like to know how you and your family can be reunited with your wife after this life and live together as an eternal family?"

The tears that streamed down the man's leathery face answered the question for him. While teaching about eternal families, the two Elders provided answers that no other religion had been able to do in four years.

After the discussion, as the Elders walked toward the main road to their next appointment, they both knew they had found a "golden" family. To prolong the Spirit that accompanied them, neither missionary said a word until they'd walked about 200 yards.

Elder Flores was somewhat caught off guard when Elder Daniels asked, "Comp, have you ever met someone for the first time, yet it felt like you'd known that person forever?"

Feeling a spiritual closeness to his companion, Elder Flores put his arm around Elder Daniels' shoulder. "That's one of the nicest things anyone's ever said to me."

"Not you!" Elder Daniels chuckled, "I'm talking about Brother Baribal. I can't help feeling like I've met him before tonight."

\* \* \* \* \*

The Elders awoke the next morning to the sound of someone knocking on their front door. Still wiping the sleep from his eyes, Elder Flores let out a loud "woohoo" when he saw who it was. Standing on their doorstep was the ward mission leader holding a large bowl of "champrado," still warm from the stove at his house. The smell of chocolate instantly made his mouth water.

This was Elder Daniels first taste of "chocolate rice," as he later called it, but it soon became his favorite breakfast food. Made of a thick blend of cocoa, sugar, and water, mixed into a pot of steaming rice, this simple meal was a welcome alternative to the usual dried fish, eggs, and rice. It also appeased his slumbering love for sweets.

After a quick stop at the ward mission leader's home to thank his wife for the delicious meal, the Elders were off to a highly anticipated appointment with the Baribal family. This would be their second appointment with them in three days and the memory of the other night's experience lingered in their minds.

Basking in the sunshine on a beautiful Saturday morning, both missionaries felt invincible. Walking down the hard-packed road of Barangay Villasis, worn smooth by the feet of daily travelers, the thought of a family with six amazing baptismal candidates was exciting and humbling at the same time.

Their excitement burst within a stone's throw from the Baribal's home as both Elders saw Jocelyn rounding the corner of their cinder-block home. Just as Elder Flores was about to call her name their eyes met. The fear that flooded the girl's face caught both missionaries by surprise. Before either could say a word she darted in the front door and shut it quickly behind her.

Surprised and confused, Elder Daniels turned to his companion. "That was weird. What was that all about?"

Elder Flores let out a long sigh. "I think we're about to find out."

José Baribal walked out the door and shut it behind him. Meeting the Elders halfway up the walk his eyes never left the ground.

"Good morning," Elder Flores greeted.

For Elder Daniels, the remainder of the conversation was unintelligible though José Baribal's nervousness was quite obvious. He spoke quickly, shuffled from one foot to the other and his eyes never left the ground.

A movement at the window behind Brother Baribal caught Elder Daniels attention. Six small faces shuffled for a position to see out of the only window in the front of the home. The sadness on each face confirmed his suspicion. They would not be teaching the Baribal family anymore lessons.

Turning back to his companion, he caught sight of a small crowd gathered next to the sari-sari store just a few dozen meters down the way. More than just the Baribal children were interested in the conversation taking place. One spectator, an older man, obviously intoxicated by the way he leaned on his friend for support, listened intently.

Just as Elder Daniels turned back to the conversation, the man yelled something in their direction that caused the entire group to roar with laughter. The outburst increased Brother Baribal's nervousness as he scowled at the ground and spoke even faster.

Throughout the conversation, Elder Flores remained calm and supportive, gently nodding as he listened. Knowing that in the present situation there was no way to resolve any of their investigator's concerns, the missionary shook the man's hand and thanked him for his time. With a quick turn and brisk walk, José Baribal returned inside and closed the door—to the spectators outside and the gospel of Jesus Christ.

As they walked home, Elder Flores explained the reason they were no longer welcome in the Baribal home. The neighborhood was not accepting of Mormons.

José Baribal had described to Elder Flores the events that occurred after their first visit. Almost the entire barangay had descended upon his doorstep protesting everything Mormons stood for. Some told stories of how Mormons prayed to a man named "Joe Smith." Others contended that Mormons had multiple wives. One elderly woman, hunched over from years in the rice patties, took a soggy, half-smoked cigar from her mouth and shook it within an inch of José's face, insisting that Mormons drank the blood of animals they sacrificed.

The immediate persecution took its toll on the small family's disposition. José Baribal was especially concerned that, not only were these his neighbors, but also the patrons of his business. Regardless of the way he'd felt when the Elders were in his home, he just couldn't throw his life's work away a second time.

\* \* \* \* \*

Standing once again at the Baribal's front door, Elder Daniels could actually hear his heart beating in his chest. The hair on the back of his neck bristled like that of a frightened cat. He felt the eyes of strangers watching their every move. The instant his companion tapped on the tattered, wooden door, Elder Daniels shut his eyes, quietly hoping no one was home.

Knowing this, Elder Daniels couldn't believe his companion had marched back to the Baribal's front door a third time, let alone in broad daylight. Tightening his hold on his backpack, he quickly figured the odds were greater that they'd be chased from the neighborhood by an angry mob than being invited into the Baribal's home. No longer was his stomach knotted by hunger—he was now completely sick with fear!

A firm rap on the door brought his thoughts back to the moment. Upon opening the door and seeing the Elders standing there, Dante exploded into a huge smile. Just as he stepped aside to let the missionaries in, a figure appeared behind him. Elder Daniels could not see the man's face but a shiver ran down his spine and he dropped back a step in hesitation.

Elder Flores didn't move. With unbridled enthusiasm he greeted José.

"Good morning, Sir."

Elder Daniels was astonished when Brother Baribal opened the front door and stepped to the side.

"Come in, please."

Elder Daniels guard was still up as he entered. In the center of the room stood a well-used table. The spindly legs made it look feeble. Around the table were three folding chairs—the same ones in which the Elders had sat during their first visit. In the chairs sat Eddie, Jocelyn, and Lawrence. The three younger children, José Jr., Regina, and Dante, sat on their older siblings' laps.

Close to the window was an old crate, which Elder Daniels assumed to be José's seat. Filtering through the tall coconut trees outside the window, a soft ray of sunlight descended on the small table, on which lay an open copy of The Book of Mormon.

José Baribal offered his chair to Elder Daniels. He gently lifted José Jr. from Lawrence's lap and asked the Elders to take a seat. Pulling another wooden crate from the corner, José made himself a place at the table after making sure everyone else was comfortable.

More surprising to Elder Daniels than the sight of The Book of Mormon was the feeling he experienced as soon as he entered the room. The Holy Ghost was so strong it reminded him of walking through the doors of the Salt Lake City Temple for the very first time.

As he collected his thoughts, a wave of guilt swept over him as he looked over the family he'd so quickly dismissed as lost investigators. His guilt intensified as he remembered how easily he'd doubted the Lord. A tear rolled down his cheek.

Brother Baribal was obviously choked up as well. His worn and callused hands brushed at his eyes frequently. Elder Daniels looked at those hands carefully from across the table. They were strong hands, the kind developed by swinging a hammer day after day in a welding shop. But to Elder Daniels, they seemed more human now as he watched them shaking .

José Baribal cleared his throat. "We were just reading…" His voice faltered as tears sprang from his eyes.

*What happened here?* Elder Daniels asked silently.

Elder Flores, who had been sitting quietly, had already figured it out. Maybe not the specific details, but he had seen enough to know that, with God, nothing is impossible. With a gentle hand he reached over and placed it on the man's hand. It was his way of saying, "It's alright…this is how it happens."

In the open Book of Mormon, Elder Flores noticed several verses lightly shaded in red pencil. Picking up The Book of Mormon, he began to read aloud in 1Nephi, Chapter 2.

*"I did go forth and partake of the fruit thereof; and I beheld that it was most sweet, above all that I ever before tasted. Yea, and I beheld that the fruit thereof was white, to exceed all the whiteness that I had ever seen. And as I partook of the fruit thereof it filled my soul with exceedingly great joy; wherefore, I began to be desirous that my family should partake of it also; for I knew that it was desirable above all other fruit."*

Skipping to the next shaded verse, Elder Flores continued.

*"And I . . . cast my eyes round about, and beheld, on the other side of the river of water, a great and spacious building; and it stood as it were in the air, high above the earth. And it was filled with people . . . pointing their fingers toward those who had come out and were partaking of the fruit. And after they had tasted of the fruit they were ashamed, because of those that were scoffing at them; and they fell away into forbidden paths and were lost."*

Elder Daniels couldn't help wonder about the persecution Brother Baribal had encountered after their first visit. He knew enough from what the Bishop's daughter had told them that people were not afraid to openly condemn José and his family. They'd boycotted his business in the past and he was sure they were doing it again. He wondered just how many sets of eyes and whispering voices were outside the door, pointing fingers and scoffing at José Baribal at that very moment.

Turning his attention to Brother Baribal, Elder Daniels wondered how much more adversity this humble man would have to endure. He wondered how difficult it must have been to have to tell his children their mother was gone; to give up alcohol; to raise six children by himself; to see his business slipping away again.

The only sound in the room was the muffled sobbing of a penitent man. After a few more moments, it was completely quiet. Long moments passed, though there was nothing uncomfortable in this silence.

"I had a dream last night," he began again, still struggling for control of his emotions. "I had a dream that I was standing on the banks of a large river. On the other side I could see the friends I used to drink with." Staring at his hands, he relived the spiritual experience he'd had in his dream.

"They called for me. They wanted me to come over, pleading for me to swim across the river. I wanted to go to them—to be with them again—so I waded into the water."

"But when I started swimming, I realized that the current was moving very fast. I tried to swim harder, kicking as hard as I could, but I was being carried downstream and I started getting tired. When I looked to my friends for help they laughed at me. They were pointing their fingers and laughing at me."

"I knew I wasn't going to make it," he continued, "so I turned around to see if I could make it back to where I'd started. On the banks of the river I saw my children. They too were calling for me and crying. I tried to swim back but I was too tired. I was having trouble keeping my head above water and I started going under water. So I prayed."

Wiping at his eyes again, he said, "I was drowning. I couldn't breathe. I was dying. But then I brushed up against something, and I grabbed hold of it." Looking up for the first time since they sat down, he said, "It was a tree branch."

"I got hold of the branch and pulled my head above water. That's when I saw the two of you standing on the banks of the river…holding the other end of the branch."

"When I woke from my dream, I opened this book, pointing to The Book of Mormon. Right to the page you just read."

The tears once again sprang from his eyes, running down his cheeks and disappearing on his dark t-shirt as they fell. The room was completely silent. The quietness only intensified the Spirit as everyone waited for him to speak again.

"That branch in my dream was a branch from the Tree of Life, which represents the love of God. And this book is the rod of iron, representing the word of God."

"Elders," he said, looking them both in the eyes. "My family and I want to be baptized."

# CHAPTER 5

*Wherefore, whoso believeth in God might with surety hope for a better world, yea, even a place at the right hand of God, which hope cometh of faith, maketh an anchor to the souls of men, which would make them sure and steadfast, always abounding in good works, being led to glorify God.*

—*Ether 12:4*

Ann Daniels picked up the stack of letters from the kitchen table. Shuffling through the bills and junk mail, her eyes lit up upon seeing a blue envelope with an airmail stamp. Dropping all but that one letter on the table, she slid a fingernail under the flap and tore it open. Inside was a two-page letter in the handwriting of her missionary son. Carefully, she unfolded the letter and stared at it a moment before reading the first line.

The corners of her mouth turned upwards as she read the embossed letterhead at the top of the page.

*Elder Aaron Daniels*
*Philippines Baguio Mission*

She smiled each time she heard her son's name spoken with that title. Since she was always the first one home, she read Aaron's letters to herself, enjoying the private moments with no one else around.

Ann Daniels' admiration for her son was not something she kept to herself. The letters often went with her to the elementary school the next day where she shared them with her co-workers who, by this time, knew Aaron Daniels well.

She cared for the severely handicapped children in the "resource room" at the elementary school. These special children, with severe mental and physical handicaps, were unable to be mainstreamed into regular classes and needed a great deal of care. Caring for others was something Ann Daniels did well. She enjoyed being needed. As her own children grew into their teen-age and adult years, she missed that part of parenting, especially when three-thousand miles separated her and her eldest son.

The initial few days after dropping Elder Daniels off at the Missionary Training Center (MTC) were long and depressing. She missed the front door slamming as he came in after school. She missed the thunderous commotion of him running down the stairs, skipping two with each step. She missed the gentle but exuberant sound of his voice as he called, "Mom, where are you," just to know she was there.

She'd handled her emotions well when they dropped him off at the curb and he walked through the front doors of the MTC with two suitcases filled with everything he would take for the next two years. But then she'd amply prepared herself for that. With a hug and a kiss, they'd said their good-byes. The fifteen-minute ride home had felt more like an hour and she'd cried the entire way. Even though he was only ten miles from her when she arrived home, he'd already felt half a world away.

She soon found that as long as she kept herself busy, she did fine. When she wasn't busy and reflected on how much she missed him, tears welled up in her eyes. She knew it would take a while for her to get used to having him gone.

On the fourth day after he'd entered the MTC, Ann Daniels had realized she needed time to grieve her loss—almost as if her son were deceased. Metaphorically, he was. The Aaron Daniels she'd raised for 19 years was gone and, even though she knew he would return, he would be quite different after 2 years in the mission field.

On one particular morning just a few days later, both her daughters were getting ready for school as Ann Daniels frantically tried to make up for lost time. She was preparing breakfast when she heard a scream from the basement. She flew down the stairs and flung open the bathroom door to find her 14-year-old daughter wrapped in a towel with the shower running. A few moments later and they were both in tears as her daughter recounted her fright at seeing a spider and calling her brother's name to come and dispose of it. It was then that reality sunk in and they all knew Aaron was gone.

She wondered what he would look like when he returned. Would he still have those dimples at the corners of his mouth? Would his voice be deeper? Would he speak with a foreign accent? Would she still see her father every time she looked at him?

Shaking the questions from her head, Ann Daniels checked the date of the letter and was surprised to see it had arrived less than two weeks after it was put in the mail. That was the quickest they'd received a letter. More often than not it took between three weeks and a month. But to Ann Daniels, old news was still new news and she was grateful for any news at all.

*Dear Family,*

*Hey! How's everybody doing? I guess it's probably starting to get pretty cool there now that it's October. I wish it were cooling off here. Instead of the leaves changing colors on the trees, they just seem to wilt more and more each day. It's so hot!*

*I never thought I could sweat so much! It doesn't help knowing that we're not too far from a beach and the ocean. Too bad we can't swim in it. Sometimes I just don't understand all the mission rules we have to put up with.*

*In your last letter you asked how the language is coming. Well, I hate to say "it sucks" but it does. I get so frustrated when I teach an entire principle and my companion has to re-teach it because our investigators have this blank look on their faces. I mean, sometimes I don't know why I even try speaking any Tagalog at all. It's not Elder Flores' fault—he's great! I just don't think I'll ever be fluent.*

*Not everything's bad though. I mean, there's a lot that I like. I wrote to you before about the Baribal family, this totally awesome family in Rosales. Well, guess what? We baptized them last Sunday! You should have seen how excited they were. Even little Dante, the six-year old boy, was excited and he wasn't even baptized. After it was all over, he asked if he could "go swimming" too, but his father explained to him it wasn't a swimming pool and why he had to wait two more years. Anyway, they are a great family and I know they'll be excellent members of the Church.*

*I don't mean to sound prideful but sometimes I think about some of my friends, like Jake, who aren't going on missions. I kind of feel sorry for him. Even though I miss Alicia, my car, and the conveniences of home, when I have days like this I begin to see things differently.*

*If nothing else, I wouldn't have met my companion, Elder Flores. He's way cool! I wish you could meet him. There's no doubt that he has more faith than anyone that I've ever met. Sometimes it's hard for me to understand how I could ever be like him. He keeps telling me I will someday, but it's hard for me to see that ever happening.*

*Anyway, I want you to know how much I love you all. I never realized before how much I took my family for granted. I wish I could tell you in person, and give you each a big hug, but I can't. This is the best I can do.*

*I also thought you might want to know that I've read half the Book of Mormon already! Cool huh? I'm finally starting to see why all my seminary teachers felt it was their mission in life to get me to read it. I kind of feel like Alma the Younger at times. I mean, I wasn't always the best kid... but I don't have to tell you that, do I?*

*Well, it gets lonely out here sometimes so keep writing, and remember...I love you all very much!*

*Love,*
*Aaron*

*P.S. We met our goal of six convert baptisms in the month of September!*

In the middle of her kitchen, Ann Daniels dropped to her knees in prayer. Unlike past occasions when she'd been driven to her knees pleading for strength, this time she asked for nothing. In the stillness of the quiet house, she spoke not a word. The lump in her throat would have made the attempt impossible.

She closed her eyes tightly in an attempt to stop the tears and she gave her Father in Heaven her heartfelt thanks. As hard as it was to have him gone, she knew her son was right where he needed to be.

# CHAPTER 6

*Because of their exceeding faith in that which they had been taught to believe—that there was a just God, and whosoever did not doubt, that they should be preserved by his marvelous power.*

*Now this was the faith of these of whom I have spoken; they are young, and their minds are firm, and they do put their trust in God continually.*
*—Alma 57:26 & 27*

The moment the power went out in their apartment Elder Daniels awoke. The oscillating fan creaked out one more half swing before it sat completely motionless on the desk next to his bed. He immediately pulled the linen sheet—his only covering—over his head to protect him from the onslaught he knew would follow. Within seconds the first mosquito circled above his head and sent a shiver down his spine. He detested the blood-sucking predators that called "his" apartment home.

As he lay in the blackness of night, he imagined the walls crawling with spiders and cockroaches. On more than one occasion he slipped out of bed only to feel something brush his foot as it scurried across the floor. It wasn't uncommon to turn on the bathroom light and see three or four cockroaches probing the walls, ceiling or floor with their long antennas. Killing one did little to help the situation because if they didn't get rid of it right away, a trail of ants would be there by sunrise, marching in unison toward the decaying corpse.

Even worse than the mosquitoes was the sound of one of these disease-carrying cockroaches buzzing his head in the dark. Elder Daniels put his hands over his ears as he remembered stories of cockroaches crawling into a person's ear to lay eggs. He really wasn't sure if the stories were true but he didn't want to find out either.

His mind soon drifted to rats—invasive vermin with beady eyes. A week after arriving in his first area, Elder Daniels awakened in the night from a loud sound coming from the kitchen. The distinctive sound of a pan hitting the floor sent his heart into tachycardia. Flipping on the light, his immediate fear was that they were being robbed and he looked to his senior companion for help. Elder Juarez didn't move, even with 100 watts of light shining in his face.

Elder Daniels had wondered if his imagination was playing tricks on him and tried to calm his nerves. A second clatter from the front room made his heart race once again. As he looked around the room for something to protect himself, he shook his head knowing that the intruder out there definitely had the upper hand. The only thing he found was a beat-up, rusty umbrella, and one that had been through quite a few rainy seasons.

As quietly as he could he opened the bedroom door and stepped into the darkness. Out of his missionary clothes, and out of character, he'd cursed whoever placed the light switch at the other side of the room. Inch by inch he tiptoed across the cold linoleum floor. Taking a deep breath he readied himself, expecting the worst as he flipped the light switch and turned around. In the brightness of the living room light he saw two beady eyes staring at him from the middle of the kitchen table.

The first thought that came to his mind was '*What an ugly cat!*' But as the creature turned and he saw the tail, he realized it was not a cat. It was a giant rat!

Eyes wide open, Elder Daniels nearly dropped his umbrella as the feline-sized beast leaped off the table, waddled across the kitchen floor and disappeared behind the refrigerator. As he crawled back into bed, he wasn't sure whether to be grateful or more frightened that it wasn't a thief at all.

Laying under the sheet with sweat dripping down his forehead, Elder Daniels wondered what things were like back home. Things were so different here—the poverty, the living conditions, the food—or lack thereof. People spent a lifetime just trying to survive. He came to the realization that most Americans had no idea how different the rest of the world lived.

\* \* \* \* \*

The rooster began its morning ritual as the first crack of light broke over the rusty tin roof. Strutting into the middle of the barren courtyard, he threw back his decoratively feathered head, thrust out his mighty chest and crowed as if the day would not began without his permission.

Elder Daniels lifted one eyelid but struggled under the weight of the other. Lying completely still he knew the alarm clock would ring in a few minutes and didn't dare go back to sleep. Every morning for the past two weeks he'd awoken just moments before his alarm clock sounded. The anticipation of its horrendous clattering brought him to life before it had a chance to scare it from him.

Knowing that he often slept through his alarm clock back home, his mother had bought him one of those clocks with a hammer that beat on the inside of a bell. Where she possibly found it, he had no idea. To his great disappointment, it lacked two important features, a snooze button and volume control! That first morning it went off in the MTC, his companion had fallen right out of bed.

The heaviness of his eyelids paled in comparison to the strength it took to lift an arm or leg. Remembering the power going out during the night, he estimated he had lay awake two hours or more in the stifling stillness of the unventilated room. To a missionary working fourteen to sixteen hours a day, with endless hours of walking, those one or two hours of missed sleep could be debilitating.

Elder Flores had slept through the "brownout" without even stirring. He'd explained to his companion that the Philippine Government regulated the power companies and shut off all electricity for two hours during the night, and each afternoon, to conserve energy. Elder Daniels had a hard time finding the logic in that, especially since most people slept during the early morning hours and worked in the rice fields in the day.

A sharp clanking noise brought him out of his daze as his clock sounded its ridiculous alarm. It didn't surprise him that the clock actually danced across his desktop as it rang. Elder Flores stirred under his sheet and cotton blanket. Elder Daniels couldn't imagine how he slept with that much covering in the sultry heat, especially without a fan.

As habit dictated, the Filipino Elder slipped out of bed and dropped to his knees. With bowed head and crossed arms, the senior companion reminded his junior companion that they were on the Lord's errand and there was work to be done.

\* \* \* \* \*

Sitting on the side of the road, Elder Daniels was a pitiful sight. Anyone passing by with a shred of compassion must have felt sympathy toward him. Without knowing him or his business, it was obvious from a glance that things weren't going well.

Elder Daniels shifted his position on his makeshift stool causing the bamboo backpack to groan under his weight. With an elbow on his knee for support, the exhausted missionary stared at the ground, his head resting in his hand. By his side, Elder Flores stood resolutely, his weight evenly distributed on both legs, obviously absorbed in the blue, soft cover book he held open in his hands. Other than an occasional peek down the road for an approaching jeepney, Elder Flores never lifted his eyes from his reading.

Elder Daniels looked at his watch, showing a little past seven in the evening. They had been proselyting ten hours with only a short break at lunch for a cold, leftover, cheese sandwich. Elder Daniels shook his head, remembering the home-cooked meals back home. Homesickness crept into his mind as the thought of his mother's delicious cooking—something he hadn't tasted in several months.

They'd sat on the edge of the broken pavement for nearly twenty minutes with no sign of a jeepney, at least not one with room for two more people. Each time they saw one coming and stuck out a hand to wave it down, the driver simply gave it the gas and barreled on by. They'd not even seen one on which they could stand on the back step and hold onto the cargo rack. Although dangerous, it was a common "seating arrangement" in the Philippines, and either missionary would have welcomed the cool breeze.

Elder Daniels watched a tiny ant traverse a fallen limb from the tree overhead. With little effort, it navigated the maze of branches standing in its path. The junior missionary noticed each time the ant came to a dead end it simply turned around and retraced its course to find a new route.

As the ant continued its hurried march, Elder Daniels felt a twinge of guilt as he contemplated the "pity-party" he'd thrown himself. Before him, a seemingly insignificant ant trudged on—regardless of the obstacle—while he sat wallowing in his own misfortune.

Elder Daniels had not received a letter from Alicia in over a month. A faithful letter writer, not a delivery had gone by since he arrived in the mission field that didn't contain at least one of her perfume-scented envelopes. After today's visit by the district leaders, three deliveries had passed without a letter from his girl.

For the last twenty minutes his mind had been preoccupied with her. Images of her long brown hair and soft hazel eyes consumed his every thought. The more he thought about her, the more he missed her.

"What are you thinking about, Comp?" Elder Flores asked, noticing the posture and forlorn look of his companion.

"Nothing much." He lied.

Elder Flores closed The Book of Mormon and set his backpack on the ground. "You're thinking about her again, aren't you?"

Elder Daniels sighed, "I just don't get it. I mean, I'm out here serving the Lord just like she wanted me to do and she's forgotten about me. How does that happen? Or a better question," he said out of frustration, "How could God *let* that happen?"

Elder Flores smiled, seeing the opportunity to teach a principle he knew was fundamental to missionary work. "That's a tough one, Comp, but I can assure you, you're not the first missionary to struggle with that question."

"Well, that doesn't make it any easier!" Elder Daniels snapped.

The gentle Filipino put his arm on his companion's shoulder for consolation, "I just meant that you're not alone here. Not so long ago I was wondering the same thing."

Elder Daniels lifted his head and looked at this companion. "You have a girlfriend?"

"Would it surprise you that much?"

Realizing how his question must have sounded, Elder Daniels interjected "No, no, that's not what I meant. It's just that I've never heard you speak of her."

Elder Flores smiled, "I was just playing with you."

Turning his back to the passing traffic, Elder Flores began, "Let me tell you how my mission started."

Elder Daniels sat in dismay as he listened to his companion's story. He told Elder Daniels about the girl he had loved since his fifteenth birthday—the girl he had planned to spend eternity with. To his companion's surprise, Elder Flores knew a thing or two about "heartbreak."

When they started dating a few years earlier she had made it very clear that for their dating to continue, he would have to meet the missionaries. Elder Flores explained that he took the discussions so that he might continue their courtship. He soon realized that much of what drew him to her was how he felt around her, which was the same way he felt when hearing the gospel message. In a month's time he had read The Book of Mormon, pondered and prayed about it, and gained a testimony of the truthfulness of the Gospel.

Elder Flores' eyes filled with tears as he spoke. He explained how their love intensified over the next two years and how they had made wedding plans for when he returned from his mission.

"You can imagine how hard it was when I received a letter after being in the MTC for only a month that she was engaged to my best friend."

"After only a month?" Elder Daniels shouted. "What did you do?"

"I was hurt," Elder Flores conceded, "but after a good bit of time on my knees, I realized that I'm not on a mission for her. I'm here for the Lord."

Elder Daniels sighed. He understood why his companion shared the story with him, even when it brought back painful memories.

"Do you still write to her?"

Elder Flores had turned back to the road and signaled the next jeepney to stop. Surprisingly, this one lurched to the side of the road and stopped.

"Yeah, we still write, but just about missionary stuff," he said. "I figure that if she's happy, that's really all that matters." Elder Flores shrugged, "Besides, I know that if I put my faith in the Lord, everything will work out the way He has planned it to be."

Elder Daniels followed his companion into the crowded aisle of the jeepney, careful not to step on anyone's toes with his size eleven shoe. "I wish I could believe that, Comp."

\* \* \* \* \*

A loud knock at the door brought Brother Baribal out of a spell. He'd been welding for six hours but thinking very little about his work. Raising the hood of his mask, he looked at his watch in amazement. The afternoon hours had slipped right on by.

A quick turn of a valve on his propane tank killed the flame from the acetylene torch, bathing the shop in darkness. Working alone, the small light bulb hanging from the ceiling did little to chase the growing shadows. Ironically, all it seemed to do was amplify the need for better lighting.

Through the dusty pane glass of the front door, he could see the silhouette of two individuals against the fading sunset. Walking to the door, he smiled as their mismatched height gave away their identity before he even opened it.

"Good evening, Sir." Elder Flores smiled and extended his hand. José finished wiping his greasy hands on a soiled rag and returned the vigorous handshake.

"Sorry we're late," Elder Daniels offered, noticing by his own watch that they were twenty minutes past their scheduled appointment, "We had a hard time catching a jeepney this late." Brother Baribal immediately noticed the weariness in the young man's voice.

"No problem," he said in Tagalog, "I lost track of time myself." Shaking his head in amazement, he explained, "I've had more work than ever these past couple of weeks and can hardly keep up with orders."

"That's great," Elder Flores exclaimed, "I'm glad to hear that business is picking up again."

Taking a deep breath, Brother Baribal explained, "It's not just picking up, Elders, it's better than it's ever been. I'm thinking about hiring an apprentice." Looking at a small picture of his late wife hanging on the wall, his voice faltered a bit as he continued, "The Lord has really blessed us."

Both missionaries smiled as a feeling of peace settled over the tiny vulcanizing shop. The acrid smell of smoke and metal was barely noticeable and all was silent as the Spirit bore witness to the sincerity of this humble man's words.

Elder Flores expressed his own gratitude silently. There was nothing sweeter than the testimony of a recent convert.

Throwing the dirty rag on his workbench, Brother Baribal broke the silence, "Come on, the children must be going crazy. They do nothing but talk about you two and their new friends at Church."

\* \* \* \* \*

The relationship that often develops between missionaries and those they teach is stronger than any simple friendship. Missionary work is truly a labor of love. For that reason it becomes very difficult when missionaries are transferred, for both the convert *and* the missionary.

By the time a family has entered the waters of baptism they have spent a considerable amount of time with the missionaries. They will have participated in many discussions about the Gospel of Jesus Christ, attended Church on at least three separate occasions and demonstrated a desire to follow Christ. Those truly converted develop their own testimony of the restored gospel. It is a missionary's responsibility to ensure these events have taken place, but these are just the minimum requirements.

Intertwined with these responsibilities is the need to help converts gain fellowship with the members of the ward to which they belong. A missionary knows that regardless of how converted a family or individual may be, if they do not receive the proper fellowship from ward members, the convert will struggle when the missionaries are transferred, too often falling into complete inactivity. The Rosales missionaries were not going to let that happen to the Baribal family.

\* \* \* \* \*

Dante, the youngest of José's children, sat the entire discussion on Elder Daniels' lap. The small boy carefully brushed his hand over the hair that grew on the Elder's forearm. By no means was Elder Daniels overly hairy—he grew an appropriate amount of body hair—but then Americans have a great deal more body hair than Filipinos. Soon after arriving in his first area, Elder Daniels had become accustomed to the fascination Filipino children had with his arms.

The six-year-old child was about to lift up the white sleeve of the Elder's shirt to see just how far up his arm the hair went when Jocelyn gave the boy a pointed look. Embarrassed, Dante went back to stroking the Elder's arms so that all the hair ran smoothly in one direction. It was the only thing keeping Elder Daniels awake.

Two stake missionaries were supposed to be with them on this new member discussion but both had canceled at the last minute. The ward mission leader had been with them on the first two discussions but little support was given by anyone else, aside from the bishop's daughter, Rachel. The lack of new-member support made this third new member discussion somewhat difficult to teach.

"Two priesthood holders are assigned to visit the home of each member at least monthly," Elder Flores explained. "They watch over the family both spiritually and temporally. They present messages and help the head of the family meet the family's needs. In addition, two Relief Society sisters visit each adult woman as visiting sisters"

"So you mean we will still have more missionary lessons?" Jocelyn asked.

"No, not exactly" Elder Flores explained, "home teachers and visiting teachers share a message that is appropriate for your family. Perhaps they might plan their visit around a Monday night and introduce you to Family Home Evening. Or maybe their message will come from one of the Church magazines, or on a particular topic you may be interested in."

"Would they teach me about passing the sacrament?" Eddie asked.

"Oh you just want to walk past Rachel in your new Sunday clothes." Jocelyn teased.

"I do not!" Eddie shot back, turning three shades of red.

"All right you two, that's enough," Brother Baribal ordered in a stern voice. For the past couple weeks he'd heard a great deal of teasing on that subject concerning his oldest son and the bishop's daughter.

"Besides," he added, "Eddie will be too tired from walking back and forth in front of her house every chance he gets!"

With that, the entire room burst out laughing. It was no secret that Eddie had a crush on the bishop's daughter and made nearly any excuse to walk the two kilometers into town to pass by her house in hopes that he might catch a glimpse of her. His younger siblings teased him relentlessly, but not until now had his father joined in the fun.

Eddie didn't think the comment was nearly as funny as everyone else and stewed a moment in silence waiting for the laughter to die down. "Well at least I don't spend an hour in front of the mirror like you do on Sunday mornings practicing my smile for all the Deacons."

Now it was Jocelyn's turn to be embarrassed, but instead of denying it, she simply smiled and looked to the Elders to bail her out.

Elder Daniels shifted Dante on his lap and began the next principle, amused by the bantering but tired and ready to head home. Paraphrasing the principles the best he could in Tagalog, Elder Daniels explained that Church members are concerned for one another and grow by serving their fellow Saints. After explaining that each member is asked to accept Church callings, he bore testimony of the growth he had experienced as President of the Teachers Quorum.

"Brother Baribal, how would you feel about accepting a Church calling?"

"Well, I really don't know what I could do," he replied."

"That's okay," Elder Flores explained. "The Lord knows where He can use your talents." After testifying of the blessings that would come through service, he asked if they could close with a prayer. Kneeling in a large circle, the missionaries were overjoyed as they heard nine-year-old José Jr., utter his very first public prayer. Nervous and fidgety, he forgot how to end the prayer and simply said, "in the name of Jesus Christ . . ." but when no one else opened their eyes, he looked around and said, "The end!" It was the perfect ending to a beautiful discussion.

The first off her knees, Jocelyn went to the cupboard and pulled out a small purse. Pulling out twenty pesos she asked, "Elders, can you stay for refreshments?"

Before either of the missionaries could object, Dante grabbed the money and was out the door, running at full pace to the nearest sari-sari store. Within minutes, he returned with two small plastic bags filled with orange soda, a straw for each, and two individually wrapped packages of soda crackers.

Graciously accepting, the Elders commenced the formality of eating the after-discussion refreshments. Although soda crackers and orange soda were not his favorite, Elder Daniels knew the simple offering, while plain by American standards, was a sacrifice for this family.

It was often difficult eating in front of them, especially when he knew how much twenty pesos meant to a family of seven with only one breadwinner among them. He also knew this was Filipino culture and, if refused, it would be taken as an insult.

After finishing their refreshments, the Elders looked at each other and nodded. It was late and they still had a long walk home.

"Thank you, Sir," Elder Flores said as he stood to leave. Elder Daniels reached for his backpack and nearly fell over as the two youngest boys jumped on his back.

"Dante! Ricardo!" Jocelyn shouted, more like a mother than an older sister. "Can't you see how tired the Elders are tonight?"

After regaining his balance and summoning all the strength he had left, Elder Daniels grabbed each child in his arms. "Oh that's all right. I was hoping for a hug anyway."

Setting the young boys on the ground, he knelt down to get hugs from the remaining small children and shook the hands of the older ones. In reality, he was just grateful he hadn't fallen over. With his energy completely depleted, he wondered if he'd have even tried getting back up.

After their good-byes, Eddie escorted the Elders from the house to the entrance of the barangay. This had become a tradition and although he had never said why, Elder Flores knew that it was for their protection.

At the end of the road stood the sign marking the barangay entrance and it was there that the Elders took leave of their companion. Cautioning them to be careful as they departed company, Eddie disappeared into the night from the direction they'd come.

\* \* \* \* \*

The moon was only a sliver as it hung in the Southeast Asian sky. It's light barely perceptible enough to outline shapes in the thick darkness of night.

Elder Daniels wondered what time it was. Holding his watch a few inches from his face told him nothing. It was past nine o'clock, as most of the lights in the houses they passed were extinguished, but how far past, he didn't know.

All Elder Daniels wanted to do was crawl in bed and sleep. Succumbing to the force that tugged at his lower jaw, he yawned and closed his eyes. He would sleep well tonight—brownout or not.

"C'mon, Comp, let's take the shortcut home."

Elder Flores looked at his companion in surprise. He was about to say, 'It's late. We need to go through town where there's more light,' but the weariness in his companion's face, made him pause. "Okay, but let's be careful."

"Sure," Elder Daniels said without thinking. "Whatever you say." He just wanted to get me home as quickly as he could. What could possibly happen anyway?

\* \* \* \* \*

Six thousand miles away, a chill ran down Ann Daniels' spine. It started at the base of her neck and crawled down her back, spreading over every inch of her body. Even with her hands in a sink of warm dishwater, every strand of hair on the back of her neck stood on end.

The egg-stained plate left over from the morning meal slipped from her fingertips and sunk to the bottom of the sink. It made an ugly sound as it landed atop a pile of dishes in the sink. Ann Daniels' sixth sense was telling her something, and the mother of four was accustomed to listening to her feelings.

As she closed her eyes she once again saw her son waving as he walked through the doors to the MTC. She recalled his white shirt, shiny black shoes and the smile he'd tried to fake. He'd appeared to be brave, but she knew her son—and she knew he was scared. That was the last time she'd seen him and that wasn't the image she wanted to remember.

On more than one occasion she had wondered if the white shirt had faded, if the shoes had lost their store-bought shine, if his missionary nametag still bore the gleam of the reflecting sun. Most of all she wondered if her son was safe.

\* \* \* \* \*

The two Elders walked in silence. A melody of cricket chirps was the only sound that disturbed the dark, still night. The shortcut took them through an empty rice field suffering to regenerate after a less-than-average rainy season. The tender blades, once long and green, were dry and withering in the summer heat.

The nearest dwelling stood over a half-kilometer behind them, and it was this environment that Elder Flores feared the most. Not only was it dark but the ground was also strewn with danger. Either of them could step in a hole and twist an ankle or even a knee. At this time of night help was a long way off and would require an unwelcome separation between the two of them.

"Be careful, Comp," Elder Flores cautioned, "try to step where I step."

Entirely wasted, Elder Daniels complied, wishing to expend no more energy than required.

They walked for 10 minutes in the dark night and Elder Flores began wondering if they were traveling across the wrong field. Soon a tree line appeared marking the end of the field. Immediately before it they came upon a road that would take them through another small barangay, eventually meeting up with the main road not far from their apartment.

Elder Flores breathed easier as they set foot upon the well-traveled road. Although there were no houses yet, he knew they would soon pass a few dwellings and a lamp post or two. Already, they were approaching a cement structure used for cover while waiting for a jeepney or a trike. As they got closer, Elder Flores could see a small amount of light coming from inside and heard a distinctly harsh laugh echo off its walls.

The waiting shade consisted of a cement slab surrounded on three sides with walls and covered by a tin roof sloping to the rear. A ledge protruded from each of the walls forming a bench for seating and the entire structure faced the open road. A large opening in each of the sidewalls allowed its occupants to see an approaching vehicle and yet be sheltered from the sun or rain.

As they approached, the two Elders heard a second and third voice from inside, then a bottle hitting the cement floor. A small candle flickered in the night. Now and again a shadow appeared on the road in front of the waiting shade.

At fifty yards out, Elder Flores knew what was going on inside. He heard foul words echoing from the walls and could smell cigarette smoke in the air. He had no doubt the loiterers were drunk.

Hoping to pass by without making them aware, Elder Flores nudged his companion to walk on the far side of the road. Growing up in a nonmember family, the young Filipino had seen the effects of alcohol in his home, and didn't need to be reminded of its effect on people's behavior.

The men's laughter grew stronger and louder with each passing step. If the waiting shade hadn't been so small, one would have assumed there were at least a dozen drunken men inside. As they approached within ten meters of the structure, Elder Flores unconsciously held his breath, hoping they would be able to pass by without being noticed.

Just then a large man stumbled out of the waiting shade, tripping on a rock and nearly falling in the middle of the road. Standing in the flickering light of the almost spent candle, the man righted himself, holding a bottle of liquor in one hand and a freshly lit cigarette in the other. Extending his arm to the side for balance, he blinked his eyes at the sight of two young men approaching and asked, "Who's this?"

Edging even closer to the opposite side of the road, both missionaries quickened their step but kept an eye on the man, hoping if they ignored him, he would grow disinterested and let them pass by without incident.

The man took a step forward, positioning himself directly in front of the Elders and facing them as they drew near. With a small ditch lining the far side of the road, the two missionaries had no room to step further left. The only way to pass was for Elder Flores to step to the right and walk around the man.

Quickly, for his impaired state, the man turned as they passed, reached into his waistband and pulled out a .45 pistol from under his shirt. The Elders caught the movement out of the corner of their eyes and both turned to see the man raise the gun in front of him. It was aimed directly at Elder Daniels but swayed toward his companion as the man attempted to keep his balance. By this time, some of the other men had seen what was happening and stood at the entrance of the waiting shade, amused by their drunken companion.

For an instant Elder Daniels thought about running. He knew he was the largest target and most likely the one who would be hit if the man pulled the trigger. Closing his eyes, the tall American began to tremble.

Elder Flores, his head half-cocked toward the man, watched out of the corner of his eyes, being sure his companion was where he could see him.

One of the men spoke from the shadows, "Go ahead. Do it."

Elder Daniels drew a deep breath. It would be many moments before he breathed again. Turning to look at his companion, he received a gentle nod. The look on Elder Flores's face was one of complete control. While Elder

Daniels' insides turned, and his hands quivered like a frightened child, Elder Flores displayed no emotion. It was all Elder Daniels could do to turn straight ahead and keep walking. In the stillness of the dark night, he knew there was nothing they could do if the man decided to kill them. The outcome of this situation was no longer in their hands. An arm placed along the small of his back was Elder Flores's way of saying, 'Don't worry. Everything's going to be okay.'

Without looking over their shoulders the two missionaries continued walking. Each praying fervently for the protection of angels they could not see. Step after step, Elder Daniels wondered if he would hear the shot before feeling the bullet take him down. Would he die in the street or make it to a hospital before he bled out? But with each passing step, the sounds of the night returned and nothing more was heard from the group of men they left behind.

Walking the remainder of the way home in silence, both missionaries filled the heavens with the sound of their prayers. Their hearts cried in relief and gratitude. Elder Daniels would never know what happened to the man with the gun, or his partners, but the one thing he did know was that in that moment he had felt true fear. It left an acrid taste in his mouth. Never in his life did he want to feel that way again.

The first thing he did when he got home was open his scriptures to a verse he'd read a week earlier in Doctrine and Covenants, Section 48, verses 87 & 88.

*Behold, I send you out to reprove the world. . . I will go before your face. I will be on your right hand and on your left, and my Spirit shall be in your hearts, and mine angels round about you, to bear you up.*

After showering and brushing his teeth, he walked to the bedroom where his companion sat at his desk writing in his missionary journal.

"Comp, can I ask you something?"

Looking up from the page, Elder Flores nodded his head.

"What happened tonight scared me to death . . . but you . . . you were so calm. Why weren't you afraid?"

Elder Flores's eyes returned to his journal. He picked up the book and handed it to Elder Daniels, pointing to the paragraph he'd just written.

*"Where doubt and uncertainty are, there faith is not, nor can it be. For doubt and faith do not exist in the same person at the same time; so that persons whose minds are under doubts and fears cannot have unshaken confidence; and where unshaken confidence is not, there faith is weak." (Joseph Smith, Jr.)*

Although there was no brown out that night and his body and mind ached with fatigue, it took Elder Daniels over an hour to fall asleep. His mind kept repeating the words of the Prophet.

*"For doubt and faith do not exist in the same person at the same time...where*

*unshaken confidence is not, there faith is weak."*

# CHAPTER 7

*Now faith is the substance of things hoped for, the evidence of things not seen.*

*But without faith it is impossible to please him: for he that cometh to God must believe that he is, and that he is a rewarder of them that diligently seek him.*
*—Hebrews 11: 1 & 6*

Elder Daniels stepped off the jeepney just as the sputtering diesel engine came to a halt. One final plume of smoke filled the air around him. Taking his handkerchief from his back pocket, he wiped his face and neck, leaving a dark smudge of dirt on the white, linen cloth.

Happy to be at their destination, Elder Daniels looked around, noticing for the first time the dozens of missionaries gathered within the chapel gates. Some were standing around talking in small groups; others were sitting on the grass. All, it seemed, were excited for transfers and the opportunities to see old friends and meet new ones. Elder Daniels was excited to see some of his friends from the MTC. He was not, however, excited to be moving to a new area. He had only spent one month in Rosales and with Elder Flores and it seemed he was just starting to understand what it felt like to be a missionary.

"Elder Daniels!" a jovial voice called from over his shoulder. It was a voice he knew well and conjured up memories of the MTC. Turning around he was immediately swept up in a huge bear hug from his old roommate.

Elder Hastings was from Taylorsville, Utah and was every bit the athlete his six-foot, four-inch frame portrayed him to be. Having played every high school sport from football to baseball to golf, he had been heavily recruited by more than a dozen colleges in four different sports. With a future like that, it was difficult for many people, even church members, to understand why he would take a two-year sabbatical to serve a full-time mission.

"How've you been?"

"Pretty good," Elder Daniels replied, "how 'bout you?"

"Excellent!" Elder Hastings declared, "Couldn't be better! I was so excited when I found out we were being transferred to the same zone!"

Elder Daniels couldn't help but smile, Elder Hastings' enthusiasm was contagious and before long a circle of missionaries were standing around listening to him telling stories in his usual, over-animated style. This one happened to recount the rainstorm in which his apartment was flooded in his first area. The zealous missionary had the entire circle hanging on his every word. His body language alone attracted attention with wide gestures and eyebrows that danced up and down. He simulated swimming through chest deep water as he described the river in the Malasiqui apartment.

"But the best thing was performing my very first baptism in our front yard!"

"You're kidding me!" Elder Daniels gasped, caught up in the excitement with everyone else.

"I'm not joking! We'd planned a baptism for that afternoon and were trying to figure out how we were going to get to the church when our baptismal candidate literally swam up the road into our front yard and said he was ready to be baptized."

Throwing his arms up in exasperation he said," I looked at my comp, he looked at me, and we both looked at the lake sitting in our front yard. It was perfect! We took two steps off the front porch, and dunked him!"

With that, the whole group burst out laughing, more at how excited Elder Hastings became through the course of telling the story than anything else. During that brief intermission, Elder Daniels looked over his shoulder, noticing another circle of missionaries, much larger than their own, formed up under a huge Banyan tree next to the chapel.

"Hey, what's going on over there?" he asked.

"That's the zone leader circle," Elder Hastings explained, becoming rather serious as he looked across the courtyard. "At each transfer the mission president gathers his zone leaders and two assistants and holds a meeting with them under that tree."

"What do they talk about?"

"Well, I don't really know…mission stuff I guess. But one thing's for sure, that's a special group of people over there. The spiritual giants of the mission." In a voice of pure admiration he added, "Twenty zone leaders, two assistants and the mission president. Can you imagine how much faith and righteousness is present in that group of missionaries? It's kind of like all the brethren sitting on that stand at General Conference. Right?"

As the smaller group turned back to their own conversation, Elder Daniels found his eyes involuntarily wandering back to the circle of missionaries under the Banyan tree. The solemnness the group itself commanded respect. It was something about the way they held themselves—tall and trustworthy—emulating the grandeur of the mighty tree overhead.

For a moment, Elder Daniels tried to eavesdrop on what was being said.

He tried to pick up on any words that carried across the chapel courtyard. He contemplated walking closer, but quickly discarded the thought. It wasn't his business. He didn't belong there.

Turing back to the missionaries at his side, he couldn't help but feel a yearning to be a part of that circle of missionaries, but the feeling soon passed as he caught sight of Elder Flores approaching.

*Forget it,* he told himself. *You'll never be a part of something like that. That's the kind of place for missionaries like Elder Flores.*

Saying good-bye to Elder Flores was harder than Elder Daniels expected. Although they had only spent one month together in Rosales, both missionaries knew their friendship would last a lifetime.

As soon as President Hart dismissed the zone leaders, the ten jeepneys that littered the chapel parking area fired up and within five minutes the last was heading out the gate. Elder Daniels was on a jeepney heading for the San Fernando zone, where he would be assigned to one of the smaller areas, called Lingsat. Next to him sat Elder Hastings who would be dropped off in his new area only three kilometers up the road.

Pulling into the driveway of the missionary apartment, Elder Hastings jumped out and met his new companion halfway up the walk. As the small Filipino stuck out his hand to greet his new companion, Elder Hastings set down his bamboo backpack and threw his arms around the surprised missionary. Realizing how much Elder Hastings worked to make his companionships great, Elder Daniels couldn't help but smile and promised himself he would do the same.

The rest of the trip was much quieter as some missionaries slept and others pulled out letters they'd received from their families back home. Since Elder Daniels didn't know anyone else in the zone, he soon found himself replaying the events leading up to transfers, events that had taken him completely by surprise.

\* \* \* \* \*

Elder Daniels had been aware of transfers approaching but since he and Elder Flores had met President Hart's challenge to baptize six people and show him the area was productive, he never expected transfers would involve either he or his companion. It wasn't until his interview with the mission president at the zone conference just two days earlier that he learned the area was being closed despite their success. President Hart simply explained that he didn't have enough missionaries in the mission to keep it open any longer.

The next day and a half was spent turning records over to the ward mission leader, moving the few furniture items they had in the apartment to that of the zone leaders, and saying good-bye to the friends and converts they made in those four short weeks. It broke his heart having to tell the Baribal family the news although they took it well and promised to send word from time to time through other missionaries. Before he knew it, it was Friday morning and he and Elder Flores were on a jeepney to Bauang with the zone leaders and the other missionaries being transferred.

As he looked back now, the process had been very smooth and efficient. The president prayed about and decided who was being transferred, they were informed either by him or through the assistants and zone leaders and assignments were made for the non-transferring companion to work with another companionship or missionary until the replacement arrived.

The morning of transfers the zone leaders rented a jeepney and driver and picked up all the transferring missionaries. From some areas it was a short ride to the central meeting place at the base of the mountains below Baguio. For others, like those in the most northern and southern provinces, the missionaries started their journey at 4:00 A.M. to get to the transfer point by 9:00 A.M.

What Elder Daniels hadn't expected was such a short good-bye with his companion at the end of transfers. He and Elder Flores had shared a quick hug, a firm handshake and a promise to see each other again. With that, each boarded their jeepney, Elder Flores heading north to Candon and Elder Daniels to Lingsat. Sitting in the jeepney as it rumbled down the highway, Elder Daniels wondered if he would ever get used to the quick pace of missionary life.

Other than what he had seen in Manila, most of what he knew of the Philippines consisted of nipa huts and rice patties. For that reason, the multistory buildings and urban streets of San Fernando seemed almost foreign as they passed by.

Along the crowded main street where the market met the business district, vendors used every square inch available to set up their stands and display whatever product or service they marketed. On almost every street corner he saw watch repair booths, bread carts, shoeshine stands and food vendors, all fighting for the space in which they conducted business.

From the large retail clothing shops to the tiny corner pharmacies, it seemed as if everyone had a hand in commerce. Stopping at the first traffic light Elder Daniels had seen in four months, mobile vendors, selling everything from newspapers to chewing gum, immediately swarmed the jeepney. Elder Daniels, one of the three remaining missionaries on the jeepney, politely shook his head at an old man dangling small bags of quail eggs in front of him. The man, as persistent as the flies that circled his face, didn't move, expecting Elder Daniels to change his mind at any moment.

Knowing no other way to say "no," Elder Daniels turned toward the front of the jeepney hoping the man would take the hint. Up in the front seat, the driver called over a cigarette vendor asking for two "sticks." Placing one behind his ear and the other between his lips, the driver looked into the rear view mirror just in time to lock eyes with Elder Daniels. Remembering his Mormon passengers, he took the cigarette from his mouth and placed it behind his ear, next to the first.

As Elder Daniels suspected, the man had been approached by more than one missionary at the transfer point and had started asking questions, at least up until the point that he lit up a cigarette and was asked either to extinguish it or walk outside the chapel gates. At that point, he had put the cigarette out on his shoe hoping not to offend those who were paying him a full day's wages for a half-day of work.

As the light turned green, Elder Daniels stretched his legs, cramped from the two-hour ride from the chapel. Taking in new sights and sounds along the way, he felt a surge of exhilaration, knowing his was the next stop along the way. Though it was difficult leaving Elder Flores, Elder Daniels had a great bit to look forward to in San Fernando. Not only was he going to have access to a real city with modern plumbing and McDonald's, he was also going to experience his first assignment as a district leader.

\* \* \* \* \*

Gelyn Nguyen frowned at the condition of her most prized possession. Its worn paperback cover had long since faded from the deep blue color she so dearly loved. Its corners were creased and torn. On top of that, the once bright, gold lettering displayed none of the brilliance it once contained and the pages bore the wear and tear of many hours of careful study. Still, The Book of Mormon was hers and was never far from her side.

Holding the book in her tired and callused hands, her eyes left its pages to gaze at the only picture hanging on the wall of her nipa hut. A picture of the Manila Temple.

Sister Nguyen knew every detail of that picture by heart. She often spent moments each day sitting cross-legged in that very spot. With her children at school and her husband out collecting wood, her eyes were continually drawn to the framed postcard given her by a departing missionary. Although with her responsibilities of caring for a family with three small boys, as well as providing some of the family's income, these moments of solitude were rare.

With a sigh, Sister Nguyen wondered if that goal would ever be realized. She had been a member for three years and was not yet endowed. No matter how many times she asked, the answer was always the same—the trip to Manila was far too expensive.

Opening The Book of Mormon to its cover page, Sister Nguyen looked at the family picture she'd taped to the inside of the front cover. The Elders had given her the picture of her baptismal day. Dressed in white, she'd stood in front of the chapel with the two Elders on her one side, and her entire family on the other. In reality the picture depicted the relationship that had remained to this day. She was always caught in the middle—pulled in one direction by her love for her family, the other direction by her burning testimony of the restored gospel.

Looking back at the picture on her wall, she mentally transposed one picture upon the other. What she saw was the same vision she'd imagined many times—her family standing in front of the temple alongside the missionaries.

The only difference was that in her mind she saw her entire family dressed in white.

* * * * *

Unlike a barangay, Lingsat is a prospering township more accurately referred to as a "barrio." Although it acts independently of the larger city, Lingsat is considered a subsection of San Fernando, and for one traveling from the inner streets of the provincial capital, it is difficult to distinguish boundaries. One may not even realize he'd left San Fernando and entered Lingsat if he didn't notice the welcome sign posted along the road.

Although the businesses thin out around that point and fields replace government buildings, the houses are still abundant with nipa huts and cinder block dwellings replacing the cement homes found in the inner city. The apartment where the missionaries lived was not at all in Lingsat, but 5 kilometers south, well into the developed sections of San Fernando.

Nestled into the urban landscape atop a small rise, the small two-bedroom house, rented to The Church of Jesus Christ of Latter-day Saints, provided more comfort than either of his two previous apartments. To Elder Daniels surprise, the Lingsat missionaries shared an apartment with the San Fernando zone leaders.

The rented jeepney came to a halt directly in front of Elder Daniels' new home. Surveying the neighborhood, he knew this was a "wealthier" area of town, even if only by Filipino standards.

The first thing he noticed was that a yard and fence surrounded each home—some having actual grass, which was considered a luxury in the Philippines.

Even the fences declared the prosperity of the inhabitants. Elder Daniels noticed that these fences were made of actual steel. At the top of each section, pointed wrought-iron spires deterred trespassing and prevented unauthorized entry. Most of what he'd seen in less-populated areas consisted of shoddy walls of hollow bricks haphazardly cemented together. Although they too were protected with pointed objects, in all but a few cases that consisted of nothing more than broken soda bottles cemented along the top edge. Nipa huts usually only had barbed wire strung around the immediate property—and only then if the inhabitants raised goats, pigs or chickens.

As Elder Daniels pulled the front gate open, a shrill cry cut through the air. The sidewalk shrieked in protest as metal scraped across concrete. Elder Daniels felt a shiver throughout his body. It reminded him of someone scraping their fingernails across a chalkboard.

A narrow walkway lined with red-leafy bushes spanned the distance between the gate and the house. At its end, three stairs lead up to a small porch extending along the front of the house.

With a large seventy-pound suitcase in each hand and his bamboo pack on his back, Elder Daniels was careful not to step off the path as he waddled up the sidewalk toward the front door. Looking at the stairs ahead of him, he soon came to the realization that he was going to have difficulty tackling them with his heavy load. Just as he dropped one suitcase to the ground, the front door flew open and a very short, and very dark, Filipino rushed to his side. Hefting the abandoned baggage on his knee, he greeted the tall American. "Kumusta Elder, ako si Elder Reyes."

Remembering what he'd seen Elder Hastings do, Elder Daniels dropped the other suitcase and wrapped his arms around his new companion.

"It's good to meet you!" he replied. "I understand this is your first area. How have you liked it so far?"

The look of confusion that appeared on Elder Reyes' face took Elder Daniels by surprise. Figuring that perhaps the small Filipino might be hard of hearing, Elder Daniels tried again, this time speaking a bit louder and slower.

"I've heard this is a good area. Who was your trainer?"

Again nothing. His look of confusion turned to one of embarrassment as the poor Filipino lowered his head, diverting his eyes from Elder Daniels' gaze. A hand on his shoulder made Elder Daniels realize that someone was standing behind him. Turning around, he inquisitively looked to Elder Neil, his new zone leader, for help.

Elder Neil took his hand off Elder Daniels' shoulder and walked over to the uncomfortable Filipino. Putting his arm around him, he whispered something in his ear at which point the young Elder smiled and walked toward the jeepney to assist Elder Neil's companion.

Turning back to Elder Daniels, he stuck out his hand and said, "Welcome to San Fernando. I guess you've met your new companion."

"Yeah, but I must have said something wrong."

"No," Elder Neil commented, "It's not what you said, but perhaps how you said it. You see, Elder Reyes doesn't speak a word of English."

# CHAPTER 8

*Ye cannot behold with your natural eyes, for the present time, the design of your God concerning those things, which shall come hereafter, and the glory which shall follow after much tribulation. For after much tribulation come the blessings. Wherefore the day cometh that ye shall be crowned with much glory; the hour is not yet, but is nigh at hand.*

*—D&C 58:4*

Elder Daniels took his time at breakfast knowing that the next hour of companionship study would be long and tedious. The past three days with his new companion had proven exhausting. Not in the fact that they had physically worked any harder than before, but the entire relationship took more out of him mentally and emotionally than he'd ever thought possible.

To this point Elder Daniels believed he was gaining ground in regards to learning Tagalog. Although admittedly slow, he had made some progress considering five months earlier he had never heard a Tagalog word spoken in his life. He wasn't exactly teaching in Tagalog, not in the sense that excludes reading translations he'd transcribed with a Tagalog dictionary from *Preach My Gospel*, but he was doing the best he could.

Now, with the entire communication process depending on it, he realized how little he knew or understood. Since Elder Reyes spoke less English than Elder Daniels did Tagalog, he found that being able to memorize discussion principles didn't equate to being able to study together as a companionship. He never expected that he'd be translating English to Tagalog for anyone else but himself.

Although he liked what he saw in Elder Reyes, the first few days of their companionship were painful. Elder Reyes was from a very remote town on the southernmost island of the Philippines. As it turned out, Elder Daniels discovered, the first time he had ever seen an American was at the Missionary

Training Center in Manila. While most schools in the Philippines begin teaching English at the elementary level, Elder Reyes came from an area so remote that English was neither necessary nor appropriate. The area his companion came from was called Jolo, and not only was it remote and secluded, it was also predominately Muslim.

In the Philippines, people are judged upon two common stereotypes. First, considering that most well educated individuals belong to the upper class, employed in air-conditioned offices, Filipinos who work under the blazing sun and have dark complexions are generally considered less affluent. Second, since the affluent are less likely to go hungry, if a person is "mataba," meaning fat, that person is thought to be rich.

Having grown up in the rice fields in the Province of Mindanao, Elder Reyes was darker than most Filipinos. Though he stood only five-feet tall and weighed close to 170 pounds, he was an exception to the rule about fat people being rich. Elder Reyes simply loved to eat.

\* \* \* \* \*

Jornacio Reyes, the second of seven children, lived a life of hard labor. From his earliest years, he knew little more than harvesting rice. At the time when other children his age were entering elementary school, Jornacio was in the fields harvesting rice. Together, with a team of untiring water buffalo, he and his father worked the land to provide income for a growing family.

From field to feast, the manner of harvesting rice in the Philippines is far from the production-line process known by the Western world. There are no planting machines, no combines, and no heated air dryers—it is all done by hand. Harvesting rice is a backbreaking work requiring just the right amount of sun, water, and patience.

As with any agricultural endeavor, rice harvesting begins with sowing seeds. Sometimes they are planted directly in the paddies, more often than not, they are sown in a small nursery field or a well-established rice patty where they spend their first thirty days sprouting into seedlings. After growing about 20 centimeters in a protected environment, the young seedlings are transplanted into the fields where they are given space to grow without overcrowding the spreading roots. Transplanting is exhausting, tiring work that requires standing in water above the ankles and repeatedly bending over to insert the small plants into the muddy soil.

As the seedlings continue to grow, irrigation is the main concern for farmers. Too little water or too much water is detrimental to growth. With enough sunshine and a growing season uninterrupted by devastating typhoons, the mature plants take on a golden-yellow color, indicating the new grains are ready to harvest. With no mechanical reaper in most areas, Filipinos use a sharp knife or sickle to cut the stalks, binding them in bundles for transporting and storage.

The edible portion of the rice plant consists only of the grain. The panicles, or rice stalks, require threshing in order to separate the grains. This can be done by first drying the bundles in the sun and then pounding them against a hard surface.

Drying rice is critical because if the moisture content is too high, the freshly harvested grains will spoil. In most places, the grains are spread out to dry wherever space is available, from outdoor basketball courts to sections alongside major highways. It is not at all uncommon to see the shoulders of well-traveled roads covered by a thin layer of grain drying in the hot sun.

Before the grains can be eaten, harvesters must separate the rice kernel from the hull, or chaff. This is most commonly accomplished by placing the grains on a mortar in which they are pounded with a pestle. The hull debris is separated from the grains by winnowing, or tossing the pounded mixture into the wind from a shallow basket. In this manner the hull drifts away in the breeze as the rice falls back into the basket to be collected in large bags for storage and transportation.

The work is demanding and tedious. At any one time a farmer may have rice in the sowing stage, some in the harvesting stage, and other in the drying stage. In that way, it is a circuitous process that only stops when the weather is uncooperative or when it's too dark to work.

When all is said and done, a kilo of rice, equivalent to 2.2 pounds, sells for about 15 pesos on the open market, or about forty cents.

For a struggling family with six children, farming provides a very meager income. However, in areas like Mindanao where educational opportunities are rarely afforded to everyone, farming was the means of income for the Reyes family and young Jornacio.

Having come from a long line of rice farmers, Jornacio's father despised the thought of another generation condemned to the soggy existence of sowing, seeding, and harvesting. Every day that he watched the younger children dress and walk to school in their green and white uniforms, an inner voice chastised him for negating the opportunity for his oldest son. Yet, although it pained him, he knew he needed his son's help.

Jornacio never complained. He understood at an early age that he shared a responsibility in providing as much help to his family as possible—even if that meant he received no formal education. For that reason when it was too dark to work, he and his father sat around the family table and studied the schoolbooks of his younger siblings. By candlelight, he learned to read, write, and do simple arithmetic. While working in the fields his father taught him all he knew about Filipino history. His father wasn't the most knowledgeable teacher, but he was patient and determined that his son would not live his life in a rice patty.

With Jornacio, there was never a question about his responsibilities—only obedience. A natural optimist, overflowing with enthusiasm, he attacked every task with his best effort. As he got older, he found himself teaching his father what his father could not teach him.

When it came time to graduate high school, although he had never attended a day of formal schooling, he was not more than a year or two behind his peers in all subjects. Because southern Mindanao is estranged from the government in Manila, English is rarely spoken and few children study it at all in provincial schools. At the age of eighteen, Jornacio wasn't behind his peers in English, but he wasn't ahead of them either.

With all the harvesting to be done and the minimal time for other subjects, neither he nor his father had the time to tackle the difficult language. In fact, aside from working the fields and home study, Jornacio had little time for anything else.

When he did get a few minutes to himself, he often headed to the tiny bamboo meetinghouse down the road. Although it consisted of only one room with partitions that were drawn shut after sacrament meeting to allow for individual classrooms, the small meetinghouse was an oasis for many of the branch members—especially the youth. Every once in a while he was able to attend a seminary class or activity, but most of the time he just showed up to see who might be there to socialize.

The only time Jornacio ever resented his situation in life was when his friends began receiving their mission calls. It was something he'd never spoken to his parents about because he knew there was no way they could support him financially. And from what he'd heard in social circles, the small branch was unable to subsidize the cost. As cheerfully as he could, Jornacio accepted this and promised himself and the Lord that if he couldn't serve a full-time mission, he would take every opportunity he could to split with the missionaries in his own branch. Though this was far less than he yearned to do, it did serve to partially satisfy his desire to preach the gospel.

It was on his nineteenth birthday that his entire life changed. Being somewhat downcast in that this birthday represented none of what it would mean to his peers who were counting the days before they left for the MTC in Manila, his father looked at his mother and said, "It's time."

So on a rainy July morning nineteen years to the day after Jornacio was born, Brother Reyes gathered his family to the same table that he and his son had studied upon for years. As soon as the family was gathered, he disappeared into the adjoining room of the two-room nipa hut.

Jornacio looked around the table at the faces of his five sisters who apparently were in on the surprise. Not one of them could sit still for a moment and their snickers and grins only made him more curious. Sister Reyes, as excited as her daughters, continually wrung her hands, causing them to go white around the knuckles.

"What's this all about?" Jornacio inquired.

"You'll see!"

After a few more minutes, his father returned with a small shoebox under his arm. Taking his place at the head of the table, Brother Reyes sat across from his son, pausing a moment before delivering the words he'd been rehearsing for years.

"Son, your mother and I couldn't be more proud of you. I've never known a better worker or one who gave of himself more selflessly. You've proven yourself worthy of being called a man, and now it is time to get you on your way." Pushing the small cardboard shoebox across the table, Brother Reyes said, "This is for you."

Unlike most youth his age that would probably have ripped open the shoebox without hesitation, Jornacio took a moment to look at the faces of those around him. Though he had no idea what was inside, their expressions alone told him of the importance of its contents.

When he could wait no longer, Jornacio lifted the lid and set it aside. Sitting on top of a brown paper bag was an envelope.

"What's this?" he asked, as he opened the envelope.

The title on the first page read, "Application for Serving as a Full-time Missionary for The Church of Jesus Christ of Latter-day Saints." The growing excitement soon turned to confusion as he looked at his parents for an explanation, but even as he did, he knew the answer lay in the brown paper bag he had yet to open.

Setting the letter aside, he slowly reached for the bag.

"Hurry and open it!" his youngest sister yelled, no longer able to withstand the suspense.

Pulling the bag from the box, Jornacio peeled the edges apart and looked inside. In less than a second, his bottom jaw dropped and a roomful of giggles and screams erupted from his five younger sisters.

With a sweep of his arm, Jornacio pushed the box aside and turned the paper bag over, spilling the contents onto the table. Before him, in a large pile lay a mound of paper bills. In every denomination from five pesos to five hundred, Jornacio beheld more money than he'd ever seen in his life.

His voice no more than a whisper, he asked. "Where did all this money come from?"

A tear ran down his mother's cheek as she said, "It's for your mission. Your father and I have been putting money aside for a very long time."

"A l-l-long time?" he stuttered. "This must have taken a lifetime to save."

"Well not our lifetime," she conceded, her hand moving to cover her husband's, "but maybe yours."

Staring at the money before him, countless memories flooded his mind. He remembered countless nights his parents had gone to bed hungry after feeding the children and having nothing left for them. He remembered the cold rainstorms he and his sisters had endured, huddling together under a single blanket while the bone-chilling wind blew rain through the thin slats of bamboo on their home. He remembered his mother working by candlelight, mending and patching the worn-out school uniforms of one sister so that it could be passed on to another.

As the memories paraded through his mind he tried to imagine what it must have taken for his parents to set aside money that could have been used to improve their family's conditions.

"I can't take this. It's not mine."

"Yes! Yes, it is!" his youngest sister cried.

"She's right," his father agreed, "you've worked your entire life for it and nobody deserves it more than you."

"But father, who will help you in the fields?"

"We will!" His sisters cried in unison.

"We'll get by," his mother said with a smile. "Especially if we have one less mouth to feed!"

A hush fell over the room as Jornacio struggled to comprehend what had just happened. His father finally broke the silence, closing the matter for good.

"Go my son, and serve the Lord. In a way, you will be serving a mission for all of us."

\* \* \* \* \*

The only way to describe Elder Daniels' mood as he approached his new companion sitting on the couch was melancholy. Slumping into the worn cushion, Elder Daniels felt about as lifeless as the donated couch which bellowed dust as he plopped down on the vinyl cushion. Moving to a new area had proven exciting and adventurous at first but the novelty had worn off quickly as the battle to communicate with his new companion began.

Looking back on his last companionship, Elder Daniels realized how spoiled he'd been. The truth was, Elder Flores spoke better English than he did. Because of that, he'd become reliant on his companion speaking English in their everyday conversations. The only time he'd spoken Tagalog was when they were teaching. No longer an option, he found himself struggling for motivation.

Simply planning the day's schedule was a difficult task. For the most part, Elder Daniels tried to let Elder Reyes lead him through the area, tagging along as if he were on a tour. After a couple days of that, the passage of time slowed and he began to feel as bored as he'd been in his first area.

From what he could gather, their teaching pool consisted of about seventeen people. Three of their contacts were single young females studying at the Lorma College for Nursing. The others were part-member families and a young couple referred to them by a stake missionary.

On a positive note, all of their investigators were strong prospective members. Part-member families were particularly favorable if those that are members are also active in the Church. Single females are not usually great candidates, but these three lived together in the dormitory and met with the Elders as a group with an accompanying female stake missionary. Furthermore, any referral by a member is a good sign, because, like all of their contacts, fellowship with an active church member was already established. It was also positive that some of them were quite far along in the discussions and had even attended church two or more times.

Closing his eyes as he sat on the couch, Elder Daniels realized the only problem of any significance was the difficulty he was having communicating with his companion. But even that, he admitted, showed some progress.

Many of Elder Reyes' attributes were promising. From his unabashed enthusiasm for missionary work, to his ever-present smile, Elder Reyes was obviously in the mission field for the right reasons. Elder Daniels had been told a little of his background from President Hart, enough to know he came from a predominantly Muslim area of the Philippines, but from a strong, two-generation member family. The part that Elder Daniels realized now had been either intentionally, or unintentionally, left out was the language barrier.

Having finished his personal study a few moments before, Elder Reyes had already turned to the page he'd dog-eared in his copy of *Preach My Gospel*. He was eagerly awaiting the start of their companionship study. Opening his own missionary guide to a page he'd tabbed from the previous day, Elder Daniels contemplated skipping the companionship study all together. Even that, however, would be difficult since he didn't know how to explain it to his companion. Just as he was about to start reading the first paragraph, the door to the zone leaders' shared bedroom opened.

"Would you mind if we joined you this morning?" Elder Neil asked.

Seeing a silver lining in the raincloud overhead, Elder Daniels brightened immediately. "Not at all," he said, answering for the both of them.

Pulling up a couple of chairs, Elder Neil's companion quickly explained to Elder Reyes what they were going to do. Nodding, his chubby face, Elder Reyes seemed pleased. For a moment, Elder Daniels wondered whether his companion was capable of expressing any other emotion.

Elder Neil was a little shorter than Elder Daniels but obviously a few years older by the dark stubble on his face. Even after shaving an hour or two before, the shadow on his face was a witness to the daily battle between beard and razor that played out in front of a mirror and a cold sink of water.

Up until now, Elder Daniels had only seen the zone leaders a few times since arriving in San Fernando, and even then, only in passing as they came and went. The zone leaders were usually out the door early to work with other missionaries in the zone. The only other time they'd seen them more than a few minutes was his first night in the area when they all returned home from proselyting at the same time.

That first night Elder Daniels and Elder Reyes had returned home at about 7:00 P.M. so that he could unpack and get situated in his new apartment. He learned that the zone leaders typically retired to the apartment a couple of hours early on days they worked with other missionaries so that they could complete their personal and companionship study.

At 9:00 P.M., Elder Neil was working out in the living room with a homemade barbell made of a steel pipe and cement. He'd made the barbell in a previous area by purchasing cement mix and preparing it in a large bucket. He'd then inserted a robust length of steel pipe in the center of the bucket before it dried and repeated the process on the other end to form the weights.

Just happy to be around another American, Elder Daniels declined the offer to join in, preferring to sit on the couch and relax. From the discussion that followed, Elder Daniels learned that Elder Neil was a native of California, but had served four years in the Army before sending in his mission papers. Elder Neil had been honorably discharged from the Army but planned to pursue an officer's commission when he returned and use his G.I. Bill benefits to earn a college degree.

From the way he spoke, Elder Daniels was certain Elder Neil was in his mid-twenties. There was an unmistakable maturity in the way he held himself that most eighteen and nineteen-year old missionaries lacked. Beyond that, there was an attitude of humility in his voice and a well-defined sense of purpose. It was apparent that Elder Neil knew why he was here, and that he served with an eye single to the glory of God.

These were the impressions Elder Daniels remembered as he slipped into bed that first night. In the quiet of the late night hour, he compared himself to Elder Neil and realized how different they really were. Drifting off to sleep, he thought again about the zone leaders gathered under the Banyan tree at transfers. As sleep stretched forth its welcome arms, Elder Daniels envisioned Elder Neil standing in the circle and it was perfectly clear why he fit in.

\* \* \* \* \*

Gathering eight semi-rigid strips of thinly sliced bamboo, Gelyn Nguyen placed them in a circle, overlapping one another to form sixteen spokes. Her delicate fingers worked quickly but purposefully. The bamboo strips formed a hub from which the crisscrossed strands extended like the spokes of a bicycle wheel. As soon as they were properly spaced, she began weaving the bamboo strips over and under one another to form the base and sides of a basket.

On one side of her lay a pile of additional bamboo strips and on her other side were three stacks of nearly finished baskets. The baskets were sturdy, beautiful, and would soon be ready to be picked up and sent to San Fernando for export. The work was painstakingly tedious and not substantially lucrative, but few commodities produced in the Philippines attracted a price worthy of the invested labor involved.

Gelyn started each day the same way—gathering the hollow bamboo shafts that lay in a pile next to the nipa hut and cutting them into one-meter segments. Taking her hatchet and splitting them down the middle again and again and again, she was left with individual strips about 1/16 of an inch in thickness. With the skill she'd learned in childhood, advanced through her adult life, and perfected in middle age, she dipped the strands in water and wove them until the almost finished basket was ready for a handle.

The Nguyen's entrepreneurial business was a joint effort, her husband, Juan, often working right by her side. His duties, however, also included gathering the bamboo that he'd haul back in a cart pulled by an old caribou. Every once in a while she'd stop her work to see if she could hear the sound of bamboo dragging behind the cart telling her Juan was nearby.

Looking at her watch, she was pleased to see how quickly she'd progressed through the stack this particular morning. She already had three nearly completed baskets sitting at her side. The only thing they needed were handles to finish them off. Having the stronger hands to pull them tight, that task was left for Juan.

Slowly, she extended her legs after squatting over her work for the past two hours. A sharp crack in one knee sent a shiver through her entire body. There was no denying it any longer—her body was simply wearing out. Already forty-years old, she recognized the physical decline of her mortality, especially whenever she sat too long in any one position.

A cheerful laugh from outside drew a smile to her face. There was no mistaking the high-pitched squeal of her youngest son, Juan Jr. Quietly, she poked her head out the open doorway to see him playing hopscotch just a few yards away. The lines he'd drawn in the packed dirt were barely visible from her vantage point, but she was pleased with how well he entertained himself with a simple game. His back toward her, he had no idea he was being watched.

With a gentle toss, the flat rock landed in the sixth box and bounced once, barely coming to rest in the intended square. With three quick jumps, alternating between feet, he landed softly with a foot firmly planted in the fourth and fifth squares. He looked at the rock in the sixth square quizzically, realizing how large he'd drawn the hopscotch pattern. It was a one-meter leap to get to the seventh and eighth squares.

Summoning all the courage his six-year-old body possessed, he bent over at the waist and threw his arms in front of him as if attempting the broad-jump. His mother watched him intently—praying he would make it. While to most children his age it was a simple game, it was anything but a game for this child. Juan Jr. was blessed with an array of physical challenges. To Juan Jr. it represented much, much more—almost as much as it meant to his mother who grew weary of the way others treated him. When he was playing with a smile on his face, they both forgot that he was the handicapped little boy with whom none of the other children wanted to play.

The jump took all the concentration he had. As he took flight, he shut his eyes, harnessing all his strength in an attempt to clear the square. A second later and it was over, but even after he touched the ground, his eyes remained closed. Balancing on his tiptoes, he arched his back and extended his arms out to the side for balance. Despite his best effort his momentum was not enough and he fell back on his heels, only then opening his eyes to see the result.

Holding her breath, Gelyn Nguyen put her hands to her face. She was just far enough away that she wasn't certain whether he'd made it or not. When his head dropped and his shoulders sagged forward, she knew. His right foot was touching the very top of the square he so desperately wanted to clear. It broke her heart to see him put so much effort into something and fail.

Fail? Was that the right word?

*'No!'* she told herself. *'He didn't fail!'*

Sensing the presence of someone watching him, Juan Jr. turned around. When his eyes met those of his mother's, he saw tears on her face and he didn't understand why. Not that it mattered if he had. There was nothing he could say that could stay her tears. He did understand the emotion and wanted to tell her it was not a big deal—that it didn't matter all that much to him if he'd made the leap or not.

Nevertheless, that wasn't going to happen. Juan Jr. had never spoken a word in all his life. A cleft palette—a birth defect leaving him with the bones on the roof of his mouth unattached—made speaking impossible.

Harnessing every bit of emotional strength she could find, Sister Nguyen pasted a smile on her face. It wasn't real and she knew it, but she had to communicate something. She didn't like showing her emotions as much as she did. Reciprocating the smile, Juan Jr. turned back around and continued with his game.

As she attempted to return to her work, her hands didn't move. She sat alone and motionless for a long time. All the progress she'd made that morning seemed inconsequential.

For what? A few pesos? The things of real importance in her life were her family and her testimony. The value of those immaterial blessings was symbolized in the picture hanging on the wall directly across from her.

To Gelyn Nguyen the Manila Temple represented something apart from this world. It symbolized all that she held dear to her. It also symbolized her Savior's promise—that one day her mortal son would take on immortality and have a perfect body to compliment his perfect spirit.

Closing her eyes to hold back the tears, Gelyn Nguyen prayed. She prayed for strength. She prayed for patience. She prayed for endurance. She knew that one day she would be able to sit with her son and have a conversation for the very first time.

\* \* \* \* \*

Elder Daniels and Elder Reyes sat on the couch and the zone leaders had brought in chairs from the kitchen. Never before had Elder Daniels had a group companionship study. It was actually turning out to be quite enjoyable. Instead of simply reading a few pages out of *Preach My Gospel* and asking each other questions, the zone leaders were telling stories from their missions to illustrate the principles discussed in the manual.

For the past forty-five minutes, they'd been discussing the importance of asking for referrals from members as well as people in their teaching pool. Elder Tolentino, Elder Neil's companion, had told about how he and his companion had opened a new area on a Friday and had fifty-two contacts by Sunday, thirty-three of them attending the sacrament service they held in their missionary apartment. Elder Neil was sharing a story about an old, expat American that they'd happened across in Lingayen who had invited them in to hear a discussion.

"So as we finished teaching about the Holy Ghost, the spirit was just overwhelming!" he said. "It was awesome. My comp and I both shared our testimonies and this old, tattooed, ex-Navy guy became so emotional I thought he was going to cry!"

"So I asked him, 'how do you feel about the message we just shared with you?' Shaking his head in amazement, he said with a deep southern drawl, 'Well now, fellas, that was just real nice. I'll say, just real nice!'"

Elder Neil sat back in his chair, shrugging his shoulders as if that sort of thing happened every day. "So we committed him to baptism right there after the first discussion."

Elder Daniels was shaking his head. "Wow! That must have been great!"

"It was," Elder Neil continued, "right up until the point that we asked him for a referral."

"What happened?" Elder Daniels pried.

"Well, I asked him if he knew anyone that we could share our message with and he just sat there. For a second I was thinking maybe he didn't hear me. He just kept thinking. Finally, he jumped up and yelled. 'I *do* know someone.'"

Elder Neil was already laughing before he could finish the story. "He said, 'My neighbor across the street,'" Elder Neil continued, finishing all but the last word, "'cause he sure is an awn'ry son of a . . .!'"

Elder Daniels and Elder Tolentino burst out in one loud roar of laughter, but Elder Reyes just sat there smiling, waiting for the interpretation. A few minutes later and he, too, was laughing with his companions.

As the laughter finally subsided, Elder Neil turned to his companion and asked, "What do you think about splitting up for the last fifteen minutes, you with Elder Reyes and me with Elder Daniels?

"Okay," Elder Tolentino agreed, going right along with the plan they'd discussed in their bedroom earlier that morning. Together, the two Filipinos rose and went into the kitchen.

Getting a little bit more serious, Elder Neil turned to Elder Daniels and asked, "So how are things with you and Elder Reyes?"

Elder Daniels let out a long sigh as the frustrations he'd momentarily forgotten about returned and deflated his spirit.

"Well, it isn't easy. I mean, I don't speak much Tagalog and he doesn't speak much English."

Elder Neil nodded, "I noticed that."

Seeing an opportunity to vent, Elder Daniels asked, "Why would President Hart put the two of us together? I mean, doesn't he know we can't even talk to each other, let alone work as a companionship and teach the gospel?"

Elder Neil chuckled. "I'm sure President Hart knows."

Throwing his arms in the air in disgust, Elder Daniels asked, "Then why is he torturing us?"

Sensing Elder Daniels' frustration, Elder Neil moved from the chair to the couch, positioning himself a little closer to the younger missionary. "Let me explain something. But before I do, I need to know something."

"What's that?"

"Do you believe that Jesus Christ is the Son of God?"

Completely caught off guard, Elder Daniels paused, fully expecting Elder Neil to crack a smile or start laughing. When Elder Neil's face didn't change expressions, Elder Daniels replied, a bit shortly, "Of course I do!"

"Do you believe your call to serve a mission came from a true Prophet of God?"

"Yes," he replied matter-of-factly, "but what does that have to do with me and Elder Reyes?"

"How did you feel when you opened your mission call and you read the words, 'you are hereby called to serve in the Philippines, Baguio Mission?'"

Not understanding where the conversation was going, but hoping that the end was near, Elder Daniels answered, "Well, I was excited, I guess."

"Did you ever think for a moment that the Prophet made a mistake? That maybe the Lord wanted you to serve somewhere else?"

"Of course not."

Sitting up, Elder Neil leaned in a bit and asked, "Then why is it so difficult to think that the Lord might want you to serve here, at this time, with Elder Reyes?"

Elder Daniels looked at him in shock, more at his forthrightness than anything else.

"Is it that hard to imagine that perhaps He knows it will be difficult for you, but also knows you can learn the language if you really want to. And that maybe, just maybe, this experience will prepare you for something greater in the future."

Elder Daniels said nothing.

"Elder, I've spoken with President Hart and with Elder Flores. I know what you are capable of becoming. President Hart knows what you are capable of doing. There's no doubt in my mind that the Lord knows what you are capable of accomplishing in you mission."

"Then someone needs to tell me, because I don't know what any of that is, or what me being assigned here with Elder Reyes has to do with any of it."

Elder Neil sat back on the couch and put his hands behind his head in contemplation. He needed to make sure Elder Daniels was ready for this next question.

"Elder Daniels, do you believe in the Gift of Tongues?"

"Excuse me?"

"Do you believe in the Gift of Tongues?"

Elder Daniels blinked. "I guess so." He was less certain than he'd been with his previous answers.

"You can't guess about something like this. Either you believe it or you don't."

Elder Daniels was staring at his feet. Never in his life had he been faced with such a question—not even from Elder Flores.

"Listen," Elder Neil said, giving him a pat on the back, "this is what we'll do. You go out today and work. While you're working, pray. Ask God if there is such a thing as a Gift of Tongues. Tomorrow morning we'll have our personal study together and talk about it. If the answer is "yes," we'll teach you how to become worthy of receiving that gift. If the answer is "no," we'll figure out how to get you through your mission without it."

As if on cue, Elder Tolentino and Elder Reyes walked around the corner. Before Elder Daniels could say another word, Elder Neil and his companion were standing by the front door, starting their companionship prayer.

Elder Daniels remained on the couch, completely in shock at what he'd just heard.

"Tayo na, Elder?" Elder Reyes asked after the zone leaders had left and shut the door.

Struggling to his feet, Elder Daniels slowly walked toward the back bedroom. "Almost. Give me just a minute."

Not sure if his companion understood him or not, Elder Daniels simply shut the door, dropping to his knees beside his bed. In solitude he rarely found anymore, he whispered, "Father, . . . I need your help, . . . I can't go on this way, . . . Please, . . . Please help me! "

# CHAPTER 9

*And if men come unto me I will show unto them their weakness. I give unto men weakness that they may be humble; and my grace is sufficient for all men that humble themselves before me; for if they humble themselves before me, and have faith in me, then will I make weak things become strong unto them.*

—*Ether 12:27*

Alicia Decker lay on her white, feather comforter as she stared at the shadows dancing across her walls. Outside her bedroom window, the branches of a tall aspen swayed in the breeze. The soft moonlight that flickered in, cast long shadows across her room.

It was her favorite time of year, when the leaves had already changed colors and the first frost of winter was in the air. It was the perfect temperature. In the evening, she could leave her bedroom window open and feel the wind blow in as it raced out of Provo Canyon, stretching its chilly fingers throughout the valley.

She always seemed to sleep better in the cool air, even though in the early morning hours she would reach for the thick, down comforter at the foot of her bed. Under the heavy blankets that kept her snug and warm, she felt safe and comfortable.

More often than not these days she was reaching for the blanket early in the night, sometimes before she even got into bed. Perhaps the nights were getting colder. Perhaps she wasn't sleeping as deeply. Perhaps she was feeling very lonely with her boyfriend six thousand miles away.

Curled up in her warm blankets, Alicia wondered what the conditions were like where Aaron was serving. She knew from his letters that it rained a lot. He had described the daily afternoon showers during these cooler months as "torrential." Apparently, every afternoon the cumulonimbus clouds built to their towering heights and dumped a steady rain on the tropic islands for hours.

Knowing that he hadn't taken an overcoat, or anything of the sort, she wondered how he stayed dry. Certainly, he'd bought an umbrella! She hoped it was big and strong, not one of those "Tote" umbrellas that women carry in their purse. She could just imagine her six-foot, two-inch boyfriend trying to huddle under a two-foot umbrella. She wondered how he dried his clothes when there was nothing more than a clothesline hanging on the porch of his apartment. And how about his shoes?

Nestled in the comfort of her parent's home, she realized how difficult a mission must be. No music. No television. No dating. She wondered how they did it.

A small envelope lay on the corner of her nightstand next to her bed. The four-page letter, written in small block letters, attested to her boyfriend's meticulous nature. Like every one of his other letters, the envelope was decorated with X's, and O's, and according to the pact they'd made before he left, the upside-down postage stamp meant "I love you." Yes, there was no doubt about it, he loved her. She knew he had since the first day they laid eyes on one another.

Having met in seminary, they'd become very close over the next few months. Her parents teased her that he was the reason she'd gotten a "B" in the class. They were right. What they didn't know was that Aaron got a "B-."

Other than their seminary grades that first semester, Aaron and Alicia brought the best out in each other—he took life less seriously with her around, and she enjoyed life more. They'd started dating casually at first, but soon found their feelings for one another growing. After going steady for nearly half of high school, they'd begun talking about college and made plans to go to BYU-Idaho.

Although her parents had been uncomfortable with their steady dating at first, they seemed to relax when she promised them that she would only marry a returned missionary. The problem was, she'd never talked to Aaron about it. When she did, he was initially surprised, but soon sent in his mission papers and left within six months.

*It's so hard! Why does time have to go by so slowly? Why can't all missions be eighteen months?*

Deep down inside, she knew it was right. She knew he should be on a mission. However, when it came right down to it, she was selfish. She wanted to hear his voice; hear him calling each night on the phone; lay in his arms next to the fireplace. There were times she regretted telling him she would only marry a returned missionary. She knew she wasn't ready to be married, but she wasn't ready to be alone either.

She did her best to support him in her letters, but it wasn't exactly easy telling him she was proud of him and that she was glad he was there when she really wanted him home. She tried to write motivating things. She tried to tell him what she was learning in her Book of Mormon class. Most of the time she just broke down and cried, spilling her emotions on paper and letting the words write themselves, regardless of the negative impact they might have on the other end.

But, then he was the same way, telling her how much he missed her, and complaining about the hardships of missionary life. Looking back, she had no idea what made him stay in the mission after such a terrible experience in his first area. From his very first letter, he'd sounded like he wanted to come home, leave his mission and never look back. However, she did notice that something had happened when he got to his second area.

All he mentioned was that he got transferred and had a new companion and that he liked him a great deal. His letters were less negative, no longer complaining about everything from the living conditions to the language. He actually sounded upbeat—even excited at times. Still, she knew he truly loved her and rarely went more than a few lines without telling her.

*Why isn't he just allowed to call me?* She would never understand some of the mission rules. *Don't they know what a sacrifice he's making as it is?*

Nevertheless, she had his letters—one each week, as sure as the morning sun. She only wished the letters in his direction were as consistent.

From what she'd read in his last letter, there was a space of about four weeks that he didn't receive a single letter. All mail delivery to his mission had been delayed and nothing had gotten through. Thinking about that, her heart ached. What a relief it must have been to get four in one day, and put an end to the terrible silence.

Closing her eyes, she drifted asleep, hoping that he would visit her still. If she couldn't see him in real life, she could still hope to see him in her dreams.

\* \* \* \* \*

The sudden braking he felt as his body lurched forward shocked Elder Daniels so much that he almost fell off the back of the jeepney. Gripping the baggage rail as tightly as he could, he held on as five tons of metal, traveling at sixty kilometers per hour, tried to stop in about forty meters. If the momentum hadn't forced his body even closer to the back of the jeepney, he might have lost his grip entirely as the overloaded jeepney swerved out of traffic onto the shoulder of the road.

As the big vehicle labored to a stop, Elder Daniels looked at his watch. It read 8:45 A.M. "Shoot!" he breathed, knowing it was his fault they were behind schedule. "Now we'll never make it there in time!"

Elder Daniels and his companion were not the only two passengers without a seat, three others squatted amidst the knees and legs that filled the middle aisle. The two missionaries in their white shirts, ties flapping in the wind, stood on the very back of a jeepney where bags of rice were strapped down. They needed to get to San Juan quickly, an area in their district about eight kilometers north of their own.

Looking down at the rusty, metal platform on which he stood, Elder Daniels cringed, thinking how hysterical his mother would be if she ever saw him riding like this—especially on a jeepney lumbering down the highway at speeds of seventy and eighty kilometers per hour. His head above the roof, directly in line with the oncoming wind, Elder Daniels closed his eyes, knowing a bug hitting him in the eye could permanently blind him.

With the jeepney full—about eight or nine people above its highest recommended capacity—it no longer slowed as it approached individuals frantically waving it down from the side of the highway. They had already traveled through their own area and now cruised down the open road with the outskirts of San Juan barely visible beyond the banana trees and rice fields.

Elder Daniels knew the sister missionaries in San Juan had been waiting on them. Although the sister's apartment was only about a hundred yards off the main highway, conveniently located next to the chapel, they still had to travel through town, which meant unloading many of the passengers and picking up a dozen more.

Glancing at his watch once again, he knew the discussion he'd had earlier with Elder Neil, had put them behind schedule enough that if the sisters had an early appointment, they may leave without them. With no appointments set for their own area, their entire morning would be wasted.

Entering San Juan, Elder Daniels was at once taken by the beauty of the small town. At the entrance of the market was a large arch welcoming travelers to the historic district just outside the provincial capital. All around the marketplace, beautiful trees towered above rooftops reflecting the age of the old municipality. Planted with foresight, the trees offered shade to the many vendors selling merchandise in the open market. Amidst the colorful tents was everything from fruits and vegetables to intricately carved wooden statues ranging in size from tiny figurines to life-sized lions and bears.

Adding the perfect touch to the beautiful setting, a small horse gingerly pulled an old wooden cart filled with empty baskets. The baskets were decorated with intricate designs and undoubtedly handmade. So plentiful were the baskets tied to the cart that the highest baskets were well out of arms reach for even the tallest customers. Though the small horse easily pulled the light, wooden cart, it looked like a Shetland pony in comparison.

Elder Daniels jumped to the ground once the jeepney stopped so that the passengers inside could also disembark. When only four other passengers climbed aboard, the jeepney driver signaled to Elder Daniels to join his companion inside. Elder Daniels shrugged off the invitation, climbing back on the metal grate and holding onto the baggage rail.

As much as he disliked trikes, Elder Daniels despised riding in jeepneys. It wasn't just that he had to duck his head the entire ride, but he truly preferred the robust view from where he now stood and the cool breeze that accompanied it. With a loud grinding of gears and a heavy rumble, the jeepney was once again heading down the winding highway, still more than five minutes from the sister's apartment.

Since he had never visited the sisters in San Juan, Elder Daniels relied on his companion to signal the driver when they approached their stop. To his surprise, the jeepney stopped right in front of the chapel without a word from his companion. A bit puzzled as he stepped down and walked to the front to pay the driver, he saw two sister missionaries climbing in the back of the jeepney. Following them inside, Elder Daniels realized the jeepney had stopped for *them*.

A tall and beautiful American missionary greeted him as he took his seat, "Have a little trouble getting up this morning?"

Not sure whether she was joking or not, Elder Daniels paused, searching her face for an expression.

"I'm kidding you," she finally relented with a smile. "I'm Sister Adams."

"Elder Daniels," he replied hesitantly as he shook her hand, "we got a little behind during our companionship study."

"No worries," she said. "It's nice to finally meet you. This is my companion Sister Joachim."

Elder Daniels shook hands with her companion and then turned back to the sister sitting across from him. "Finally meet me? What do you mean?"

"Oh I've heard a lot about you," she said, "Elder Hastings told me all about the kinds of trouble you got into at the MTC."

"Trouble? I don't remember getting in any trouble."

"What about the pillow fights?" Sister Adams asked.

"Oh, . . . well, . . ."

"And sneaking food back to your rooms?"

"I . . ."

Laughing as Elder Daniels turned three shades of red, Sister Adams said, "It sounds like you two had a good time together."

"How do you know Elder Hastings?"

"We were in the Bayambang zone together." she replied, "That was his first area. I was transferred up here after his first month in the mission, you know the month it rained nonstop!"

Recalling the story Elder Hastings had told at transfers, Elder Daniels asked, "Oh, so you were down there when it flooded?"

"I certainly was!" She replied. "That's why I was transferred up here. Our apartment flooded so badly President Hart had to close the area and move us out."

"Really?"

"Oh yes!" she said, her eyes getting big. "We had no food in the apartment, no drinking water, and no dry clothes. We were put on the first jeepney that could get over the Dagupan Bridge and the zone leaders packed up our belongings and sent them up a few days later."

"That must have been crazy!"

"It was interesting. I'll say that much. The hardest thing was leaving the area when the work was going so well. We'd just baptized the Castillo family the week before—a future stake president, a young women's leader and three prospective missionaries, for sure!"

"Why wouldn't they let you go back?"

"Well," Sister Adams reasoned, "I guess President Hart didn't feel it was safe. To be honest with you, I've never questioned him about it. I've learned enough to know that President Hart doesn't make hasty decisions. He approaches missionary assignments prayerfully and does what the Spirit tells him to do."

Elder Daniels eyes lowered, having heard similar words only an hour before from Elder Neil.

"But great things came of it," Sister Adams added, her voice ringing with optimism. "Especially being here in San Juan with Sister Joachim. She's the best companion a missionary could have!"

Elder Daniels could already tell that he liked Sister Adams. She was the kind of missionary every district and zone leader loved to have—her attitude was as lovely as her smile.

Sister Adams had ignited the mission from the first day she arrived. Straight out of the MTC she was assigned to the hardest of all the areas in the mission—one that hadn't seen a single baptism in months. Together with her native companion, they taught and baptized eight people in the first four weeks. No one worked harder, provided more service, or loved their mission more. It was impossible not to feel good around her. When she entered a room, people noticed—and it wasn't just her sparkling personality that grabbed attention.

If her smile and persona didn't make people take notice, her long blonde hair did—flowing to the middle of her back and glittering like straw in the morning sun. In fact, all of her feminine American features—from her sapphire-blue eyes to her prominent cheekbones—made her stand out in any crowd. There just weren't many like her in all of Asia.

But if Sister Adams could turn heads just walking down the street, her companion made people's heads spin. Sister Jornacio had beautifully light skin and silky black hair that fell to her waist. She'd started a career in modeling only to find her high moral standards in contrast with the expectations of her agent. Passing up the opportunity for national and international fame, Sister Jornacio had turned to a future in television broadcasting, but one that would have to wait until after she'd served a mission.

As Elder Daniels stole glances between them, his first thought was that they were certain to never lack in potential Melchizedek Priesthood-holder investigators. It didn't take long to observe their inner beauty either. Conversation with them came easy and they made a point of taking time to talk with almost everyone in the Jeepney. As if sisters in more than just missionary title, they complemented one another in gracefulness and unconditional love.

Both sisters wore white blouses accenting the nametags that identified themselves as ambassadors of Jesus Christ. Their modest skirts came down to their ankles, careful to cover the slim figures they adorned. Their shoes, though neatly polished and free of dust and dirt, were simple, nothing of the sort that would attract inappropriate attention.

As the jeepney traveled north, Elder Daniels wondered how difficult it must be for them to keep up their appearance as they did. With few of the conveniences of home, such as hot water, makeup, or even time to get ready in the mornings, he wondered how they looked so amazing sitting on dusty seats with chickens scrambling to stand upright on the metal jeepney floor.

Though he'd known them for only a few minutes, Elder Daniels immediately felt comfortable around the two sisters. They spoke with enthusiasm, telling of the two discussions planned for that morning and the young couple they planned to baptize next Sunday.

As the jeepney pulled to the side of the road and the four missionaries disembarked, Elder Daniels looked around. There was no sign of a house, nipa hut, or any sort of dwelling as far as he could see. The only thing in sight, other than banana trees and leafy foliage, was a small trail leading through what appeared to be the densest jungle in Southeast Asia.

Without a word, Sister Adams disappeared into the trees, followed by her companion. It was obvious from the look on his face that Elder Reyes was as surprised as he. Instead of following them, the two Elders just stood on the side of the road until Sister Adams appeared again a moment later.

"What are you two waiting for? We've got a lesson to teach!"

For the next fifteen minutes, Elder Daniels and his companion followed as closely on the sisters' heels as the mission rules permitted. It wasn't just to avoid lagging behind, they were truly afraid of losing their way. Never before had Elder Daniels seen more difficult terrain.

The trail they had initially started on had already grown thin, barely discernible against the thick underbrush that made every step precarious. At times, they left the trail completely, wading through knee-length grass that sent chills up his spine. It didn't take much of an imagination to think of the many snakes, spiders, rats and other creatures that were surely scurrying around just out of sight.

Twice they crossed rope bridges spanning deep chasms to a raging river below. Each footstep was placed as carefully as possible on the wood planks, each roughly the size of a normal stair step but spaced eight to ten inches apart. Below them, great torrents of brown water churned, breaking the silence with a deafening roar that caused Elder Daniels to grip the rope handrails with knuckles white as his halve-sleeved shirt. Rather than belie his fear and anxiety, he simply shook his head in wonder at how the sisters moved so gracefully from one step to the next.

To make things even more interesting, most of the terrain was anything but flat. At one point Elder Daniels had to pull himself up a steep embankment using the branches of an overhanging tree.

The sisters, dressed in skirts, blouses and thin-soled flats, made their way over the obstacle course with little difficulty. The manner in which they traversed the slippery trail left Elder Daniels and his companion shaking their heads.

As the vegetation began to thin out, Elder Daniels could see houses coming into view. He could already smell the acrid smoke rising from a cooking fire. Stepping out into the open, he was thrilled to finally leave the arduous jungle behind.

Without the jungle canopy overhead blocking the sun, Elder Daniels got his first good look at himself since leaving the jeepney. The first thing he noticed was that, from his knees down, his pant legs were covered with burrs. Beyond that, it was nearly impossible to see where the cuffs on his trousers ended and his shoes began—both being covered in mud. At once he began stomping his feet, remembering the effort it had taken over the past few months to keep them clean.

As they approached the cinder-block houses that stood on the edge of the clearing, a group of small children charged them when the sisters came into view. In no time at all, dirty little faces surrounded both sisters with hands reaching out for "high fives."

Elder Daniels stayed a few steps back, watching the events unfold. It was obvious the sisters were well known in this tiny village. After making sure she got a high-five from each child, Sister Jornacio reached into her bag and pulled out a small paper bag. Shouts of glee erupted from the children who pressed forward with outstretched hands.

The sisters gave each child two pieces of candy, the kind that came from the United States and were made of chocolate. It reminded Elder Daniels of trick-or-treating at Halloween—sans costumes, of course. The children instantly shoved the candy in their mouths and a few of them dropped the empty wrappers on the ground only to receive a disappointed look from Sister Adams. One by one, the children bent down, picking up the empty wrappers and shoving them in a pocket.

Elder Daniels had never seen anything like this. Many children had taken an interest in him—having white skin and hairy arms—but never had he been received with such joy. He knew it wasn't just the candy either. These children had developed a special bond with the sister missionaries. In areas Elder Daniels had previously visited, many of the adolescents, and even some adults, just called out "Hey Joe"—a non-endearing term referencing the American occupation of the Philippines and "GI Joe." The term never sat well with him.

As the children began to disperse, Elder Daniels noticed the sister's shirts. Once beautifully white and neatly pressed, they were now covered with dirty handprints from the children. Looking down at themselves, the sisters simply brushed off what they could and took the rest with them as their own souvenirs.

A few minutes later, Elder Daniels was sitting on an old wooden bench listening to Sister Jornacio introduce them to their investigators. Sitting cross-legged on the floor across from him was an old woman with long, gray hair braided down her back and dark skin as wrinkled as a raisin. She looked to be in her nineties but then Elder Daniels was not good at guessing ages. Harvesting rice on a daily basis, coupled with a poor diet made premature aging inevitable in this part of the world.

The old woman, closer to 55 years old was hunched over at the waist, no longer able to persuade her ailing bones to stand erect. Her thin, gnarled hands were rough and callused. Unwilling to take one of the few chairs she owned for herself, she sat on the floor next to Elder Reyes who offered his chair to Sister Jornacio so that both sisters would have a seat.

The small concrete structure contained very few furnishings but from those present it was obvious the old woman was very devoted to her Catholic faith. On one wall hung a picture Elder Daniels had seen in many homes and was appropriately named "The Sacred Heart of Jesus."

Depicting the crucifixion, Christ hung on the cross with his heart visible in his chest. The heart, with flames shooting from the top, was wrapped once over with a branch of thorns, much like the crown of thorns placed on his head by Roman soldiers. His side bore the mark of the soldier's spear but the wound was open and as long as a man's hand. His expression—sad and gloomy— always gave Elder Daniels' a chill. The picture was not like those pictures of the Savior to which he was accustomed. Nothing in this picture depicted the love and sacrifice associated with the Son of God or the Redeemer of all mankind.

While his eyes wandered over the various articles in the room, Elder Daniels could hear the voice of Sister Jornacio teaching about the attributes of Heavenly Father. He heard the words but he did not listen. He'd heard and taught the lesson more times than he could count and developed a bad habit of paying little attention while another was teaching.

Throughout the room, he noticed many crosses, some standing alone, others draped by rosary beads. In one corner was a shrine to Mary, the mother of Jesus with tiny figurines of saints and angels. To tell the truth, Elder Daniels was impressed by the woman's devotion. Every decoration had something to do with Christ or Christianity. In a country where Catholicism was once not only the national religion but also required by law, Elder Daniels could see that this woman still embraced the Catholic beliefs and traditions voluntarily.

Sister Jornacio concluded her teaching by saying, "Elder Daniels will now share with you how Jesus Christ plays the central role in our Heavenly Father's Plan of Salvation."

So caught up was he in surveying the room that Elder Daniels barely heard Sister Jornacio's closing statement. But having taught the discussion many times, he jumped in and began rattling off what he remembered. Before long, he resorted to reading the remainder from his Tagalog translation.

"Without the help of our Father in Heaven," Elder Daniels began, "we could not benefit from the Plan of Salvation. In mortal life, each of us sins and falls short of perfection. Our sins make us unworthy to return to our Father in Heaven. In addition, each of us will die to end this mortal life."

Looking up at the old woman, Elder Daniels was pleased to see her following along. Although her expression showed no emotion, she was intently listening.

"God provided a way for us to overcome sin and death so that we can return to his presence. The central figure in the Plan of Salvation is Jesus Christ."

Elder Daniels opened his scriptures to a page he'd specifically marked for this part of the lesson and handed the open Bible to the woman. "Sister, would you mind reading John, 3:16?"

Without even looking at the page the old woman said, "For God so love the world that he gave his only begotten Son, that whosoever believeth in him should not perish, but have everlasting life."

Caught off guard, Elder Daniels buried his head in his discussion booklet, trying to find his place again. Regaining his composure, he continued.

"Jesus fulfilled His part of the plan. Through his sacrifice and resurrection, we can overcome the effects of sin and all men will live again after mortal death." Without looking up, he asked, "How is Jesus Christ, important to you?"

Had Elder Daniels listened, he would not only have heard the words the old woman said in response to the question, but more importantly he would have felt them. She bore powerful testimony that Jesus Christ was in fact her Redeemer and Savior. As it was, Elder Daniels was too busy reading ahead in his teaching manual.

As soon as she finished speaking, he continued reading. "The Plan of Salvation is simple and easy to understand, but we must choose to follow it." Finishing the rest of the principle in the same manner, Elder Daniels bore testimony of Jesus Christ, word for word as he'd written it in his notebook.

After introducing Elder Reyes, Elder Daniels closed his discussion booklet and resumed his study of the small room. His companion taught the next principle explaining how God reveals the Plan of Salvation through prophets.

"But prophets haven't been around since Bible times."

Elder Reyes asked her to open her Bible to Amos, Chapter 3, verse 7.

She read, "Surely the Lord God will do nothing, save he revealeth his secret unto his servants the prophets."

"Sister, do you believe that God loves his children today as much as he loved them in the time of Moses?"

"Yes."

"If God loves us also, why wouldn't he want us to know about the Plan of Salvation and how to return to him?"

Having no explanation, the woman simply shook her head.

"Sister Fuentes," he asked tenderly, "if the Bible says that God will do nothing without revealing it to his servants, the prophets, how do you think he would tell us about His plan?"

Nodding her head, the old woman understood. "By calling a prophet."

"Exactly," Elder Reyes confirmed. "Sister Adams is going to share with you how God called one of His prophets in our day."

Gently, Sister Adams stood up and pushed the chair on she'd been sitting against the wall behind her. She then sat on the floor directly in front of the woman so they could be at eye level with one another.

Putting her hand on the old woman's arm, Sister Adams spoke softly to her in perfect Tagalog. "Sister Fuentes, I want you to know that our Heavenly Father loves you very much. As Elder Jornacio said, we are all His children. We are all brothers and sisters and we want you to know that we love you very much."

The old woman, nearly expressionless to that point, visibly softened. Before long she began blinking rapidly trying to hold back tears that made her eyes glisten. No one had told her they loved her in a very long time.

Without taking her eyes from the woman's gaze, Sister Adams began to teach. Every set of eyes in the room was upon her. Other than her voice, it was perfectly quiet in the small home.

"Our Heavenly Father does call prophets, even today. He chose a prophet who learned about the Plan of Salvation from firsthand experience. His name was Joseph Smith."

"In the spring of 1820 Joseph Smith was a fourteen-year-old boy. He lived in a small town in the United States where there were many different churches. Young Joseph was very confused by the many different ideas being taught about religion and about God. He described his feelings in these words."

Opening her scriptures to a page with more shading and notes than Elder Daniels had ever seen before, she began reading and translating the scripture from the Joseph Smith History that explained the uneasiness he felt at a time when the question of religious preference was of great concern.

Letting her words hang in the air briefly, Sister Adams asked, "Sister Fuentes, how have your feelings been similar to those of young Joseph?"

Sighing heavily, the old woman looked up with tears forming in the corner of her eyes. Trying to speak, her voice faltered, "I, . . . I . . ." Too emotional to express her feelings in words, she simply nodded, wiping away the tears that now fell freely.

Sister Adams reached out, taking the woman's hands in her own. She had answered the question perfectly.

Taking advantage of the Spirit that filled the room, Sister Adams continued. "One day Joseph read a passage in the Bible that helped him overcome his confusion. Let's have Sister Jornacio read that for us."

Opening her scriptures to James, Chapter 1, verse 5, Sister Jornacio read aloud.

"If any of you lack wisdom, let him ask of God, that giveth to all men liberally, and upbraideth not; and it shall be given him. But let him ask in faith, nothing wavering. For he that wavereth is like a wave of the sea driven with the wind and tossed."

Caressing the old woman's gnarled hands, Sister Adams explained, "When young Joseph read that scripture he knew that if he asked God, that God would answer him. Joseph decided to do just as the Bible said. He would ask God in prayer."

Inching a bit closer to the old woman, Sister Adams's voice became even softer.

"One spring morning Joseph went into a nearby grove of trees. He knelt down and began to pray. Because of his great faith, he knew that God would hear and answer his prayers." After pausing slightly to make sure the old woman understood, she continued. "In his own words, he said, . . ."

It was if only two people were in the room. The old woman's eyes were locked on Sister Adams,' waiting on the next word as if it provided the very the air she breathed. Having been teaching entirely in Tagalog until this point, Sister Adams's voice became very quiet and her speech more deliberate and slow as she switched from Tagalog to English, quoting the very words the Prophet Joseph used in describing the First Vision.

"I saw a pillar of light," she began "exactly over my head, above the brightness of the sun, which descended gradually until it fell upon me. When the light rested upon me, I saw two Personages, whose brightness and glory defy all description, standing above me in the air. One of them spake unto me, calling me by name and said, pointing to the other—This is my Beloved Son. Hear Him."

As her voice trailed off the Spirit testified to the woman of the truthfulness of the Joseph Smith story. For a moment no one spoke. The Spirit in the room so powerful that no one wished to disturb it.

When Sister Adams did speak, she switched back to Tagalog and said, "In answer to his prayer, God the Father and Jesus Christ appeared to young Joseph." Then, after letting those words find place in her heart, Sister Adams asked, "Sister Fuentes, how do you feel right now?"

Again, the room was perfectly still, not even her sniffles interrupted the serenity that prevailed. When she did speak, her voice was barely audible. "Peaceful," she said, needing only one word to convey her feelings

Reaching up with a soft hand and brushing a tear from the old woman's cheek, Sister Adams whispered, "The feelings you have are from the Holy Ghost, witnessing to you that what we have shared with you is true. Through this and other experiences, Joseph Smith was called as a prophet of God. Much like Moses and other prophets in the Bible you've read about, Joseph Smith was called to do the Lord's work."

As Elder Daniels sat on the wooden bench, he felt his cheeks moistened by his own tears. He'd taught that principle a hundred times, and had heard the Joseph Smith story a couple hundred times more. Never in his life had he heard the story, or felt it rather, the way Sister Adams shared it that morning.

As Sister Adams shared her testimony of the First Vision and the Prophet, Joseph Smith, Elder Daniels made his own discovery—that for the first time in his life, he knew with absolute certainty the Joseph Smith story was true.

# CHAPTER 10

*And neither at any time hath any wrought miracles until after their faith; wherefore they first believed in the Son of God.*

*—Ether 12:18*

*For it is by faith that miracles are wrought; and it is by faith that angels appear and minister unto men; wherefore, if these things have ceased wo be unto the children of men, for it is because of unbelief, and all is vain.*

*—Moroni 7:37*

*Wherefore I would exhort you that ye deny not the power of God; for he worketh by power, according to the faith of the children of men, the same today and tomorrow, and forever.*

*—Moroni 17:7*

The cold water Elder Daniels poured over his head did little to help his somber mood. The chill made his chest convulse involuntarily, cutting short his breath until the initial shock subsided and he was able to look at the plastic barrel of water without cringing. It was amazing how quickly he could bathe these days, lathering and rinsing, using less than two gallons of water—eight quick scoops from the "bucket shower."

Stepping out of the shower room, Elder Daniels reached for his towel hanging on the clothesline that stretched between two nails on opposite sides of the wall. The towel was still damp from the previous day's shower. The humidity rarely allowed items to fully dry if they were not placed outside in direct sunlight.

Just as he finished drying his legs, he felt a painful sting on his wrist—and then another on his chest. Within seconds, his legs were stinging, as well as his torso and arms. Realizing his towel was filled with ants, he dropped it and began jumping around the room, slapping and brushing all over his body. He felt his skin crawling as more ants bit him in places he couldn't quite reach. Resorting to the only other option he could see, he reached for the quart-sized ladle and doused himself again and again. The cold water took his breath away once more but at least it rid him of the ant problem and took his mind off the pain.

Now wet and frustrated, he stood motionless on the bathroom tile dripping from head to toe. He had no way to dry himself so he grabbed the shorts and T-shirt he'd slept in, put them back on and stepped to the bathroom door to figure out where the ants had come from.

One glance down the clothesline revealed a trail of ants leading from a small crack between the window and windowpane high up on the bathroom wall. From there, the trail crossed where his towel had just been hanging and continued to the other side where it disappeared down the wall behind the bathroom door. Closing the door, Elder Daniels found the attraction—a dead cockroach that was now little more than an empty shell.

He ate quickly, trying to make up for the lost time of having to shower twice. Knowing Elder Neil would be ready and waiting promptly at 7:00 A.M., he grabbed a couple bananas and some juice from the refrigerator. Just as he was peeling the last banana, Elder Neil opened his bedroom door.

"Good morning. Ready to get started?"

Elder Daniels crammed the banana in his mouth and nodded. As the two sat down, Elder Neil offered to say an opening prayer.

"Dear Father, as we come before thee this morning, we do so with humble hearts and open minds. We know, Father, that we are missionaries and we know why we are here. Please send thy Spirit to teach us the things we need to know. Help us to be better missionaries, better teachers, and better examples than we've been in the past. We thank thee for thy love and blessings and know that if we have faith, that thou will bless us with the things that we need. Please help us this morning, Father, to be more faithful, to be more obedient and to be more like thee."

As Elder Daniels knelt beside his zone leader, he noticed something about the way his zone leader prayed. Elder Neil spoke to God as if He were right there in front of them. It was a simple prayer, but it came from his heart. Never once did he lose sight of whom he was speaking with, it was always "Father," as if it had been someone whom he'd known for a very long time. As Elder Daniels continued to listen, he became even more aware of the beautiful relationship Elder Neil had with his Father in Heaven.

"Father, please help Elder Daniels and I to be better teachers—to learn the language of our Filipino brothers and sisters so that we can teach them the gospel in a clear and simple manner. And most of all, Father, bless us that we may teach with the Spirit. The scriptures tell us that without the Spirit we cannot teach. Please help us to qualify for thy blessings, especially when we need thy help most."

Elder Daniels also noted that Elder Neil was very specific for those things in which he gave thanks and those things for which he asked. He even justified receiving particular blessings by referencing things the Lord had promised or taught in the scriptures.

And, Father," he continued, "let us draw on the Powers of Heaven and be more successful as missionaries. We love thee with all of our hearts and we know we are nothing without thee. Please bless us we pray, in the name of our Savior, Jesus Christ, Amen."

Elder Daniels arose from his knees as a peace fell over him. After the experience of working with the sisters in San Juan, he knew he needed help. At no other point in his mission had he been more aware of his inability to teach effectively than when he witnessed Sister Adams' teaching skills. For the first time since that experience, he felt that there was hope.

As he took his seat next to Elder Neil he asked, "What did you mean when you just said something about . . . drawing on the Powers of Heaven?"

"Elder Bruce R. McConkie once said that we need to learn how to pray 'boldly and efficaciously, not in word only but in spirit and in power, so that we may pull upon ourselves the very Powers of Heaven.'"

"*Efficaciously?*" Elder Daniels asked.

"Sure, meaning that we do it in the proper way so as to produce the desired effect."

Pulling one leg under him so that he could turn and face Elder Daniels, Elder Neil explained, "You see, the Powers of Heaven are any influence of God's power operating in our behalf."

When Elder Daniels lifted his eyebrows, scrunching his forehead into a bunch of tiny wrinkles, Elder Neil knew he was going too fast.

"Okay," he said, "Let me ask you this. Have you ever had an investigator who was really struggling with something and it seemed like no matter what you did or said, your investigator just couldn't get over his or her concern?"

"Sure."

"Okay, now have you ever had something happen—you know just completely out of the blue—that made the difference for your investigator so that he or she understood the truth and was converted?"

"Yeah," Elder Daniels replied, thinking of the Baribal family.

"That's the Powers of Heaven!" Elder Neil explained. "Anytime the Lord intervenes on our behalf, we see the Powers of Heaven in action."

"But why wouldn't God always help us? I mean we are missionaries right? Why is it only sometimes that we see these 'Powers of Heaven' when we're supposed to be baptizing the whole world?"

Flipping through his scriptures Elder Neil opened to a page in The Book of Mormon that had a bright red star in one corner. Handing it to Elder Daniels he said, "Read what the Lord says here in 2nd Nephi, Chapter 27, verse 23."

"For behold, I am God, and I am a God of miracles; and I will show unto the world that I am the same yesterday, today, and forever; and I work not among the children of men save it be according to their faith."

"What does that mean to you?"

Reading the verse again, this time to himself, Elder Daniels took his time before answering. "Well, he says that He won't work miracles if we don't have faith."

Taking the book from him, Elder Neil turned back a few pages and asked, "Do you think it's because He won't work miracles, or because he can't?"

Elder Daniels was about to say, 'Well, nothings impossible for God,' but when he saw Elder Neil opening up to another scripture he just reached for the book instead.

Elder Daniels began reading from the verse Elder Neil had marked with another red star. "Yea, and how is it that ye have forgotten that the Lord is able to do all things according to his will, for the children of men, if it so be that they exercise faith in him?"

Elder Neil waited before saying anything, giving Elder Daniels the chance to formulate his thoughts.

"So what you're saying," Elder Daniels concluded, "is that the Lord can't help us if we don't have faith in Him?"

"That's not what *I'm* saying Elder Daniels, that's what the *Lord* said. You see there are certain laws that even God has to obey."

"Laws?"

"Yes, some very important laws. I mean think about it, no matter how much our Heavenly Father wants us to live with Him again, the Law of Justice says that if we don't repent of our sins we *can't* live with Him again. It's the same with the law concerning faith. We have to exercise our faith *before* the Lord can work miracles"

"I've never thought about that."

"Think about how you would feel if police officers didn't have to obey traffic laws, I mean they could just drive as fast as they wanted, or run stop signs, or whatever. How much trust would you have in them? How inclined would you be to obey those laws yourself?"

"I get what you're saying" Elder Daniels responded. "If God didn't obey these laws we couldn't put our trust in Him." Realizing he'd inched forward in his seat, he sat back again against the cushion and admitted, "I guess I always figured that since God made the laws then He can do anything He wants."

"That's the best part Elder Daniels. You see, although God is subject to certain laws—laws that He voluntarily subjects himself to—it doesn't make Him any less powerful. In fact, it makes Him greater. When He says He is the same yesterday, today, and tomorrow we can believe it. If, instead, God was unpredictable, sometimes doing this, sometimes that, well, you can see how that would make it impossible for us to put our trust in Him, right?"

"Yeah, I see what you're saying."

Elder Neil was already reaching into his bamboo bag. Pulling out a small booklet he turned to a page near the beginning and said, excitedly, "Listen to what Joseph Smith said in the Lectures on Faith."

"Had it not been for the principle of faith the worlds would never have been framed, neither would man have been formed of the dust." Reading slowly, emphasizing each word, he continued, "It is the principle by which Jehovah works, and through which He exercises power over all temporal as well as eternal things. Take this principle or attribute—for it is an attribute—from the Deity, and He would cease to exist."

"Isn't that awesome!" Elder Neil asked energetically.

"Uh, . . . I guess so." Elder Daniels replied, shifting in his seat a bit. "But what does it mean?"

"It means that God does all the wonderful things He does, like create worlds, and be everywhere, and all those things all through the power of faith. It's saying that without faith, He couldn't do any of it."

Cocking his head to the side, Elder Daniels asked, "But doesn't God know everything?"

"Sure!"

"So why does He need to have faith when He has a perfect knowledge."

"Oh," Elder Neil responded, "I see what you're getting at. You're thinking of the scripture in Alma that says 'faith is not to have a perfect knowledge of things.'"

"Exactly," replied Elder Daniels, very matter-of-factly.

Elder Neil rubbed at the stubble on his chin that already looked a day old. "That's a good question," he said, searching for the best way to explain the concept, "because a lot of people misunderstand that scripture—even though it's one of the most often repeated scriptures about faith."

"Alma was saying that we don't need to have a perfect knowledge of things to have faith. In other words, you don't need to know everything about astronomy, physics, and stuff like that to know that the sun will rise tomorrow morning, right?

"Right."

"So all it takes is a hope for things which are not seen, which are true. Are you following me?"

"Sort of."

"Okay, so most people read that verse and say 'If I don't need a perfect knowledge to have faith, then if I have a perfect knowledge I don't need faith.' Is that what you're thinking?"

"Yes."

Opening back to his notes on the Lectures on Faith Elder Neil said, "Listen again to what the Prophet Joseph said. " Faith is the principle by which Jehovah works, . . . Take this principle or attribute—for it is an attribute—from the Deity, and he would cease to exist."

Turning back to Elder Daniels, he explained, "Faith is how God does what He does. Having faith is one of His attributes just like the attributes of being kind, all knowing, merciful, and so on. Without faith, He would not be God!"

Elder Daniels blew out a deep breath. This was complicated. Up to this point in his life he'd never thought about this kind of thing before, just imagining that God had some magical power to create the worlds, and him, and everything else. Now, Elder Neil was telling him that it was through the power of faith that God worked miracles.

As if being able to read his mind, Elder Neil turned the page in the small booklet and continued reading. "Faith, then, is the first great governing principle which has power, dominion, and authority over all things; by it they exist, by it they are upheld, by it they are changed, or by it they remain, agreeable to the will of God. Without it there is no power, and without power there could be no creation nor existence."

Putting the book aside, Elder Neil paused, knowing that Elder Daniels was feeling a little bit overwhelmed. It was time to simplify things.

"You see, Elder Daniels, faith is something much greater than a positive attitude. It's more than just believing in something. Faith is *power*! It's the very power by which God, Himself, operates. And knowing how to exercise that faith is the key to drawing on the Powers of Heaven."

"Why is this important for you, you ask?" Looking Elder Daniels straight in the eye, his voice becoming almost hushed, he said, "Because I'll testify to you, Elder Daniels, . . . that the Lord is very eager to send his angels and minister to you personally. When that happens, what might take one missionary six months to become fluent in Tagalog, it will take you much less time."

Edging a bit closer, he continued. "And Elder Daniels, not only that but you will have the Spirit so strongly in your life that when you walk in a room your investigators will say, 'I know whatever you tell me is true.' And when that happens you will be able to teach the principles of the Gospel in about ten minutes."

Searching Elder Daniels' eyes, he asked, "Is that what you want, Elder Daniels?"

Remembering the way Sister Adams had taught the afternoon before, he nodded his head. "That is what I want."

"Then," Elder Neil said with a slight pause, drawing nearer with his unwavering stare, "you first have to know how to call down the Powers of Heaven."

\* \* \* \* \*

A phone ringing in the next room made the large man jump a bit as his mind was brought back to his task. For the last 30 minutes he'd studied the 168 pictures that hung on his office wall. But having been a mission president for over a year, he knew that he could not rush inspiration. It simply came when it came—sometimes quickly, other times less quickly—but it always came.

*Who do I send to Pozorrubio with Sister Bennett?* That was the question on his mind at the particular moment the phone rang.

His method for receiving inspiration was very deliberate. One day a month he fasted and prayed to know the Lord's will concerning his missionaries. He studied their pictures and visualized them working with specific companions in specific areas. When he could clearly see in his mind the companionship, and when the Holy Ghost confirmed that his pairing was correct, he moved the pictures to a whiteboard divided into 10 zones and 84 areas. When all the pictures were removed from his wall and assigned to areas by missionary companionships, he got down on his knees and prayed for confirmation that the assignments were correct. From time to time he received revelation that told him something wasn't right and he would rework the board until it was correct. This didn't happen often, but he knew to trust in the Lord and if it didn't feel right, he changed it.

As his eyes passed over each missionary, he paused momentarily on the face of one young sister who had recently entered the mission. She was a native Filipino who had come from a small branch in Cebu. Knowing that she had only been a member of the Church for just over 2 years, he had to make sure she was assigned with a more seasoned missionary who could help in her development as a missionary and as a recent convert to the Church.

*No*, he thought, *we won't send Sister Tubo to Pozorrubio. That's too difficult an area for a new missionary—let alone a new convert.* As his eyes continued searching the faces of the other sister missionaries, they kept coming back to Sister Tubo. And there it was—the impression that Sister Tubo should go to . . .

A knock at the door interrupted his thought in mid-sentence.

"Come in," he said.

"President, there's a call for you." Elder Marshall said, opening the door and stepping in the doorway.

"Thank you Elder Marshall," he said, as the elderly office assistant closed the door. President Hart knew the phone call was important without even asking. Elder Marshall and the rest of his staff knew that he was not to be disturbed during the few hours he had to look over transfers.

Picking up the phone, he could tell by the background static that it was a call from overseas.

"Good Morning, President Hart speaking."

A soft voice was barely heard above the static in the line. The voice seemed very distant as it lagged a bit, leaving a two-second pause between exchanges. "Hello President Hart. This is President Colvin, from the Orem Utah East Stake."

Hoping to get right down to business, President Hart asked, "How can I help you?"

The voice on the other end became somewhat strained and serious as he said, "Well, I have some difficult news I need to share with you, President, about one of the missionaries from our stake currently assigned to your mission."

"Oh, who would that be?" President Hart asked.

As he listened to the voice on the other end, President Hart's eyes scanned his missionary board for the missionary in question. He found the picture in the San Fernando zone and then his heart fell as he was given the news.

"She was a very strong woman," the stake president said, "and having known her for many years, it pains me deeply to have to pass along the news of her death."

"What a tragedy!" President Hart responded, expressing his grief at hearing of the mother's death.

"The funeral service will be held on Thursday morning," he continued. "President Hart, I don't know how you would normally handle this sort of thing, but I thought someone breaking the news in person would, perhaps, be better than any of us could do with a phone call."

"I agree," President Hart said before regretfully adding, "As you know, the Church's policy is not to let a missionary return home for the funeral, but I'm sure a phone call home will be in order."

"Yes, I understand," the stake president replied. "We'll take care of everything on this end."

President Hart nodded, "Thank you. We'll do our best here as well. Good-bye."

After hanging up the phone, President Hart stepped away from the pictures and knelt by his desk in prayer. He'd hoped never to have to tell a missionary of a family member's death but it had happened twice now in just over a year. Remembering his own mission 37 years earlier, he wondered how he would have taken the news if he had learned of his own mother's death.

"What a tragedy," he said again.

Standing up, he walked back over to the missionary board with his arms folded behind him. Studying the smiling face of the young American in the picture, he shook his head, knowing how difficult the news would be to pass along.

"Elder Marshall," he called.

"Yes, president," the elderly missionary answered as he entered the office.

"Could you please get me the phone number for the zone leader's apartment in San Fernando?"

\* \* \* \* \*

"What do I have to do?" Elder Daniels asked.

"Well, once you have a clear understanding that faith is a principle of power and know that the Powers of Heaven are governed by your individual faith, you'll want to go to the Lord in prayer and let him guide you in selecting your righteous desires."

"So you're saying I need to set my goals by inspiration?"

"Exactly!" Elder Neil confirmed. "You have to clearly state what it is that you want the Lord to help you with. Until you determine that, you will never have access to the Powers of Heaven."

"Okay, so let's say after fasting and praying I decide that I want to learn Tagalog. What do I do next?"

Elder Neil reached into his missionary bag and pulled out a small notebook. Turning past several pages filled with scrupulous notes, he found a blank sheet and handed the notebook to Elder Daniels. "That's a good start but you'll be missing a very important aspect if you leave it at that."

"What's that?" Elder Daniels asked.

"Well, if you just say you want to learn Tagalog, assuming you are mentally capable, which we know you are, how much faith is that going to require?"

"I don't know," Elder Daniels shrugged.

"What I mean is, isn't that something you could do on your own?"

"Yeah, I guess so."

"So let's just say that after fasting and prayer you decide your goal is to be fluent in Tagalog in two months. Is that going to take some faith?"

Letting out a long breath, Elder Daniels answered, "Uh, yeah. That would take a lot of faith...and a miracle!"

"Perfect! And that's what you have to do. You have to distinguish which of your goals you can do on your own, and those that you need the Lord's help with. If you can clearly see in your mind's eye how you will accomplish the goal then if doesn't take much faith. But, if your goal is one that you *cannot* clearly see how you will achieve, then that's the type of goal that will require you to draw on the Powers of Heaven. Do you follow me?"

"I do now."

"Good. Now write this down because there are specific steps you'll need to follow."

Elder Daniels began writing frantically, filling up the page with some of the basic principles he'd just learned. The first step was prayerfully selecting a righteous desire that would require him to exercise faith.

Elder Neil coached him, saying,, "Be specific and set a date."

"Okay," Elder Neil continued, after making sure all the important points were written down. "Once you've selected your righteous desire, and a date that you want to have it accomplished, your next step is to commit yourself."

After writing 'Commit yourself' on the next line, Elder Neil instructed him to make three separate columns down the page and label them: *My Resolves; Help I Will Need from the Lord; and My Commitments.*

"All right. So you've got your goal, now let's figure out how to achieve it."

"But I thought you said this would have to be the type of goal that you can't see how to achieve."

"Right. But that doesn't mean you go at it without a plan. In order to draw on the Powers of Heaven you're going to need to do your part."

"Start by listing everything you will need to do to accomplish your particular goal. That'll probably include how much time you will spend each day studying the language, how you will discipline yourself to open your mouth and trust that the Lord will help you. When you will practice your language skills, and how you're going to keep all the mission rules."

"Keep the mission rules? But I already do that." Elder Daniels complained.

"I know you do, but probably not to the degree that this will require."

Before Elder Daniels could rebut, Elder Neil said, "Don't worry, we'll get to that a little bit later. Let's get on with the next column."

Elder Daniels relaxed, but only a little. That comment about keeping the mission rules' had struck a chord with him a bit. What was he doing that was wrong? He didn't sleep in late. He was never separated from his companion. What could he be doing wrong? What would Elder Neil know about his obedience anyway? He'd only known him a few days!

"The next thing you want to do is to make a list of the things you will need the Lord to do. In other words," he explained, "the specific blessings you desire, which will require the Powers of Heaven to obtain."

"Like what?"

"Like helping you remember what you study, or facilitating the learning process through the Holy Ghost. Or, . . . you may even be so inspired as to ask for the Gift of Tongues."

"Okay," Elder Daniels replied as he continued writing.

"And be specific as you write these things down too. Tell the Lord exactly what you will need."

Elder Daniels finished scribbling his notes and asked, "So what's this column about commitments? Isn't that the same as resolves?"

"No. Your resolves are the things *you're* going to do to meet your goal. Your commitments are the things you're going to do specifically to qualify for the Lord's help. What I mean is that through prayer and inspiration, you need to demonstrate to the Lord just how dedicated you are, as well as how worthy you are, to receive his help. This might include your commitment to study the scriptures for an hour each day, or fast and pray more often for your goal. Whatever you feel you will need to do to qualify for his help."

"I get it. It's like going 'the extra mile.'"

"Pretty much," Elder Neil agreed. "That's what sets apart those who receive blessings from the Lord on a consistent basis with those who don't."

Elder Daniels filled the last column with the examples Elder Neil had just given him and said, "So that's it? That's how you draw on the Powers of Heaven?"

"Not quite. There are just a couple more steps. But what you've just written down is the part that most people neglect, and a big reason they never achieve their righteous desires."

Elder Daniels looked at the page and a half of notes and shook his head. "Man, I had no idea there was so much to do. Where did you learn all this?"

"Well, from other missionaries and reading a lot of books about faith."

"So what's next?" Elder Daniels asked.

"Now you've got to plead your case before the Lord."

"You mean through prayer?"

"Yes. You want to explain to the Lord what your goal is, and most importantly, explain your rationale for wanting your desire to be realized."

Elder Daniels sat for a moment, thinking. "But wouldn't the Lord already know that?"

"Well sure, but think about how many hundreds of times the scriptures say 'ask and ye shall receive, seek and ye shall find, knock and it shall be opened unto you.' You see the Lord wants us to ask and he wants us to be specific in stating our desires. Think about how many times we say 'please help us,' 'please bless us' and never really tell Him what we need help with or what blessings we are in need of. Of course, He knows what we need, but He's commanded us to ask. This shows that we are earnest and have given thought to what we need."

Elder Daniels nodded again, remembering how rarely he prayed like that, and how repetitious his prayers were most of the time. Just that morning when he'd knelt in prayer by his bedside he'd been very vague in the help he requested. Perhaps that was a big reason why it seemed his prayers were rarely answered in the way he expected.

Elder Neil continued, "When you plead your case, explain to the Lord how your desires will bring about His purposes. Explain to Him that learning the language will make you a better missionary by being able to teach the gospel in a clear and simple manner, that it will help in your companionship with Elder Reyes who speaks little English. You see, you want to tell Him specifically how it will help in each instance."

Elder Daniels looked at his watch. He knew Elder Reyes was at his desk doing his personal study and would soon be ready to begin their companionship study. Eagerly he wrote faster, hoping to get more recorded before their time was up.

"Okay, so after I plead my case, what's next?"

"Now begins the real test of your faith," Elder Neil explained. "First you have to make sure you're living your life in harmony with the gospel."

Ensuring that Elder Daniels was listening closely, he continued, "Elder Daniels, I mean *every* aspect of your life. This is what I was talking about before about the mission rules."

Opening his Doctrine and Covenants to Section 121, Elder Neil handed the book to Elder Daniels and pointed to the 36th verse. "The Lord has said that 'the Powers of Heaven cannot be controlled nor handled only upon the principles of righteousness.' You have to make sure that you are earnestly striving to obey every commandment, every mission rule, and every aspect of the gospel."

"I'm doing that!" Elder Daniels blurted out in self-defense.

Elder Neil smiled, "I know you are. Honestly. I'm not accusing you of anything. All I'm saying is that your faith, to a large part, can be measured by the degree of righteousness to which you live. For example," he continued, "when you step into a jeepney what's the first thing you notice?"

Just as Elder Daniels was about to say, 'I don't know,' a jeepney passed in front of the apartment with its radio blasting a popular hit Elder Daniels recognized. "The music I guess."

"Right. But what do the mission rules say about worldly music?"

"Not to listen to it." Elder Daniels said sheepishly, remembering how often he found himself singing a song that was stuck in his mind after stepping out of a jeepney.

"Okay, so in order to exercise your faith you have to block out the music. When you're sitting in a member's home and they have the TV on, you have to exercise discipline not to look at it. When you pass by a newspaper vendor, you have to control your eyes so they don't glance at the headlines. Why? Because that's what the Lord has told us to do. You, see," he explained, "it's these little things—just as much as fasting and prayer—that shows the Lord that you are willing to pay any price in order to see your desire realized."

Letting out a deep breath, Elder Daniels put his hands behind his head and stared at the ceiling. This was going to take some work!

He had never thought of himself as a disobedient missionary, not that he felt Elder Neil was insinuating such, but, at times, he knew he had justified breaking some of the mission rules that seemed trivial. Were those little things like glancing at a TV, or looking back at a pretty girl that walked by, really keeping him from seeing the Powers of Heaven manifest in his life?

As he contemplated his actions he thought back at the past four months and how often he really did fall short of precise obedience to the mission rules. He had regularly come in early in the evening with Elder Juarez, taken a drink of water halfway through his fasting with Elder Flores, and recently stayed longer than they should at member's houses with Elder Reyes. No, he realized, he wasn't really a disobedient missionary. He just wasn't completely an obedient missionary either.

When he thought about it, he'd seen the Powers of Heaven at work in his last area with the Baribal family. But he also knew it wasn't because of his faith, but because of the faith of Elder Flores. In fact, the thought went through his mind on whether or not he'd been the reason more blessings had *not* come when they were truly needed.

"You all right, Elder Daniels?"

"Yeah, I was just thinking," Elder Daniels replied. "Having faith is harder than I thought."

"I know how you feel. It's definitely something you have to train yourself to do. Probably the hardest thing is the mental aspect of living faithfully."

"You mean controlling your thoughts?"

"Yes" Elder Neil remarked, "Joseph Smith said that when a man works by faith, he works by a mental exertion rather than a physical force. But it's less about controlling which thoughts enter your mind than it is which thoughts you let stay there. There are thoughts that are constructive to faith and those that are destructive to faith. And, Elder Daniels…there are no other thoughts in between."

"One of my most favorite passages in the scripture is in Matthew where it tells of the Savior walking on water. When Peter asked if he could venture out on the water the Lord invited him, saying, 'Come,' but even when Peter was out there walking on the water, when he saw the wind, he began to be afraid and as he began to sink, he cried out, 'Lord, save me.'"

"We're often just like Peter. When we see the wind or some other small test of our faith come along, our faith begins to waver. We begin to doubt, and as we talked about earlier, 'Where doubt is, faith is not.'"

"I mean, how many times have you gone to a door and said to yourself as you knocked, 'I know there is someone here that is ready to hear the gospel.' Instead, we go to the door and say 'I'll bet no one is even home,' or 'I hope this person doesn't slam the door in my face.' That's not exercising faith, right?"

Elder Daniels shook his head.

"We'd better wrap this up," Elder Neil said as he looked at his watch.

As he and Elder Daniels slid off the edge of the couch to their knees, he said, "No matter what you think, Elder Daniels, you are capable of having great faith. All you need to do is learn how to increase your faith and exercise it. When you do, you'll see how much you become preoccupied with your desire, to the point that every prayer, every action, every thought will be geared toward achieving your righteous desires. When that happens, there is no limit to what you and the Lord can do together."

Elder Daniels didn't move. He was transfixed by what he'd just learned.

Elder Neil put an arm around him. "Great things are about to happen, my friend."

As Elder Daniels bowed his head to pray, Elder Neil surprised him by saying, "Someday, when you're a zone leader you'll look back on our discussion and say, 'Elder Neil was right about faith.'"

# CHAPTER 11

*Now behold, a marvelous work is about to come forth among the children of men. Therefore, O ye that embark in the service of God, see that ye serve him with all your heart, might, mind and strength, that ye may stand blameless before God at the last day.*

*Therefore, if ye have desires to serve God ye are called to the work; For behold the field is white already to harvest; and Lo, he that thrusteth in his sickle with his might, the same layeth up in store that he perisheth not, but bringeth salvation to his soul;*

*And faith, hope, charity and love, with an eye single to the glory of God, qualify him for the work. Remember faith, virtue, knowledge, temperance, patience, brotherly kindness, godliness, charity, humility, diligence. Ask and ye shall receive, knock, and it shall be opened unto you.*

*—D&C 4*

Alicia Decker walked in the front door of her family's two-story home just as her mother was hanging up the phone. "Oh, that was a call for you," her mother said disappointedly.

"Oh really?" Alicia said nonchalantly as she flipped through the stack of mail that lay on the kitchen table. "Who was it?"

"I'm not sure, I think he said his name was *David*."

Alicia's heart jumped in her chest!

"He didn't leave a number," her mother continued.

Alicia dropped the letter she held in her hands and put them in her pockets, not wanting her mother to see how she was shaking. Just the mention of his name made her short of breath and sent a tremor all the way down to her knees.

*I can't believe he called! I can't believe he called!*

Picking up her book bag, she turned to exit the room as quickly as she could, trying hard to avoid the questions she always got from her mother whenever any boy's name was mentioned, other than Aaron Daniels.

"Do you know a *David?*" her mother asked.

*Rats!* She'd almost made it. Stopping at the bottom of the stairs, she turned, "Oh, he's just another student in my American History class."

She lied. The fact was that if her mother knew she'd met this guy for lunch every day that week, she'd have to explain some things she really wasn't ready to talk about.

As she hurried up the stairs trying to avoid eye contact with her mother, she nearly tripped on the third step, only making her want to disappear even faster. She had never been able to lie well to her mother. Although she'd escaped it for the moment, she knew at some point she would have to tell it all, especially if things kept moving as fast as they were.

Dropping her bag as she entered her bedroom, she turned and locked the door, not wanting any of her nosy sisters barging in on her. Kicking off her shoes, she fell back on her feather comforter and pulled the pillow over her head.

*What are you doing?* She screamed at herself. Things were just getting so complicated.

David Holloway was the kind of guy that made girls melt at the very mention of his name. With wavy, blond hair and green eyes, he belonged more on a movie set than in her boring American History class. Upon first seeing him, she immediately noticed his deep, golden tan from which she correctly assumed he was a native of California, and had lived near the beach with surfboard in hand nearly his entire life. He wore loose fitting clothes but she could tell he had an athletic figure. More than once she caught herself picturing him in his surf trunks paddling out to catch a wave. It seemed she never came out of American History with more than a line or two of lecture notes—none of which she could even remember scribbling.

He'd sat two rows in front of her every day since the beginning of class, but on Monday of that week, he'd come in late and taken the seat right next to her.

"Do you mind if I sit here?" he'd asked.

"Not at all," she'd managed to say, although she knew she must have turned red as a strawberry when she looked in his eyes. The rest of the class they'd sat in perfect silence, wondering if the other was going to say something more. By the end of the class, she'd totally given up the idea that he might have sat there because of her, but at the last moment, he'd turned to her, introduced himself, and asked if she wanted to join him for a bite to eat. That meeting had started what became a ritual every day after class since.

*What am I going to do?* She asked herself, contemplating how she would tell him about Aaron.

*What am I going to tell Aaron?*

For now, she'd told no one, not even her closest friends. In some ways, she was too embarrassed to say anything at all. She and Aaron had dated for almost three years and she didn't expect anyone to see how she was doing anything but cheating on him, especially when he'd only been in the mission field only four, or was it five, months?

Was it really cheating? It wasn't like they were married or anything. Besides, who could blame her for wanting to meet new people and make new friends? After all, he hadn't even kissed her yet.

*Yet?*

Even as she finished the thought, she knew that wasn't far away.

\* \* \* \* \*

The sound of a ringing phone stopped Elder Daniels in his tracks as he was heading out the door with his companion. He hadn't heard a phone ring in nearly four months. There were only a few missionary apartments in the entire mission with telephones and this was one of them. In a way, it sounded almost unreal, as if someone was rattling a spoon in an empty glass bottle.

"San Fernando Zone Leaders' apartment," Elder Neil said as he put the receiver to his ear. "Good Morning President Hart, . . . We're doing great, Sir! How are you?"

Elder Daniels didn't know if a call from President Hart was something unusual or not, but one thing he was sure of was that he'd lived there almost a week and had never even noticed the phone sitting on the floor next to the old sofa. That was just one of the many conveniences of home he'd learned to do without. After all, who was he going to call?

"Yes he is, President. He was just walking out the door, let me get him for you." Turning to Elder Daniels, he shrugged his shoulders and said, "It's for you."

At that moment, a thousand thoughts went through his head. *Why would President Hart want to talk to me? Did I do something wrong? Did he find out I broke my fast early last week with that sip of water at church?*

Taking the phone in his hand, he cleared his throat, trying to get the lump that had just appeared out of the way so he could talk.

"Hello, . . . this is Elder Daniels."

A deep voice greeted him from the other end, recalling vivid memories of his first night in the mission field and the anxiety he'd felt toward his mission president.

"Good Morning Elder. How are you finding your new area?" President Hart asked, getting right down to business.

"Just f-fine, Sir."

"Good. Listen son, I've got something that I need to speak to you about, . . ."

Standing beside him, Elder Neil and their two Filipino companions saw a visible change come over Elder Daniels as he spoke to President Hart.

Although they heard nothing of the conversation from the other end, it was obvious by the color of Elder Daniels face that it was not good news. "Yes, President, I will, . . . . Yes, . . . thank you for calling. Yes, we'll leave right now, . . . Okay, goodbye."

Elder Daniels let the phone slip from his fingers. Feeling dizzy and weak in the knees, he fell into the cushions of the couch and put his hands to his face,

"Oh no!" he said, hiding the anguish that contorted his features.

\* \* \* \* \*

Tucking the end of the bamboo strip under the last row of the basket she'd just woven, Gelyn Nguyen looked around for another strip, only to find the pile she'd been taking them from exhausted.

"Could you pass me one more?"

Those were the first words either of them had spoken in almost an hour. The silence had been almost unbearable at times but the air was too heavy with bad feelings now to say anything more. Though they sat within a yard of each other, they were kilometers apart inside.

She'd asked a question that violated the unspoken agreement they'd honored for the past three years concerning religion. Would he consider listening to the missionary discussions again?

In the dim light of the nipa hut, the husband and wife sat in silence, trying to avoid any more contention. Although he was still angry that she even broached the subject with him, he knew from the way she'd wiped at her eyes that his sharp words had cut her deeply. He also knew how much her faith meant to her.

\* \* \* \* \*

Walking over to Elder Daniel's side, Elder Neil asked, "What's wrong?"

Taking his hands from his face, Elder Daniels explained, "There's been an accident, . . . Sister Adams's mother was killed in a car accident yesterday, . . . and President Hart wants me to relay the message to her."

Standing up, he felt light-headed and nearly fainted as the thought of telling a missionary in his district the news. And Sister Adams at that. He saw her smile in his mind and then saw it vanish, knowing how she would react to the news.

*Why her? Why did this have to happen to Sister Adams?*

\* \* \* \* \*

"Listen Gelyn," her husband said after a few moments, "I'm sorry for snapping at you like that, but you know how I feel about the Mormons." Without looking up, Gelyn nodded, pressing her eyes together tightly as the tears began to fall once again.

Although he was still upset, the sight of her crumbling emotionally made his heart sink. Life had been difficult for her as it was: a mute son; despicable living conditions; hours upon hours of finger-numbing basket weaving. As he sat and pondered, he could see few things that brought her joy. The question he was left with was what right he had to infringe upon those that did?

Setting his basket aside, he crawled over on hands and knees until he was directly in front of her. From that position, the shiny streaks of tears down her face could not be hidden. He inwardly kicked himself for causing her more grief. He was tired of fighting—tired of arguing about something he knew nothing about.

"Okay dear," he said in a quiet voice, taking her hands in his so that she finally quit working, "If it means that much to you, I'll listen to the missionaries again."

Throwing her arms around him she sobbed even more, finally letting out some of the inner turmoil she'd harbored internally.

She knew that didn't mean that he'd go to church, or be baptized, but it was a step in the right direction. A big step! Having to choose between her husband and her faith was harder than any trial she'd ever encountered. She'd spent many sleepless nights on her knees trying to draw comfort from the one source on which she could always count.

\* \* \* \* \*

Elder Daniels took a seat on the jeepney next to his companion. Normally, he would have hung off the back even with empty seats inside. Not today. His task weighed far too heavily on his mind to enjoy any of the scenery along the way.

Although they had planned to work in their area in the morning and with the Bacnotan Elders that afternoon, the call from President Hart had changed everything. In a two-minute conversation with his mission president, Elder Daniels had been given the biggest challenge of his mission—he had to tell one of the missionaries in his district that her mother had died.

As the road twisted and turned along the sandy shoreline , Elder Daniels stared out over the deep-blue ocean that sparkled like silver in the morning sun. The irony of the moment didn't even register. Nothing contrasted more with the beautiful scene before him than his troubled mind.

It was a long ride from San Fernando to San Juan. His entire concentration was on trying to figure out how he would break the news to Sister Adams, a missionary who was only a few months away from going home.

*How do you tell someone her mother is dead? How can I break that news to her without crushing her soul? Why did President Hart ask me to do it? Elder Neil would know just what to say.*

Such were the questions that had raced through his mind as the over-crowded jeepney barreled down the road toward San Juan. For Elder Daniels, the most difficult question was 'why would the Lord let such a thing happen?'

However, he knew that question would not be answered on the ride to San Juan. Remembering what Elder Flores had said about his asthma, he now understood that question wasn't his to ask?

With a prayer in his heart and his companion at his side, Elder Daniels paused at the sister's front door. Searching for the courage to knock, it took many moments before his knuckles found the surface of the old wooden door. He felt sweat run all the way down his arms, dripping off his fingertips. Even as the sun beat down upon his neck, he knew the perspiration had nothing to do with the heat. Clearing his throat, he tried to swallow. His mouth was as dry as parched sand.

He actually hoped the sisters weren't home—that no one would come to the door and he could put the matter aside. But that was not to be. Within seconds of knocking, Elder Daniels found himself face to face with the effervescent sister missionary.

Inviting the Elders in, Sister Adams's smile soon faded when Elder Daniels asked if they could begin with a word of prayer. Having been in the mission field well over a year, Sister Adams knew that when district leaders show up without notice and ask to start with a prayer, something was definitely wrong.

\* \* \* \* \*

On the jeepney to Bacnotan, Elder Daniels closed his eyes. All he could see was the heart-broken face of a young missionary who'd just learned that her mother had been killed in a car accident. But even that expression was short-lived.

There had been no screaming, no sobbing, no outward show of emotion other than a stream of tears that mirrored his own. She had just sat there, letting the tears fall down her cheeks onto her white blouse and black missionary nametag.

"The Lord is my Shepherd," she'd said, wiping her eyes. "I shall not want, . . ."

Elder Daniels had watched as her persona changed and he could see that she visibly drew strength from a reserve somewhere deep inside of her. Thanking him for bringing the message, she'd stood up and went to her room to pray. Moments later she'd reappeared, completely together as if nothing was amiss at all.

"So I guess I need to call President Hart and see what he wants me to do. I'm sure he'll let me call home, but there's really not much I can do from here."

As Elder Daniels sat on the jeepney pondering Sister Adam's reaction to the news, his mind cleared and a shiver ran from the back of his neck. On his arms, and even under his pant legs, he felt every hair stand. At that moment, he finally understood the true meaning of the Gospel of Jesus Christ.

As he thought back on it, he realized he'd misjudged Sister Adams completely. What had he expected her to do? Yell? Shout? Lie on the floor kicking and screaming? No. Not Sister Adams. She knew too much for that.

Was she surprised by the news? Yes! Was she hurt by the news? Of course! Did she love her mother? Absolutely! But Sister Adams also understood the gospel she was teaching. She knew that Christ had defeated death on that holy Sabbath Day in the meridian of time. She knew his willing sacrifice and miraculous resurrection promised eternal life.

It wasn't something she simply taught in discussions with investigators. It wasn't just something she just *believed*. Sister Adams *knew* that her mother was in the arms of her Heavenly Father. It was an infallible truth that swallowed her pain and allowed her to see things from an eternal perspective.

Closing his eyes once again, Elder Daniels said a prayer of thanks. It was then that he understood why President Hart asked him to deliver the news. He was learning what it felt like to have a real testimony—something he didn't know how he'd done without for all this time. After all, what business did he have preaching about the Plan of Salvation if he didn't believe it himself?

Drawing a deep breath and exhaling slowly, Elder Daniels relaxed for the first time all morning. Sister Adams would be all right. She and Sister Jornacio were going to teach a discussion that morning and then head to the mission home to speak with President Hart. She would then make a call home to her family.

Would she go home? Elder Daniels assumed she might be given the choice since she only had a few more months in the mission. But he already knew that she would call home, she would express her love and support for her family, but she would finish her mission.

Staring out the window, he recalled a scripture that he'd learned in seminary. Under light of these circumstances, he finally understood its meaning.

*And every one that hath forsaken houses, or brethren, or sisters, or father, or mother, or wife, or children, or lands, for my name's sake, shall receive an hundredfold, and shall inherit everlasting life (Matthew 19:29).*

\* \* \* \* \*

"What are you going to do?"

"Go out with him!" Alicia replied sharply. "I mean it's not like Aaron and I are engaged or anything!"

"Almost! I mean isn't that what you've been saying for the past year? When Aaron gets off his mission you two are getting married? I mean...," she almost didn't say it. "...didn't you tell him you *wouldn't* marry him if he *didn't* go on a mission?"

Alicia sat in silence. As much as she hated admitting it, her best friend was right. They had talked about marriage. They'd talked a *lot* about it. She was the one who always brought it up.

"Yeah, well, what am I supposed to do?" she asked, her voice a little louder than she'd expected. "Just sit home every night for two years?"

"Shhhhssh."

Diverting their eyes from one another, both girls returned to their assigned reading. The school library probably wasn't the best place to have this conversation. Reading the first couple lines of her civil war history book, she was halfway into the third sentence before she was at it again, justifying in her mind the decision she'd made to go out with David.

*After all,* she thought, *it's only a date. What could happen in just one date?*

\* \* \* \* \*

Elder Reyes stepped off the jeepney and pointed toward a distant house sitting on the beach. In awe of the view before him, Elder Daniels stared in the direction his companion was pointing. Directly in front of him lay a newly sprouted rice field completely blanketed in emerald green. In sharp contrast to this emerald expanse was an electric blue ocean just beyond. The ocean drifted far into the distant horizon where the sparkling water merged with the baby blue of a cloudless sky. The only thing that broke the horizon was a row of coconut trees and a tropical beach house sitting alone on a gentle rise. Elder Reyes said, pointing to the house, " Bacnotan Elders."

The landscape astounded him. Elder Daniels stood motionless, transfixed by the majestic colors upon which he gazed. For a moment he felt like he was looking at a postcard. Setting his backpack down, he pulled out his camera, snapping a quick picture before running down a small road to catch up with his expeditious companion.

It was already mid-morning and the Bacnotan Elders were sure to be out working. Elder Daniels needed to leave them a note to check on Sister Adams each day for a week or so. They'd planned to surprise them and split with them that morning, but that plan had fallen through when he received the call came about Sister Adams's mother.

Unable to take his eyes off the beautiful vista, Elder Daniels didn't even see the two bicycles leaning against the beach house. Nor did he notice the young boy squatting near a washbasin scrubbing at the dingy collar of a white shirt.

"Good morning!" greeted the hired househelp in Tagalog as the missionaries approached.

"Good morning."

Letting his companion do the talking, Elder Daniels listened as Elder Reyes explained the reason for their visit and produced the note he had scribbled on their way from San Juan.

"Why don't you just talk to them inside?" the young man asked.

Elder Daniels looked to his companion who stood by his side with a puzzled expression on his face.

"What did he say?"

Elder Reyes paused, searching for the right words in English. "She say," he began, erring in his use of the feminine pronoun, "Elders inside."

"Huh?" Elder Daniels asked, looking back to the young boy for clarification.

Pointing to the bicycles, he repeated his earlier statement, this time in English. "Elders inside."

Elder Daniels turned around and looked at the two red bikes leaning against the house. *That's strange,* he thought, looking at his watch. *I wonder why they're back so early for lunch.*

Walking to the front door, he turned the doorknob. Finding it unlocked, he opened the door and stepped inside.

Elder Daniels had only met the Bacnotan Elders one time and his first impression of them had not been good. They'd arrived twenty minutes late for his first district meeting. Elder Sullivan and Elder Torres had expressed their lackadaisical attitude toward missionary work by walking in and sitting down without so much as a word of explanation.

After an opening prayer and a somewhat pitiful rendition of "Called to Serve," Elder Daniels had asked Sister Jornacio to lead them in reciting Doctrine and Covenants Section Four. During both the opening hymn and recital of the section every missionary had memorized, the tall, overweight Elder Sullivan stared blankly out the window as his companion mouthed the words.

Their weekly report was no better. Expected to meet or exceed the standard of 70 proselyting hours, 30 contacts, 20 discussions, and 7 church investigators, the Bacnotan Elders reported 61 proselyting hours, 13 contacts, 7 discussions, and 1 church investigator. Elder Daniels had looked at the report and frowned. Things weren't going well in that part of his district.

As Elder Daniels entered the beach house, it took a moment for his eyes to adjust to the dim lighting. With the blinds on every window pulled down, he had a difficult time figuring out the layout of the two-bedroom apartment.

The sparsely decorated room contained nothing more than two wicker chairs, a small bistro-style table, a plywood bookcase full of Books of Mormon, and an old mesh hammock strung between two supporting wood pillars in the middle of the room.

As he surveyed the room he wondered why the lights were out if the Elders were inside. And if they were inside, where were they?

Noticing three doors spread out along on the far side of the room, he peeked into the first to find a simple bathroom complete with a bucket shower and a dingy porcelain toilet. He figured the door to the other must be one of the bedroom areas and confirmed his suspicion finding an odd assortment of dusty workout equipment and a full-length mirror.

Without a sound in the entire apartment besides his own footsteps on the linoleum floor, Elder Daniels already knew what he would find behind door number three.

Elder Daniels knocked once and pushed the door open. A surge of anger exploded within him. There, in two separate beds, lay the Bacnotan Elders snoring away as their electric fan lazily oscillated from side to side.

Elder Torres stirred slightly as the door opened but quickly relaxed again and continued snoring. Elder Sullivan lay motionless, lying on his back with one leg hanging off his bed.

On a small table between the two twin beds sat a stereo. Not a stereo, really, a "boom box." With twelve-inch speakers, a five-disc CD changer, and more dials and buttons than he'd ever seen. This stereo was built to play music at high volume—the kind of music the mission rules prohibited. Stacked next to the stereo were a dozen or more CD's. The titles of many of the bands were familiar to Elder Daniels and "Explicit Lyrics" warning labels reminded him of his own wayward past.

Against the wall across from the beds, Elder Daniels saw a large desk. Upon the desk were two decks of playing cards and a copy of *Sports Illustrated*. Nowhere to be found was a missionary journal or a set of scriptures. The only item that reminded him that he was in a missionary apartment was a black missionary nametag he saw on the pocket of a white shirt balled up on the floor next to the desk.

Elder Daniels stood in the doorway confused and angry. It was almost 10:00 A.M. He wanted to rip their sheets off and jerk them out of bed.

The thing that made his blood boil most was the contrast between the earlier events of that morning and what he saw before him. Somewhere, out proselyting in San Juan, was a sister missionary who had just learned of her mother's passing yet was still out teaching a discussion before she attended to her personal affairs. The Bacnotan Elders hadn't even gotten out of bed.

Turning around, Elder Daniels noticed his companion standing just behind him. He, too, was shocked at what he saw. But the look on Elder Reyes' face was not one of anger or frustration, it was a look of utter disappointment.

For Elder Reyes, the opportunity to serve a mission was equivalent to winning the lottery. Up until six months ago, it had only been a dream. It had taken his parents years to save enough money to support him on a mission and what he saw in that room stole something from his mission experience..

Elder Daniels took the note in his hand and scribbled a couple of lines at the bottom. Leaving the note next to the stereo, he turned around, walked out and shut the door.

On the bus ride back to San Fernando, Elder Daniels could think of only one thing. He'd just seen two ends of the missionary spectrum—two sets of missionaries who were as opposite as they could possibly be. Elder Sullivan wanted to be anywhere else but on his mission and Sister Adams couldn't be persuaded, even by the death of her mother, to leave hers.

Elder Daniels also knew that he was somewhere in the middle of that spectrum of dedication. He didn't see himself as an Elder Sullivan, but he certainly wasn't a Sister Adams either. The more Elder Daniels thought about it, the more he realized how ridiculous it was to find himself so noncommittal.

He hated the position he found himself in—a position he'd placed himself in by months of just getting by. As he watched the rice fields pass by outside his window, he realized he was at a decision point himself—a decision point that would define the rest of his mission—and perhaps the rest of his life.

*What kind of missionary are you going to be?*

Thinking back to his conversation with Elder Neil earlier that morning, he knew he could continue to struggle with faith or he could exercise exact obedience and reap the blessings. He was at a fork in the road.

The bus was only a kilometer from San Fernando when Elder Reyes turned to him and asked, "What write on paper?

"I told them that we would be back tomorrow with the zone leaders to pay them another visit."

# CHAPTER 12

*Ask the Father in my name, in faith believing that you shall receive, and you shall have the Holy Ghost, which manifesteth all things which are expedient unto the children of men.*

*And if you have not faith, hope, and charity, you can do nothing.*
*—D&C 18:18 & 19*

"Okay, the scores tied," Elder Hastings huffed, bending over to catch his breath. Smiling, he took the ball from Elder Daniels and bounced it to his companion. "Next basket wins and it's our ball."

Elder Daniels looked at Elder Reyes, giving him a wink. "All right, Comp. Let's hold 'em here. We can't let them score." It had been a long game and he wasn't about to let go of the win easily, especially not to his old "batch mate" from the MTC.

With a quick step—especially for a big man—Elder Hastings faked left then cut right, creating some room between he and Elder Daniels. As if they'd practiced the play his companion tossed the basketball over the outstretched arms of Elder Reyes, right into the hands of Elder Hastings who had easily beat Elder Daniels down the lane toward the basket.

Taking two large steps, he bounced the ball once and was airborne, jumping off his left leg from just inside the foul line. Seeing the inevitable, Elder Daniels stopped short, knowing this would not only be an easy dunk for Elder Hastings, it would also mean the end of the game.

With little effort, the big American was a meter in the air and coming down for a two-handed dunk when the ball hit the back of the rim and ricocheted out of bounds.

Laughing hysterically, Elder Daniels ran after the ball. "That'll teach you for showing off!"

Elder Hastings stood with his mouth open, dismayed at missing the game-winning shot. "Sorry, Comp, we'll get 'em here," he said, walking to the top of the key where Elder Daniels was waiting to check-in the ball.

Just as Elder Daniels was just about to pass the ball, he noticed a woman standing near the entrance of the chapel watching them. Having been the only ones at the Lingsat chapel since their district meeting, he was surprised to see someone else there on a Monday afternoon.

"Hello." the woman said as he approached.

"Sorry, we didn't see you there," he said in English, hoping she understood. Tucking the ball under his arm, he extended a hand but quickly withdrew it when he realized he was dripping sweat.

Blushing a little behind her dark complexion, the woman said something in Tagalog that Elder Daniels didn't understand.

"Uh, . . . wait just a second," Elder Daniels said, waving his companion over.

"Hey, are we going to finish this game or not?" Elder Hastings yelled, still waiting under the basket in the church parking lot.

"Hold on!"

Elder Daniels turned back to the sister he recognized now from the Lingsat Ward. Although he'd only seen her twice, both times at the sacrament service, he remembered her because she now wore the same blouse and skirt she'd worn on both occasions. Somewhere in her late forties, Elder Daniels had noticed her sitting alone, quietly worshipping without a word to anyone else.

Wiping the sweat out of his eyes and enjoying a moment to rest in the shade of the large steeple, he listened carefully as the woman introduced herself. Her name was Sister Nguyen. Instead of tuning out the conversation as he'd often done when English wasn't spoken, Elder Daniels listened intently to piece together the conversation.

He learned that she was a convert to the Church of about three years. He also recognized the names of one of the missionaries that had taught and baptized her. An American, with a poor reputation in the mission, had fallen in love with a young Filipina they were teaching and had been transferred to another area when it was discovered they were passing notes to one another.

Sister Nguyen spoke softly but quickly. She, explained that she had much work to do back at the house, and even this brief departure from her work might jeopardize things. As she spoke, the words came faster and faster until she had to stop for several moments to catch her breath.

After a brief pause, she went right back to the story of her conversion and the difficulty she'd had getting her husband to agree to the missionary discussions. It had already been a week since he'd agreed to meet with the Elders but work had prevented her from coming sooner and a sick child at home had kept her from attending the service the day before. That one week had felt like an eternity.

An impatient inquiry from the basketball court reminded Elder Daniels of the interrupted game. "Hey, what's up?" Elder Hastings shouted. "Let's finish this. There's only one basket to go!"

Turning briskly, Elder Daniels tossed the ball onto the basketball court and immediately turned back to the conversation. Elder Reyes was getting directions to the woman's home and setting an appointment for the following morning when they could meet her husband for the first time.

Elder Daniels experienced a surge of excitement and felt like running home and changing into his missionary attire right that moment. P-Day or not, he was ready to meet their new investigator right away. But knowing these days were meant for preparing mentally and physically for the week ahead, he let the idea go and settled with knowing they had a great referral from a part-member family.

As quickly as she'd appeared, the woman was gone, practically running out the gate and hailing the first trike she could find. Elder Daniels high-fived his companion, congratulating each other on the new contact. Having taught only a handful of discussions in the last week, both missionaries knew the value of a member referral, especially one where there would be instant fellowship and the uniting of a family in the Gospel of Jesus Christ.

"Hey what's gotten into you, man?" Elder Hastings asked as the two missionaries walked back on the court.

"What are you talking about?"

"Well, . . . I don't know," Elder Hastings shrugged, tossing the ball back to Elder Daniels. "I mean I hear you guys are working like eighty hours a week and doing this "speak-your-language day" like we did in the MTC."
Elder Daniels bounced the ball a couple of times through his legs, "We're just trying to be better missionaries."

"We all are!" Elder Hastings shot back.

"No, I mean we're just trying to get into the "pure blessing zone."

"The *what* zone?" Elder Hastings asked, bouncing the ball back to his batch mate.

With a wink, Elder Daniels bounce-passed the ball to his companion, saying, "Let's finish this game, then I'll explain it to you."

Catching the ball off the bounce, Elder Reyes posted up against his own defender only to find the lane well-guarded. Elder Hastings' companion had a hand in his face no matter where he turned. Dribbling once he faked a turnaround jumper only to pass the ball off at the last second to Elder Daniels who hadn't moved from the spot where he'd brought the ball in at the top of the key.

Seeing his man left open, Elder Hastings lunged forward, reaching high in the air to block the shot. It was too late. Elder Daniels, who hadn't made an outside shot all game, let go of a three-point "hail-Mary." The ball arced high over the out-stretched arms of his taller batch-mate and fell through the net with a "swoosh."

"That's it! The game-winner!"

Elder Hastings caught the ball as it fell through the net and grimaced, "That was a lucky shot. I'll bet you couldn't make that again if you had ten more tries."

Knowing it had been more luck than skill, Elder Daniels replied, "Yeah, I guess the blessings are flowing today! Right, Elder Reyes?"

\* \* \* \* \*

Looking in the mirror, Elder Daniels ran a hand through his hair. Although it wasn't growing as quickly as he'd hoped, it was better than the quarter-inch bristles he'd been left with by a barber in his last area. He was actually able to style it now, combing it in a way that the natural curl made his bangs stick up in front and then droop to the side. It wasn't a thick, wavy hairstyle out of *Men's Health*, but the missionary standards didn't allow for that. Alicia had always liked him with longer hair, but she wasn't here to comment on the way his hair looked now.

*I wonder what she's doing right now.*

"Stop it!" Elder Daniels said aloud, berating himself for letting his mind wander. "Heart, might, mind, and strength," he reminded himself. Keeping his mind focused was definitely the hardest part of being an obedient missionary.

Glancing at the corner of his bedroom mirror, Elder Daniels saw the three-by-five index cards he'd taped there to remind him of the goals he'd set. On the first card he'd written his goal: *Become Fluent in Tagalog in Two Months*. Below that he'd taped three more index cards that listed the specific steps he would take to achieve it—steps Elder Neil taught him to draw upon the Powers of Heaven.

Coming up with the goal had been the easy part. After realizing how poor a teacher he was in that discussion with the sister missionaries, he'd known immediately that in order to teach the gospel effectively he would have to learn the language quickly. Sure, he'd seen other missionaries baptize who didn't master the language, but he'd also seen how Sister Adams taught. He'd seen the way she brought gospel principles to life—how she taught from the heart—how she communicated not only by voice, but also by feeling. Elder Daniels attributed much of that to her fluency with the native language of her investigators.

Elder Daniels was going to learn Tagalog and he wasn't about to wait the year or longer that most missionaries took to master the skill. After his study with Elder Neil, he knew, or at least wanted to believe, that God would make that possible if he asked with enough faith. But what was *enough* faith? Even though he didn't know the answer to that question, he knew that having a desire to believe was enough to plant the seed of faith and by his obedience, that seed would receive nourishment.

On the top of the index card was also a date. The date was December 31st, not because it had anything to do with New Year's Eve, but solely because it marked the exact date two months from when he'd written down his goal. Putting his desire on paper had marked the beginning of his journey, and that journey began on October 31st.

Back in the States his family had celebrated Halloween on October 31st, a strange holiday he'd never really understood. In the Philippines, however, that day signified preparations for a different holiday—All Saint's Day.

Among Western Liturgical churches, November 1st is celebrated as the Christian feast in honor of all the saints. Having a very Roman Catholic heritage, this national holiday is widely celebrated throughout the Philippines and many other countries throughout the world.

Similar to Memorial Day, Elder Daniels found that large masses of people visited cemeteries where their relatives were buried, decorating the graves with ornamental flowers. Beginning the night before, he'd seen long parades of people holding candles on their way to the cemetery, which coincided with All Soul's Day, another holiday, on November 2nd. All Soul's Day was a melancholic celebration during which masses gathered to pray for the souls of the faithfully departed.

To Elder Daniels it all seemed very strange. Although he'd visited the graves of relatives on Memorial Day, it didn't make much sense feasting over the departed and then praying for their souls. Instead, this was one of those times the gospel really made sense to him. From his companion he learned that Filipino Latter-day Saints did genealogy work instead.

Since he didn't have the resources, or the time, to do genealogy work on his mission, it seemed like the perfect time to put his old ways and habits into the grave and celebrate his own new beginning. This would be a beginning, in which he would learn to exercise his faith, even to the point of drawing on the Powers of Heaven.

On the second card he'd listed the things he would do himself in order to achieve his goal.

---

### My Resolves

1. Study the missionary discussions in Tagalog for 1/2 an hour each day and study Tagalog for 1/2 an hour in our companionship study.
2. Alternate Speak Your Language days with my companion.
3. Open my mouth and believe that the Lord will fill my mind with the things that I should say.

---

Elder Daniels knew he would have to make a concentrated effort to learn the language. Except for his two months in the MTC he really hadn't set aside any particular time to study Tagalog. Sure he'd gotten by so far memorizing most of the discussions in Tagalog but that had been done out of necessity rather than desire. He also knew, reciting the discussions without comprehending what he was saying made teaching with the Holy Ghost quite difficult. As a result, he dedicated time each day to study his language books, in his self-study and with his companion. He'd even decided to write down and translate ten words from English to Tagalog and then use each one in his conversations with others.

His second resolve had to do with discipline. In his first two areas, Elder Daniels had been blessed with companions who spoke English well enough that he never had to worry about speaking Tagalog with them. But in Lingsat things were different. Elder Reyes was learning English but the communication process was difficult at best.

Elder Daniels initially planned to never speak a word of English to his companion again. A single morning of that had made him change his mind. Explaining his resolution to his companion, Elder Reyes had soon decided that he too wanted to help, both himself and his companion.

Aside from teaching and working with members, it was agreed that each day was either an "English day" or a "Tagalog day," alternating between the two. In this way, each missionary got a chance to practice his language skills as well as help his companion with his.

His third resolve was where Elder Daniels struggled most. Severely self-conscious of his grammar and use of Tagalog, it was difficult to know if what he was about to say was correct. At those times he often just shut his mouth and said nothing. Remembering what Elder Neil had said about faith, he resolved to open his mouth—trusting the Lord to help him. It was a big step, and one that he wasn't all that comfortable with much of the time. By now, however, he knew enough about faith to know that he would have to step out of his comfort zone to do so.

On the next index card he'd listed the things he would need the Lord to do—the things he could not do himself.

## Help I Will Need from the Lord

1. Facilitate my learning by the power of the Holy Ghost, and through the power of the Holy Ghost, help others understand me.
2. Help me retain the things I study and be able to recall them when needed.
3. Bestow upon me the Gift of Tongues.

Probably more than any other time in his life, Elder Daniels was completely aware of his own limitations. Though he hadn't tried very hard to learn the language on his own, he knew that no amount of study would yield the results he wanted in only two months. The only way to achieve this goal would be to qualify for, and receive, specific blessings from the Lord.

As he'd learned very clearly, he needed the Spirit to help quicken his mind. The Holy Ghost would "teach him all things, and bring all things to his remembrance" just as it was promised in Section 8 of the Doctrine and Covenants. He didn't really understand how that worked, but he knew that he needed to tell the Lord the specific blessings he desired—and one of those blessings was the Gift of Tongues.

On the last card he'd written four steps he would need to take in order to qualify for the blessings for which he was asking. This card differed from the second in that the list had nothing to do directly with learning Tagalog. Instead, this card outlined how he would show the Lord just how desirous and committed he was to achieving his goal.

---

**My Commitments**

1. I will obey every mission rule.
2. I will wake 1/2 an hour early day to study scriptures about faith.
3. I will fast twice a month and pray continuously about my goal.
4. I will control my thoughts, letting only positive thoughts dictate my actions.

---

Perhaps more conscious of his own weaknesses than before, Elder Daniels found the majority of his effort spent in this last card. He had never been a rebellious missionary but he certainly had room for improvement in his obedience to the mission rules.

Never again could he justify writing letters on days other than those permitted by the mission rules. That meant that only on P-Days could he write to his family and girlfriend. Never again could he allow himself to look twice at a pretty girl walking down the street. Instead, he began a practice of humming the melody of "Called to Serve" whenever he was tempted to turn around. Never again could he become absorbed in the music played on jeepneys. Instead, he would begin a conversation with someone or pull out a copy of The Book of Mormon and read until they arrived at their stop.

This was also the area that Elder Daniels knew was most important. Too many times he'd justified the little things, thinking they made little or no difference upon his spirituality. He now understood that whether he achieved his goal of becoming fluent depended upon being able to draw upon the Powers of Heaven.

Looking back at the image reflected in his bedroom mirror, he finished putting on his tie and pulled his white collar down. As he looked in the mirror he liked what he saw. It wasn't that his hair was finally growing back. It wasn't the new tie he'd received in his last care package. What made him smile was the reflection of the man he saw standing there.

Blinking twice, Elder Daniels looked around the room, making sure he was still alone. For a moment, he thought he'd seen another's reflection in the mirror.

It was the man who had baptized him as an eight-year-old child. The man who ordained him a Deacon, Teacher, and Priest. The same man who'd taught him how to give his first blessing as an Elder in the Melchizedek Priesthood. The man who had set him apart as a missionary and then gathered him in his arms and held him tight, letting the warm tears stream down his face and onto his shoulder as he said good-bye at the front doors of the MTC.

Elder Daniels had never really realized how much he resembled his father. He had the same square jaw, the same dark hair, and the same deep blue eyes. He was beginning to look more and more like him which each day that passed.

Oh, how he wished his father could see him now—that he could see the man he was becoming. Turning away from the mirror, he felt his own tears well up inside his eyes, clouding his vision and making it difficult to see. Yet even as he brought his hand up to wipe his eyes, he knew there had never been a time in his life when he'd seen things more clearly.

\* \* \* \* \*

"Hello," Elder Reyes called, his voice rising melodically on the last syllable.

The two missionaries stood next to a small bamboo hut on stilts, far out of reach of the summer monsoons that often flooded the "lowland" plains. A thin nylon curtain hung in place of a door making it difficult to knock. Smelling cigarette smoke in the air, he and Elder Daniels stepped back from the hut and waited, knowing that at least their investigator, Juan Nguyen, was home.

"Good morning, Elders," Sister Nguyen greeted, pulling the curtain back for the Elders to enter.

Letting his companion climb the steps first, Elder Daniels took off his pack and set it in the entranceway before gingerly testing his weight on the first step. The bamboo ladder leading into the hut was old and worn, except for the first step which was crisp and new.

The creaking and sagging of the ladder brought back agonizing memories of the previous morning when he'd thoughtlessly stepped on the bottom step and felt it break under his weight. Crashing to the ground, he didn't know who had been more embarrassed—the young couple or himself. He'd felt terrible about causing the rather insignificant damage, but the blushing faces of their hosts told him that their own embarrassment was even greater than his.

The young couple apologized again on this morning for the condition of their home as the Elders entered the one-room hut. When they'd been invited inside to meet Juan Nguyen the previous morning, Elder Daniels has been so distracted by the commotion his misstep had caused that he hadn't noticed very much about the furnishings inside. A quick glance around the room now told the same story he'd seen in many of the other homes he'd visited in the Philippines.

There was a small dresser, a rickety table, a couple of bedrolls, and some blackened cookware in the corner—all rudimentary possessions that revealed not so much what they had as it did what they did without.

A picture on the small table caught his eye this morning with its ragged edges and faded color. Elder Daniels knew the picture was not new but the frame certainly was. He was sure of that by the price tag still attached.

It was a photo of a young family standing in front of the San Juan chapel. Dressed in their Sunday best, with the exception of Sister Nguyen who was clothed in white, the family was accompanied by two missionaries. It was a beautiful picture of her baptismal day, and from the look on her face, one that brought her much joy.

On her left stood the missionaries. On her right, her four small children—all under twelve years old and each bearing a strong resemblance to their father. On the very edge of the group was her husband, Juan. In the picture, the small man's face was void of any facial expression whatsoever and seemed out of place with the rest of the family. With his arms crossed and looking nowhere near the camera, it was apparent he had not shared the same emotions as the rest of his family. As he stood farthest from the Elders and the church in the picture, so had he remained.

On the far wall hung the only other picture in the room. There, carefully framed and centered, was a picture of the Manila Temple. Draped in the glorious white glow of lights from the temple grounds, the tall spires reached high above any other buildings in that area of Makati, Metro-Manila. In beautiful gold lettering the words—*The House of the Lord, All Holiness to the Lord*—left no room for interpretation to whom the sacred edifice was dedicated.

Elder Daniels' attention returned to the young couple and the conversation they were having with Elder Reyes. His companion was asking the young couple more about their children. Remembering his goal to become fluent in Tagalog, Elder Daniels began following the conversation more intently as Sister Nguyen highlighted their recent accomplishments in school. There was no holding back her affection as she spoke of her greatest blessings.

The only thing that darkened the moment was the way her smile vanished when asked about her youngest son Juan, Jr. Her joy was replaced by hurt and anger as she related the teasing he faced nearly every day. Born with a cleft palette, the bones of his upper mouth had never fused together preventing him from forming words and syllables. In all his six years, she explained, he'd never spoken a word.

Although the missionaries wanted to come at a time when the entire family was home, Sister Nguyen felt that all efforts should be focused on her husband. She had explained that the missionaries had visited many times and the children often accompanied her to church and were ready to be baptized if her husband would only allow it. What she didn't explain was her fear that her husband might openly object to the missionary lessons and embarrass and emotionally scar the children if they were present.

Apologizing once again for having no chairs, Juan Nguyen pushed the basket he'd been weaving aside and sat down on the hard floor, next to his wife.

"Thank you for letting us visit you this morning," Elder Reyes began in Tagalog as he and Elder Daniels took their place across from them. "We know you are very busy."

Respectful of where they were, he asked, "Brother, since this is your home, would you mind if we began with an opening prayer?"

Brother Nguyen shook his head.

Not wanting to offend the man, Elder Reyes asked further, "Who would you like to give the opening prayer?" Not having said more than a handful words the day before, and only a few since they'd arrived, Brother Nguyen pointed to Elder Daniels.

If anyone else noticed the look of fright that suddenly came over Elder Daniels, they didn't give any indication. This was one of those moments he wished he could crawl under a rock and hide. Having resolved to speak Tagalog at every opportunity, Elder Daniels froze, knowing he wouldn't be able to rely on anything he'd previously memorized to get through this prayer.

The last to bow his head, Elder Daniels took a deep breath to calm himself. Summoning as much concentration as he could find, he forcibly pushed a stream of negative thoughts from his mind—thoughts that placed doubt and disbelief before his faith.

He began by opening his mouth and speaking the first word that came to his mind. After that word he said the next, and then the next—whatever words came to mind without thought of meaning, grammar or pronunciation. It wasn't a perfect prayer—neither was it a long prayer—but it was a prayer spoken in Tagalog and Elder Daniels' first!

The remainder of the discussion progressed smoothly and the Spirit was present in the small nipa hut. The missionaries took turns teaching about two obstacles that stood in their way of returning to our Heavenly Father: death and sin. They taught about Christ's role in the plan of salvation and how He overcame both these obstacles through His death, resurrection and atonement for our sins. They taught that all mankind would live again after this life but that each will have to choose to follow the Savior in order to dwell in the presence of our Heavenly Father.

Elder Daniels introduced the first four principles and ordinances of the Gospel: faith, repentance, baptism by immersion, and receiving the Gift of the Holy Ghost, explaining that Christ taught that these principles and ordinances were necessary for salvation.

Elder Reyes asked if Brother Nguyen had any questions.

"No," he responded.

Very surprised at how well both discussions had gone so far, Elder Reyes looked at his companion, his eyes searching for confirmation to proceed with the next question. This wasn't at all like Sister Nguyen had warned them it might be.

"Brother Nguyen," Elder Reyes continued, "are you willing to follow our Savior's example by being baptized a member of The Church of Jesus Christ of Latter-day Saints?"

It was the perfect lesson—almost *too* perfect, Elder Daniels thought to himself. No questions. No concerns. No hang-ups he wasn't willing to put aside. For a man who had adamantly told his wife he never wanted anything to do with the Mormon Church, things were going almost *too* well.

Gelyn Nguyen bit her lip, half wishing the Elders hadn't moved so quickly. Maybe this was a mistake. Maybe he wasn't ready. She was already very surprised that he had gone this far in the discussions without working himself into a fit of anger. So many times before he'd blown up at the slightest mention of the Church.

What would he say now? Would he laugh at the invitation to be baptized? Would he explode into a frenzy of hate and rage? Half turning to see him out of the corner of her eye, she tasted blood as she realized she'd bit her lower lip in anticipation of his response.

Without a moment's hesitation, Brother Nguyen opened his mouth and spoke a single word.

"Yes."

For a moment the entire room was silent. Not a single person spoke. Not a single strip of bamboo creaked. Nothing. It was perfectly silent as everyone waited as if to verify they'd heard his answer correctly.

Finally, realizing what her husband had said, Sister Nguyen jumped to her knees and nearly knocked her husband over as she threw her arms around his neck. She began sobbing uncontrollably. For three long years she'd dreamt of this moment—hoping, waiting and pleading that this day would come.

Turning back toward the Elders, Brother Nguyen struggled under the grip of his wife. "Okay! Okay!" he said as he tried to loosen her hold just a little. He knew she'd be pleased with his decision but never to this extent.

"Wonderful!" Elder Reyes exclaimed joyfully.

Rising up on his knees, Elder Daniels reached forward to shake the hand of their newest baptismal candidate. Still encumbered by the weight of his wife, Brother Nguyen reached out and took the hand of the large missionary, trying to balance himself with his other hand.

Not wanting to pass up this perfect moment, Elder Reyes asked, "Brother Nguyen, how would you feel if we set November 25th, the Sunday after next, for your baptismal date?"

With a look of surprise, Brother Nguyen replied, "I want to be baptized today."

Explaining that they had more to teach him, both missionaries grew concerned when the corners of their investigator's mouth dropped into a frown.

"I don't understand." Brother Nguyen explained, "I'm ready now. Why do we have to wait?"

Reassuring him that these were the mission rules, Elder Reyes did his best to put the man's worries to rest. Finally content that a week and a half was not too long to wait, Brother Nguyen agreed to the goal date and promised that he would do his best to attend church with his wife and family the next Sunday.

As Sister Nguyen offered the closing prayer, Elder Daniels felt a cold chill run down his spine. Surprised by the sensation, he couldn't help wondering why he felt so strangely in the midst of such great news. A nagging little voice inside his head was telling him that something didn't seem quite right. Elder Daniels brushed the thought aside, forcing himself to remain positive and full of faith.

Halfway through the prayer he stole a glance at the man sitting across from him. Head bowed and eyes closed, the man sat motionless. Dismissing the strange notion from his mind once again, Elder Daniels closed his eyes, attributing his skepticism to his lack of faith and experience in the mission field.

*Everything will work out,* he said to himself. *I'm sure of it!*

* * * * *

"You're not cold are you?" he asked, noticing her rosy cheeks.

"Just a little," Alicia admitted, trying not to sound too pitiful as the biting wind cut through her ski parka.

"I guess I should have warned you it gets pretty cold up here, especially this time of day when the sun hides behind the peaks of those mountains to the West."

Alicia lifted her eyes to the skyline where the broad-faced peaks of Snowbird Ski Resort towered over the skiers and snowboarders zigzagging their way down the mountain. Under the backdrop of the majestic monoliths, the people looked like tiny ants scurrying along a frozen blanket of white—only the blanket was on such an angle that the only direction the ants could go was down.

Her first time skiing, Alicia had fallen more than her share. The only thing that took her mind off the chilling cold was her aching body begging her to put a stop to the abuse. Between the numbness in her extremities and the throbbing pain in her muscles, she wondered why so many people flocked to the mountains of Utah to ski "the greatest snow on earth."

"You're really picking it up quick!" David offered enthusiastically. "But I still can't believe you've lived in Utah nineteen years and never learned to ski!"

Alicia smiled, "I guess I've always been the summer type, you know, believing that winters are made for sipping hot chocolate next to a warm fire." Even before she finished the sentence she wished she'd never said it. It sounded so corny! If it hadn't been for her rosy cheeks, David might have seen her blush.

But that wasn't the only reason she wished she'd never mentioned cozy fires and hot chocolate. Memories of Aaron flooded her mind. They'd watched countless hours of TV in front of the fireplace at her parents' house on evenings just like this one.

Shaking her head, she did her best to chase the thoughts away. Aaron was half a world away and that she didn't need to be thinking of him at that moment—not with David sitting only inches away from her.

It happened so casually that she almost didn't notice. With a slight lean and a shuffle, David was sitting right next to her, actually touching her arm and leg with his. After a half-dozen trips up the mountain, David Holloway finally made his move. With one easy motion, he swung his arm over her head and around her shoulder, gently pulling her close as the chair lift climbed toward the summit.

The flutter of butterflies tickled her stomach. So many nights in the past two weeks she'd dreamt of this moment. Even through parkas and layers of sweaters, she could almost feel the warmth of his body next to hers.

Turning her head slightly, she was instantly mesmerized by his emerald green eyes. Just as quickly, she forgot about her aches and pains. She felt her heart beat rapidly as she drew her next breath and leaned forward and kissed him.

* * * * *

Elder Neil was bench-pressing his third set when Elder Daniels came out of his room. With a plop and a sigh, he was sprawled out on the couch staring at the plasterboard ceiling.

"You want to work in with me?"

"No, not tonight. I'm not really in the mood to work out."

Wiping the sweat from his forehead, Elder Neil sat down on the wooden end table he was using as a bench. He reached for a pair of dumbbells made out of cement-filled coffee cans. If the coffee cans didn't look strange enough being used as weights, they sure seemed out of place sitting in the missionary's apartment.

"You look like you've got a lot on your mind. What's up?"

"Oh, I was just thinking about Sister Adams and what she must be going through right now. I can't imagine how I would feel if my mother died."

"Me neither. That's got to be tough."

Still staring at the ceiling, Elder Daniels asked, "Would you have gone home?"

"What do you mean?" Elder Neil grunted between curls with the dumbbell.

"I mean if your mother died two months before you were going home. You said it yourself, she could have gotten an early release, right?"

"I'd imagine." Elder Neil replied.

"So what would you do if you were in her situation? Ride it out or go home?"

Setting the barbell down between his feet, Elder Neil rubbed his chin. "I don't know," he finally admitted. "It'd be a tough decision."

"See, I don't think it would be." Elder Daniels confessed, "I'd go home in a heartbeat."

Elder Neil picked up the dumbbell and started working on his other biceps. "You say that now, but wait until you hit your hump day."

"Hump day? What the heck is that?" Elder Daniels asked.

"One year into your mission. You know, . . . the hump. It's all downhill from there."

"You mean it gets *worse?*"

"No! I mean like on a bike—once you reach the top of a hill and start down the other side, the time starts going way *too fast.*"

"Oh, I get it." Thinking of the Bacnotan Elders, he added, "I guess some missionaries just stop pedaling and coast the rest of the way!"

"That's true!" Elder Neil agreed.

"So why doesn't President Hart send missionaries like Elder Sullivan and Elder Torres home? I mean, they don't seem like they want to be here."

Elder Neil finished his last set of curls and returned the dumbbells to their spot under the end table.

"Well, that's probably got to be one of the toughest decisions a mission president has to make. I mean sending someone home with a dishonorable release. Right? I'm sure there are some cases when that's the only choice, you know? Like when morality issues are involved or the missionary's behavior brings discredit upon the Church. But in some cases it does more harm to the missionary to send them home than to leave them in the mission."

"How's that?"

"Well, say for example that Elder Sullivan was sent home dishonorably. What's he going to do when he gets home?"

"I don't know."

"Chances are he'll go inactive and fall away from the church."

"Yeah, you're probably right," Elder Daniels admitted.

Sitting back down on the table, Elder Neil continued, "As sad as it is, it takes some missionaries their entire two years to figure out why they're out here. Some even go home after two years *not* knowing why they came. That's why it's our responsibility as leaders to make sure we set a good example and help them strengthen their testimonies of the gospel. When they realize why they're here, they won't need as much attention. They'll do it on their own."

Closing his eyes, Elder Daniels asked, "Are you saying I need to work with the Bacnotan Elders more?"

"I'm just saying don't give up on them. I'll bet there was a time in your own life that someone was worried about your testimony. Just keep working with them and it'll come. The Spirit will direct you."

Elder Neil stood slowly, feeling the effects of his workout. "But don't worry, that's part of our responsibility as well."

Heading to the bathroom for a quick shower, Elder Neil looked forward to a restful night sleep. Just as he was turning the corner, Elder Daniels sat up on the couch and asked, "Can I ask you one more question?"

"Sure, what is it?"

"What do you do when you've got an investigator that wants to get baptized for the wrong reason?"

Elder Neil paused, standing in the doorway searching for the right answer. "Peter said, 'Repent and be baptized every one of you in the name of Jesus Christ for the remission of sins, and ye shall receive the Holy Ghost.' I guess that's the deciding factor, if your investigator is penitent, then he's not being baptized for the wrong reason."

"Yeah, I guess you're right." Elder Daniels acknowledged, wondering why he was so worried about Brother Nguyen.

# CHAPTER 13

*And our hope of you is steadfast, knowing, that as ye are partakers of the suffering, so shall ye be also of the consolation.*

*—2 Corinthians 1:7*

*Watch ye, stand fast in the faith . . . be strong.*

*—1 Corinthians 16:13*

Elder Daniels and his companion were just crossing the street when a large Philippine Rabbit stopped in front of them. The large, red bus with the speeding jackrabbit on the side came to a halt with a hiss, liberating the pressure of the pneumatic suspension.

Grabbing his companion by the arm, the way a small child would pull his mother toward the candy aisle, Elder Reyes excitedly tugged at Elder Daniels.

"This one! This one!"

"Okay!" Elder Daniels relented, tired of waiting for a jeepney to come along. The large commercial bus was faster and more comfortable, but his mind was not on comfort as much as it was on the man he'd met and administered a blessing to that morning.

Waiting for two elderly women to disembark, one with a basket of roasted peanuts, the other with small bags of quail eggs, Elder Daniels frowned at the sight of each chewing a thick cigar. It was simply shocking to see women with cigars hanging out of their mouths!

Turning back to his companion, Elder Daniels winked and nodded. "This is nice!"

The larger bus would make for a much better ride back to San Fernando than changing jeepneys in each small town along the way. Destined for Manila, the Philippine Rabbit would take them directly through San Fernando without stopping. Even better, these buses were air-conditioned!

As Elder Daniels took the empty aisle seat in front of his companion, his thoughts turned back to the events of that morning. He'd not looked forward to working with the Bacnotan Elders, but knew they needed extra help in their area. Strangely enough, it was he who was blessed more than they.

He and his companion had gone on splits with the Elders to double the effort—Elder Daniels with Elder Torres, and Elder Reyes with Elder Sullivan. Each companionship had a discussion planned but both fell through when the contacts were not at home. For Elder Daniels and Elder Torres, that meant a morning of asking members for referrals while the other companionship followed up on the few other contacts the Elders had in their teaching pool.

Aside from a couple names they wouldn't be able to follow up on until later that evening, Elder Daniels and his companion learned of only one individual they could pay a visit to that morning. It was their last stop before meeting back at the missionary apartment.

\* \* \* \* \*

In a small barangay three kilometers north of town, a part-member family had been asking to have the missionaries visit their father for many months. The father was not a member and was in very poor health. Having not been able to attend services in months, the referral had finally been relayed to the Elders the previous Sunday by a less-active neighbor.

According to the neighbor, the family of three had taken the missionary discussions about a year before but only the mother and thirteen-year-old daughter were baptized. The father, suffering from diabetes, glaucoma and a number of other ailments, had not been baptized. It wasn't because of a lack of desire, but simply because the man had not been able to get out of his bed for three years. Rather than appearing like they were just trying to run up their numbers, the Elders had told him it was best to wait, promising his work would be done in the temple at a later date.

Unlike most of the homes in the barangay, the Valdez home was simply four walls of aluminum siding and a roof of similar construction. As Elder Daniels approached the "house," he couldn't take his eyes off the structure.

The patchwork of corrugated aluminum contrasted sharply with the thick vegetation growing alongside. Every piece of aluminum that covered the structure was painted a different color. The conglomeration of tin roofing had been collected as scraps from various other structures. Sporadic words hinted at the origin of some pieces while graffiti camouflaged others. One piece read, "Do not urinate here." He assumed that piece came from a fence or building lining a street where people commonly relieved themselves.

Elder Daniels sensed a wonderful spirit as he entered the humble dwelling. With little else to decorate the house, the family had cut out pictures from the *Tambuli*, the Filipino version of the *Ensign* magazine, and taped them to the wall. As if members of their own family, pictures of the First Presidency decorated the walls, along with pictures of Joseph Smith and a half-dozen temples. The pictures provided a visual depiction of the family's tremendous faith.

Sister Valdez was a small woman, full of energy and beaming with the missionaries' presence in her home. Her high-pitched voice added a spark of life to the dirt-floor house. The thing that Elder Daniels found most noble was the way she spoke to and cared for her husband of twenty-six years. As he watched her in the first five minutes, he knew there were few women more compassionate than her.

If Elder Daniels could have pictured misery in human form, Ronaldo Valdez was it. He was the Biblical Job in modern times. Lying on a thin mattress made of three folded blankets, Brother Valdez heard the Elders' voices and immediately called them closer. As he approached, Elder Daniels immediately noticed the white tissue that clouded the lenses of both eyes, obstructing the passage of light into his retinas. Between cataracts and an extremely severe case of glaucoma, Brother Valdez was completely blind. He could no longer distinguish between the passage of light and shadow.

Ronaldo Valdez weighed no more than sixty pounds and was the skinniest man Elder Daniels had ever laid eyes on. Suffering from kidney disease that left him bedridden, he lay in a loincloth diaper leaving all other portions of his body exposed. Elder Daniels winced at the sight of the man as he felt his skin crawl. Little was left of him but skin, bones and bedsores. It was immediately obvious why the Elders had not baptized him.

The bedsores stretched from head to toe. No portion of his exposed body was untouched by discoloration or blisters. Portions of his hips and lower back were covered in blisters—some filled with fluid, others ruptured and oozing at the edges. Heels, ankles and knees were nearly indistinguishable as yellow patches of dark and crusty skin disguised their form. The tissue—either dead or dying as a result of limited blood flow—looked so painful that Elder Daniels had to look away.

Calming himself sufficiently, he squatted down next to Brother Valdez as the man began to speak. His voice was weak but surprisingly coherent and he thanked the Elders for visiting his home. As his eyes stared toward infinity, he spoke of his family's love for the Church and bore his own testimony of the restored Gospel of Jesus Christ. Reaching toward Elder Daniels, he clasped the large American's hand in his and asked that they pray for him.

In the dimly lit interior of the aluminum-sided home, the two nineteen-year-olds laid their hands on the feeble man and administered unto him a blessing as holders of the Melchizedek Priesthood. With wisdom beyond their years, they listened to the Spirit and asked not that the man be healed, but for peace, comfort, and strength to endure. After visiting with him only a few moments, both missionaries knew that if the Lord wanted Ronaldo Valdez to "take up his bed and walk," the man's faith was sufficient that he would have already done so.

\* \* \* \* \*

Sitting on the Philippine Rabbit as it hurled down the provincial highway, Elder Daniels couldn't shake the memory of Brother Valdez, or the question that had been eating at him since they left his side.

*Should he not be baptized?*

It was a question that was tearing Elder Daniels apart. On one hand, if he desired to be baptized, every possible effort should be made to see that it was done. They were missionaries for heaven's sake!

On the other hand, the circumstances made that logic a moot point. The man hadn't been out of his bed in three years! How could they possibly baptize him? Would the Lord really expect them too or require it of a man in his condition?

Debating every possible argument from Bacnotan to San Fernando, Elder Daniels sighed as he came to the same conclusion as the Elders a year ago— Brother Valdez was willing but simply not able—his spirit was strong, but his flesh was weak.

\* \* \* \* \*

All the lights in the San Fernando zone leaders apartments were out but one. With only a reading light, Elder Daniels sat at a small desk next to his bed with a book open in front of him. Picking up his chair as he stood, he carefully pushed the chair back so as not to wake his sleeping companion. He'd already been sitting at the desk for over two hours and needed a good stretch before continuing his study. Having gone to work with the Bacnotan Elders that morning, he and his companion had left the house at 8:00 A.M., setting aside their personal study until that evening.

After working in their own area all afternoon and evening, they'd returned home an hour early to make up for their lost study time. Since it was a Tagalog day, Elder Reyes had led the study with Elder Daniels following along as closely as possible and fighting to keep his eyes open.

Progress was slow, especially when Elder Daniels had to stop his companion mid-sentence to explain the meaning of a word. Still, they'd committed to this course of action and were following through with their plan.

After a quick stretch and a drink of water, Elder Daniels was back in his chair with a half an hour left of Tagalog study. The hour was late but this was something he'd resolved to do in order to learn the language.

Two weeks had already passed and he didn't need anyone to tell him he had a long way to go. At times, he wondered if he could do it. In those moments of frustration, he tried to block out the negative thoughts and replace them with positive, faith-filled thoughts. He envisioned himself teaching entire lessons in Tagalog. He visualized himself approaching people on the street and sharing with them an invitation to hear about the restored Gospel of Jesus Christ taught in their own language. He pictured himself standing in a baptismal font with Juan Nguyen and reciting the baptismal prayer in Tagalog.

Turning the page in his notebook, he spent the next ten minutes translating and conjugating a list of verbs that he'd written earlier in the day. When the list was complete, he began building sentences using each verb in its past, present and future tense and repeating each sentence multiple times. Although he wasn't sure he was pronouncing everything correctly, he knew there would be plenty of people who would correct him if he made a mistake.

"Saan pumunta si Juan?" He said aloud, although almost in a whisper. "Where did Juan go?"

"Alin ba ang bahay ninyo? Which is your house?"

"Ilan ang anak ninyo? How many children do you have?"

Looking at the clock on his desk, he closed his eyes briefly, knowing he would pay for the lack of sleep in the morning. Something Elder Flores had said early in their companionship came back to his mind: the Lord promised a renewing of the body for those who magnify their callings. It was a scripture his earlier companion read to him from Doctrine and Covenants, Section Eighty-Four.

Closing the book, Elder Daniels dropped to his knees next to his bed. After thanking his Heavenly Father for the experiences that morning with Brother Valdez, he once again pleaded with the Lord for help in reaching his goal. It wasn't a long prayer—he and his companion had prayed for their investigators by name in their companionship prayer—this was a personal prayer about his goal. He also prayed to know what to do with Brother Valdez.

Climbing into bed, Elder Daniels reached over to his desk and turned out the light. As his eyes passed over the 5 x 7 picture of Alicia, his thoughts turned to her and what she might be doing right then. Although he hadn't received a letter from her in a couple of weeks, he knew the mail system was unpredictable and figured the mail was hung up somewhere.

*Never mind,* he thought confidently. *It won't be long before I get another stack of her letters.*

\* \* \* \* \*

Elder Daniels stepped out of the trike slowly. Turning his head from side to side, he tried working out the kinks the fifteen-minute ride with his chin on his chest had given him. There was never enough room in a trike.

After setting his bamboo pack on the ground, he reached into his pocket and pulled out a small leather bag shaped like a miniature taco shell. With a zipper that ran down the middle, the "change purse" contained all the money he had. Never in his life did he imagine carrying a "purse" but he had to admit it was a lot easier than trying to keep coins in a wallet.

Unfolding a worn twenty-peso bill, he handed it to the trike driver who took it and stuffed it in his shirt pocket. The small 125cc engine sounded like a chainsaw as the driver turned the motorcycle handlebars in the direction of the highway and started forward.

"Hey! Hold on! What about our change?"

The driver shook his head, pretending not to understand the big American.

"Change!" Elder Daniels repeated as he held out an open palm, forgetting the Tagalog translation.

Just then, Elder Reyes stepped between the two, pushing Elder Daniels back a step. "I do, . . . me talk him," Elder Reyes struggled, trying to calm Elder Daniels.

Not understanding the full exchange between the two Filipinos, Elder Daniels kicked at the dust gravel, spewing pea-sized rocks into the empty road. It was a childish act but he had no other way to vent the frustration that had built over the past hour. Although the sun hadn't been in the sky more than a couple hours, it had already been a long Sunday morning.

From the moment he'd stepped out of bed Elder Daniels knew it was going to be a rough day. They'd forgotten to stop by the market the evening before and, therefore, he and his companion woke to nothing but an egg and a half of a cup of rice in the entire house. It had been an easy decision at that point to begin a fast.

Sacrament meeting started promptly at 9:00 A.M., so the Elders were out of their apartment by 7:30 A.M. As usual, the missionaries dropped in on their investigators to fetch as many as they could for church. Some were ready, others had forgotten, and the remainder had an excuse for why they couldn't attend.

The most frustrating thing that Elder Daniels had yet experienced on his mission was being "punted." Having no idea where the term had originated, the only thing Elder Daniels knew was that being "punted" had nothing to do with football and everything to do with "getting stood up" for an appointment. He'd been punted when it came to discussions. He'd been punted when it came to fetching church investigators. He'd been punted when it came to baptisms. He'd even been punted when he and Elder Juarez showed up at the city municipal building to get a mother and father legally married after they'd lived together for eighteen years.

On this particular morning, he and Elder Reyes had already been punted three times. At their first stop, a young lady who'd met with them five times but not yet come to church, said she had to study for a test at the nursing academy.

The second stop yielded the same results when they stopped to pick up an elderly man they'd committed to baptism just the day before. No one came to the door.

The last contact they were to pick up was home and willing to go but promised to meet the Elders at the church. Elder Daniels knew she wouldn't show up. Her shifting eyes and nervous laugh told him she was just too uncomfortable to tell them she didn't want to go. After as many Sundays as Elder Daniels has spent in the mission, he was painfully aware that people in Asian cultures dislike saying "no."

As the angry trike driver sped off, Elder Daniels and his companion walked through the church entryway empty handed. After ninety minutes and six trike rides, they'd not been able to bring a single investigator to church. The only hope of having even one church investigator was if Brother Nguyen kept his promise of accompanying his wife to the service. Right about now neither missionary had much faith that even that would happen.

As they strolled up the walk with their heads hanging low, a friendly voice greeted them. "Good morning!" Without even seeing her face, Elder Daniels knew whose voice it was.

"Hey, Sister Adams" Elder Daniels replied despondently, hiding none of the self-pity he felt inside.

"Something wrong?"

"It's been a tough morning."

Picking up on the fact that the two Elders were alone, Sister Adams started to say something about being punted but thought better of it. The first and second rows in the chapel were filled with her and Sister Jornacio's contacts and any attempt at consolation may have come across wrong.

Searching for something else to brighten the mood, she asked, "How's Brother Nguyen doing?"

"I don't know, we haven't seen him yet. He's supposed to come with his wife."

"Excellent!" Sister Adams shouted, "He's going to make a great convert. You'll be uniting a part-member family, right?"

"Yeah, I guess so," Elder Daniels nodded, still not sure what to think of Brother Nguyen's baptismal commitment.

Sister Jornacio walked out the front door toward them with her backpack on her shoulder.

"Hey, Elders. We're glad you're here. We're going to have seven baptisms next Sunday. Do you think you could baptize them for us?"

"Sure." Elder Daniels agreed, thankful that someone in his district was baptizing. "By the way, how's your family doing?"

Tossing her blond hair out of her face with a shake of her head, Sister Adams smiled, "They're doing okay. My dad's really strong and he's holding the family together."

Turning to join her companion, Sister Adams started down the lane toward the gate. Three steps from where she'd started, she stopped and turned back to Elder Daniels. "Elder Daniels, . . . thanks for asking. That was very kind of you when you have so much else on your mind."

Watching the two sisters walk down the lane, Elder Daniels felt butterflies in his stomach. They caught him completely off guard. Turning back toward the church, a smile appeared. Maybe it wasn't going be such a bad day after all.

# CHAPTER 14

*Which of you by taking thought can add one cubit unto his stature? And why take ye thought for raiment? Consider the lilies of the field, how they grow; they toil not, neither do they spin: And yet I say unto you, That even Solomon in all his glory was not arrayed like one of these.*

*Wherefore, if God so clothe the grass of the field, which today is, and tomorrow is cast into the oven, shall he not much more clothe you, O ye of little faith? Take no thought saying, What shall we eat? or, What shall we drink: or, Wherewithal shall we be clothed? . . . For your heavenly Father knoweth that ye have need of all these things.*

*But seek ye first the kingdom of God, and his righteousness; and all these things shall be added unto you.*

*—Matthew 6:27–33*

"The law of chastity says that we are to have no sexual relations with anyone except our husband or wife," Elder Daniels explained in Tagalog, as best he could. "The Lord also taught that we must avoid impure thoughts and actions." Even though he'd memorized much of the lesson, he tried his best to change the wording in order to practice his language skills. He wasn't sure he said everything correctly but no one was laughing or appeared too confused, so he guessed he'd at least gotten the message across.

Elder Daniels watched the man's face as he sat quietly across the room. Weaving a small basket, the man only looked up after a long pause where nothing was said. Halfway through the fourth discussion, Brother Nguyen still hadn't vocalized a single concern about the Gospel teachings. That would normally have made the Elders happy but something seemed out of place. Even what they'd just taught him about the pre-mortal life, the purpose of our mortal life and life after death—none of it brought even a spark of interest to the man's face.

"We must keep our thoughts clean and be modest in our dress, speech, and actions. The procreative power is sacred, and our bodies must also be kept clean." As his voice trailed off, Elder Daniels waited to see if Brother Nguyen would ask any questions.

Nothing.

It wasn't that anyone expected that Brother Nguyen had any concerns with obeying the law of chastity—he was happily married. The question on their minds was that for someone who had openly resisted his wife joining the Church for the past three years, why was he now accepting *everything* the missionaries shared with him?

"Brother Nguyen," Elder Daniels asked, "how do you feel about the law of chastity?"

Without raising his eyes from the basket, Brother Nguyen answered almost immediately.

"Good."

There was no emotion in the voice, no feeling, just a one-word answer that told nothing about what might be going through his mind.

Looking at his companion, Elder Daniels shrugged his shoulders. They'd discussed their concerns over Brother Nguyen's sudden acceptance of the Gospel, yet one fact remained—he was the only contact that had visited the church with them that past Sunday and their only investigator with a firm baptismal date.

As hard as both missionaries were trying, there was very little of the Spirit in the room. Hoping that by bearing his testimony would help diminish the man's non-verbal apathy, Elder Daniels testified of the sacredness of the power of procreation.

Brother Nguyen..." Elder Daniels began again, this time waiting until the man looked up. "Will you continue to live the law of chastity in your actions, your thoughts, and your speech?

"Yes"

Elder Daniels sat in silence, confused by the misgiving that lingered in his heart. Here was their best contact, at least the one closest to baptism, with no more enthusiasm than a quorum of deacons in Fast and Testimony meeting.

In a way, Elder Daniels wanted the man to flat out reject their teachings. He wanted to hear him question them! He wanted the man to say, 'No, I don't believe what you are saying'—anything that would show he was internalizing their message. Instead, Brother Nguyen went right back to weaving and waited for Elder Reyes to begin the next principle.

Turning to his companion, Elder Daniels brightened considerably as he remembered the next principle they would teach: the Word of Wisdom. Anticipating a confrontation over this principle because he knew the man smoked and drank, Elder Daniels sat back to watch the fireworks.

As if on cue, Brother Nguyen pulled out a pack of cigarettes and prepared to light it.

"During our discussion today, we have discussed precious gifts that we have in this life: our physical bodies and our freedom to choose," said Elder Reyes. "We have also discussed how we use these gifts determines our blessings in this life and in the life to come."

Watching the man pull out a matchbook, Elder Daniels smiled. This was just what he'd been waiting for. Just as the man struck the match and cupped his hands to light a cigarette dangling from his lips, Elder Reyes said, "Among his commandments is a law of health known as the Word of Wisdom . . ."

The match froze a half-inch from the cigarette. Brother Nguyen's eyes rose to meet those of the missionaries. There was no mistaking his recognition of this principle.

Pausing briefly, Elder Reyes watched as Brother Nguyen drew in a deep breath. With a gentle pull, the flickering flame bridged the gap between match and cigarette and a bright orange glow appeared. As he continued to inhale, the glowing ember crawled up the cigarette stick sending a crackling sound into the air along with a heavy odor of smoke.

Holding his breath for a brief moment, the man took the cigarette between his finger and his thumb and crushed it out on the bamboo floor. Slowly exhaling a cloud of billowy smoke, he dropped the remainder of the cigarette between two of the bamboo strips to the ground below. Never once breaking his gaze with Elder Reyes.

Juan Nguyen sat motionless waiting for the Elders to continue.

Caught entirely off guard, Elder Daniels' couldn't believe what he was seeing. *Are you serious?*

"This law teaches us not to take alcohol, tobacco, coffee, tea or harmful drugs into our bodies. As Elder Reyes continued teaching, Elder Daniels sat dumbfounded. He had not expected that response. As he intently watched Brother Nguyen, he heard a sniffle to his left. As he turned his head toward the sound he remembered Sister Nguyen was present.

At the sight of her tearstained cheeks, he realized she'd been crying for most of the discussion. Although his initial reaction was one of concern, he soon realized just how important this moment was to her.

An overwhelming sense of guilt and remorse enveloped Elder Daniels. He'd been so caught up in his reservations of Brother Nguyen that he'd completely immersed himself in doubt and suspicion of the man's true intentions. He quickly realized that the enmity he'd developed toward the man had driven the Spirit from the room. It wasn't Brother Nguyen who had been the source of discontent—it was himself.

Shutting his eyes tightly, a feeling of guilt and shame enveloped Elder Daniels. Here he was teaching the Gospel of Jesus Christ to a man who had committed to be baptized, and in his heart, he didn't even want to see the man baptized.

*What's your problem?* He screamed internally. *Why are you so pessimistic? What has Brother Nguyen ever done to you? Maybe he doesn't need to look you in the eyes to pay attention! Start acting like a missionary!*

Opening his eyes, Elder Daniels' heart melted. Shuffling her way over to her husband on her hands and knees, Sister Nguyen embraced him, her body heaving as she sobbed. In front of Brother Nguyen lay a pack of cigarettes, crumpled in a ball.

He'd voiced no concerns because he didn't have any.

\* \* \* \* \*

"All right," Sister Hart said, as she stepped out into the chapel courtyard. "Who's next?"

A chorus of "not me's" greeted her as a dozen missionaries looked at their shoes. Behind the mission president's wife, Elder Neil stepped out of the makeshift infirmary and grimaced at the cowering group.

"Oh, you guys are a bunch of babies! In the Army we had to walk down a line our first day in basic and get three shots in each arm! That was before we started giving them to ourselves," he added, taunting the group even more.

"How about you Elder Daniels?" Sister Hart asked. "You ready for your shot?"

Matching the gaze of his zone leader, Elder Daniels pulled up the sleeve of his white shirt and flexed his biceps, "only if you're sure you won't break a needle on this python."

Elder Neil laughed heartily, "You'd better make sure he's got enough muscle there to put a needle in, Sister Hart."

"C'mon, you jokers," Sister Hart replied, pushing Elder Neil out the door as she took Elder Daniels into the Relief Society room and shut the door.

Hearing the 'click' of the door close behind him, Elder Daniels' machismo vanished. Freezing in mid-stride, he took one look at the table in front of him and felt more like a prisoner in a torture chamber than a missionary getting a routine booster shot.

"Relax Elder, you act like you've never had a shot needle before."

Sister Hart lead him over to a green folding chair sitting in the middle of the room. Next to the chair was a small table on which sat six vials of yellowish fluid, a small stack of three-by-five gauze pads, a bottle of rubbing alcohol, and a row of the biggest shot needles he'd ever seen.

Elder Daniels took a good look at the shot needles as he sat down and squeamishly turned away. Even through their protective caps he could see the size of the needles sitting on the table. It wasn't the length of the needle, but the girth, that made him feel sick.

He'd written home about the gamma globulin inoculations more than once. So far, he'd found no better way to describe them than by calling them "the peanut-butter shots." The most painful part wasn't the near toothpick-sized needle entering his skin, but the thick, gel-like substance that was injected through the large-bore hole. It felt like peanut butter entering in his veins.

"Do we have the option of declining?" Elder Daniels asked, hoping the mission nurse would take pity on him.

Sister Tucker, a gentle black woman who had worked as a nurse back in Alabama, winked at Elder Daniels. "Honey, the only option you got is where you want me to stick this needle!"

Elder Daniels pulled up his shirtsleeve once again and shut his eyes.

Rubbing his shoulder with a gauze pad saturated with rubbing alcohol, Sister Tucker chuckled, instructing her patient in her slow Southern drawl, "Ya know sugar, the more you flex that arm, the harder I got to push to get it in."

Elder Daniels opened his eyes, realizing there wasn't a muscle in his body that wasn't strung tighter than a guitar string. "S . . . sorry," he stuttered, "I just don't like shots."

Her soft features curling into a sympathetic smile, the mission nurse comforted him. "Elder, I've been doing this since your momma was a child. Y'all just relax and we'll be done in no time."

Consciously trying to calm himself, Elder Daniels drew in a deep breath just as he felt the sting of the needle entering his shoulder. Beads of sweat burst on his forehead the moment the gamma globulin entered his bloodstream. Feeling a burning sensation, he instinctively turned to look at his arm, only to have the burning sensation replaced by a light-headedness that left him dizzy.

"You doing all right, child?"

"I...I...I think so," Elder Daniels replied, fighting the growing darkness in his vision.

"Sister Hart, you better get over here!"

\* \* \* \* \*

Ann Daniels sat at her desk at Timpanogos Elementary School staring at the clock. It was only a little past nine and she was already counting the minutes before she could meet her husband for lunch. It had been a particularly difficult morning and she'd convinced him to push back a meeting so that she could take her mind off work.

Although she loved the special children in her class dearly, there were moments that tested her patience. Her black eye was the result of a wrestling match with an eleven-year-old and that had not been a great start to her day.

Taking a moment to herself, the tears came quickly as she contemplated the unfortunate circumstances many of these children were under. It was impossible to get angry, since none of them would be in her class if they had complete control of their emotions. The majority came from homes with parents struggling to raise "normal" children, let alone a mental- or physically-handicapped child who needed so much additional care.

Joey, the young boy who'd thrown a temper tantrum when she helped him take off his coat, was one of her most beloved. He was also the most dependent on others. Confined to a wheelchair with practically no motor control, she not only changed his diapers, but also fed and clothed him, in addition to reading him books, singing songs, and other responsibilities that came by way of her job as the resource room director. But Ann Daniels did what she did, not because it was her job, but because she loved these children nearly as much as her own.

Unfolding a letter she'd received from her son only the day before, the tears fell even more rapidly, wetting the pages as she re-read it for the fourth time. The story about an old man with glaucoma, kidney disease and bedsores, who wanted to be baptized, hit her especially hard. Her heart nearly shattered when she thought of him lying there waiting so long to be baptized, yet undaunted in his faith. She sympathized for him greatly since she had many children in her class with similar physical challenges.

Living in Orem, Utah, the majority of her students were LDS, and for those whose mental capacity allowed it, when it came to watching their siblings be baptized at eight years, many of them wanted to be baptized as well. While a few were baptized, others were attached to medical apparatuses and physically unable to be immersed in water. They were the hardest for Ann Daniels to watch, for even these physically-challenged children had the mental capacity to understand the place baptism held in their faith.

Hearing a distant bell down the hallway, Ann Daniels refolded the letter and put it in her purse, readying herself for those who would be returning from their recess break. She dabbed at her eyes with a tissue, trying to fix the mascara that ran with her tears.

*Oh, how I miss him!*

Walking to the doorway, she met her first student who was returning with a fourth-grade student who had pushed her wheelchair around the playground.

"Hi Julie, how was your walk?"

A small grunt from the twelve-year-old girl with cerebral palsy told her everything was okay.

"Good, then let's get ready for story time."

She took the wheelchair from the volunteer student and thanked her.

"Did I ever tell you about a young man who used to help me in my class before he left on his mission?"

\* \* \* \* \*

"Elder Daniels! You scared us!"

A familiar voice grew louder and more distinct as his eyes adjusted to the lights directly above him. Even before he saw her face, he recognized Sister Tucker's voice.

Feeling as if he were awaking from a deep, dream-filled sleep, he blinked away the last of the black spots in his vision and tried to sit up.

"No, no, honey, you lie still." The mission nurse gently pushed his head back down to a folded towel she'd placed under it.

Relaxing slightly, Elder Daniels looked around, recognizing the slated glass windows and wall-hanging fans that told him he was in the church house.

But why was he lying on the floor? And why did he have a painful bump on the side of his head?

Hearing a shuffle to his left, he turned his head just enough to see a door open and Sister Hart rush in with a worried look on her face.

"Oh good! He's coming around John," she said over her shoulder as a large-framed man filled the doorway. Kneeling by his side, Sister Hart placed a cool, wet handkerchief on his forehead and felt his cheek with the back of his hand.

"He's feeling a bit cooler as well."

Telling the growing crowd of missionaries that everything was fine, President Hart shut the door behind him and walked over to join his wife at Elder Daniels' side.

"I'm guessing you don't like shots very much," President Hart said with a deep chuckle.

Although his mind was still hazy, Elder Daniels recognized the humor and smiled briefly. He was grateful the mission president was able to dispel some of the tension in the room.

"I want him to see a doctor," Sister Hart proclaimed out of concern.

"Now, now, dear, let's not get carried away, I'm sure Elder Daniels is just fine."

"John!" she protested, "We need to make sure he's okay. It looked like he hit his head pretty hard. What if he has a concussion?"

Once again Elder Daniels started to sit up, saying, "Really, I'm fine, I just don't like needles much," only to be pushed back down again.

"Just rest. There's no reason to get up right now," Sister Tucker instructed.

Realizing that there were two mothers here that wouldn't stop worrying until they were completely sure he was okay, Elder Daniels rolled his eyes and lay back down. He was at their mercy—any effort to resist was going to be met with more mothering.

Just then, a soft knock turned the room's attention to the door as it opened just a couple inches.

"I, uh, . . . brought some water," a quiet voice explained, pushing the door open enough for a slim figure to squeeze through. Sister Adams held out a small glass of water, trying to see around the other figures in the room to Elder Daniels.

"Is he going to be okay?"

Elder Daniels pushed aside the hands and sat up, "I'm fine," he said, extremely embarrassed. "I just need a little room to breathe."

At that, President Hart stood and ushered everyone from the room, except for Sister Hart and Sister Tucker. "C'mon, let's get on with this zone conference. I've got more interviews to do." Before he shut the door behind him, he winked at Elder Daniels and said, "If any of these women start talking about rectal thermometers, yell for me!"

"Oh hush!" Sister Hart scolded, pushing him out the door. "You two can compare stories later. Right now we've got to figure out how to give twenty more shots without anyone else passing out."

Elder Daniels used the chair next to him for support as he rose to his feet. There was still a little bit of dizziness floating around in his head, but he wasn't about to tell anyone in this room about it.

"Sorry, 'bout that," he said to Sister Tucker as he turned toward the door. "If it's any consolation, it didn't hurt much."

"Oh, child, don't you worry none, I'll just remember next time you come in for a shot to let you lie on the floor first."

Opening the door, Elder Daniels was greeted by a chorus of cheers. His closest friends and companions loved the opportunity to taunt him after his earlier statement.

"It sounds like those pythons were no match for an immunity booster," Elder Neil started in.

"Not so much," he agreed. "I hate those things."

Scanning the crowd, Elder Daniels shook his head, embarrassed, but glad the incident was over. His eyes finally locked on those of Sister Adams. Receiving a quick wink from the sister missionary, he realized who'd gathered the group and organized the teasing.

Taking it all in good fun, Elder Daniels returned the smile, knowing that a few moments ago, that face had been filled with genuine concern for her district leader.

# CHAPTER 15

*That the trial of your faith, being much more precious than of gold that perisheth, though it be tried with fire.*

*—1 Peter 1:7*

With the first crow of the rooster, Elder Daniels slipped from his sweat-drenched sheets just as the first speck of light crested the neighboring house. Like a weary traveler forced to the ground by wind and rain, he collapsed next to his bed, driven to his knees by the storm raging within. He still couldn't believe what had transpired the previous day.

In a fitful daze, he'd tossed and turned all night, chasing the elusive sleep that seemed just out of reach. He knew he hadn't slept at all—robbing him of the chance it had all been some ill-fated dream. With barely an audible sound he prayed.

*"Father...why? What did we do wrong?"*

As he waited for an answer he replayed the previous day's events in his mind. The day had started with such promise.

\* \* \* \* \*

Elder Daniels and his companion were up and out the door fifteen minutes before their scheduled departure. They both felt as if electricity coursed through them as they set off to fetch their investigators for church.

A northern breeze had brought an early morning shower that washed clean the dust and pollution of the crowded city streets. As the sun peaked above the trees, the streets of San Fernando glistened like gold. It would be nothing short of a glorious morning.

The air still carried with it the scent of rain. Elder Daniels loved that smell. It was clean. Renewing. Sanctifying.

As they waited to catch a jeepney down the street from their apartment, Elder Daniels rejoiced in the thought of what this day represented. The cleansing rain and sparkling sun were a prelude to Brother Juan Nguyen's baptism. It was November 25th, the day Brother Nguyen and three of his children would become members of The Church of Jesus Christ of Latter-day Saints!

Hoping to fill out the baptismal recommend early, the two Elders arrived at the small nipa hut to find only Sister Nguyen dressed and ready for church. She too was as excited as the Elders and greeted them with a joyous smile and an energetic handshake.

Her children, Ernesto, Ronaldo, Gilberto, and Juan Jr., scurried around hurriedly, trying their best to get ready for church. The two smallest children stood at the water pump, taking turns with the soap and bucket. Non-bashfully, they bathed themselves in the front yard. Only Brother Nguyen was absent from the preparations.

Caught up in the excitement of the day, Elder Daniels soon found himself tying shoes and combing hair as the smaller children bounded around, loving every minute of extra attention given them by the big American. Although they had not been present at any of the formal discussions with Brother Nguyen, the two missionaries had re-taught them the basic principles of the Gospel as a Primary teacher would do.

A few visits with a Book of Mormon Reader and a short discussion about baptism and the missionaries and the children had developed a bond as close as any to whom they'd taught all the discussions. Some of the older children had attended church on a regular basis with their mother and understood many teachings as well as her.

Sister Nguyen looked over the preparation and couldn't help but smile. After three years of patiently waiting, the day had finally arrived. Her family would be united in the Gospel of Jesus Christ.

Many sleepless nights Gelyn Nguyen had knelt silently next to her sleeping husband, pleading for a softening of his heart. For three years she'd endured slighting comments about "Mormons." She'd paid as much tithing as she could without her husband knowing about it and secretly put a few pesos aside each month for an eventual trip to the temple. She'd also put up with his smoking and drinking for more years than she cared to count.

But all that was behind them now. As she often quoted from the Doctrine and Covenants, "after much tribulation come the blessings." That tribulation had passed and the blessings were materializing right before her eyes.

For the first time in her life, she felt perfectly content. Even Juan Jr., her youngest son with the cleft palate, was as happy and excited as the rest of the children. Although he was only six, she knew he understood what the Gospel of Jesus Christ promised him. On many nights, she'd tucked him into bed and reminded him of the Savior's resurrection and that one day he too would have a perfect body and would speak the things that she knew he carried in his heart.

Slipping away briefly to stand in front of her most beloved picture, Sister

Nguyen felt the stirring of emotions deep within her bosom as she stared at the Manila Temple. She was already making plans for a visit to the temple in a year. The trip would require many more sacrifices but she was certain the Lord would bless them and make it possible to get to Manila.

There had already been an announcement that a new Temple would be constructed in Urdaneta, Pangasinan, but the Manila Temple had always been her favorite and she wasn't about to wait any longer. She could picture her family standing under the towering precipice of the Manila Temple, dressed in white and sealed together for time and all eternity.

Elder Daniels couldn't have been more pleased. This was what missionary work was all about. Thinking back on the matter things couldn't have gone any better. Brother Nguyen was present at every discussion, committed to living the law of chastity, the word of wisdom, and even to pay a full tithe. He'd also attended church two weeks in a row. Just the day before, he and the three children over the age of eight had been interviewed by the zone leaders and found ready to enter the waters of baptism.

Finished with the children, Elder Daniels and his companion entered the small hut. Sister Nguyen had invited them in to escape the sun. The day was heating up quickly, especially since the air was still partially saturated with moisture. Taking a seat on his bamboo backpack, Elder Reyes began gathering information for the baptismal record.

"What is Brother Nguyen's full name?"

"And his birthday?"

Elder Daniels stood next to an open window, listening as his companion asked about hometowns, ages, and middle names. In the cool morning breeze he wondered how many other investigators they would have at church this day. The ward mission leader had promised to follow up on as many as he could, especially those who had been unsure whether they could make it. In all, he hoped to have five or six investigators attend the meetings, and hopefully, the baptismal service following the last hour.

As Elder Daniels stood at the window, something in his peripheral vision caught his attention. He turned his head instinctively toward the source. Amidst the thick vegetation a single leaf of a banana tree moved against the otherwise still backdrop of the jungle.

Scanning the distance, only about 20 meters away, he caught sight of something else—something moving in the trees. Because of the shadows from the overhanging trees, Elder Daniels figured it was a bird, or other small animal, and nearly turned away. Just then, a small red dot, barely visible, drew his attention further within the emerald-green vegetation.

At first he thought his eyes were playing tricks on him, watching the red glow fade. Within a few seconds it was there again. Shifting his weight to the other foot, he bent forward trying to narrow the gap and get a closer look at whatever was there.

As the banana leaf moved a few inches to the left, he saw him. A shaft of sunlight entered the enclosed area and brought a face into full view. Elder

Daniels nearly fainted as his heart dropped to the bottom of his stomach. Closing his eyes, he whispered, "Oh no!"

Hidden in the shadows of the overhanging banana trees, Brother Juan Nguyen sat on a stump smoking a cigarette.

\* \* \* \* \*

Without hearing his companion slip out of his own bed to his knees, Elder Daniels sat motionless kneeling in prayer. He wasn't even aware that twenty minutes had slipped by as he replayed the events of the previous day. Neither was he aware that his morning prayer had thus far consisted of only seven words.

The entire afternoon and evening he'd been dumbfounded by what had come of their five baptismal candidates. He was finally relinquishing his hold on his thoughts—letting his mind replay the events as they'd happened, rather than block out the memories he'd tried to forget.

Elder Daniels once again saw the face of Brother Nguyen sitting in the shadows of the banana trees, dressed in no more than a cutoff pair of shorts and flip-flops. He'd sat on a stump, puffing away at a freshly lit cigarette, unaware that he'd given away his hiding place.

At first, Elder Daniels had just wanted to turn his head—pretend he didn't see their baptismal candidate breaking the Word of Wisdom—and go on as planned. After all, he reasoned, he wasn't even a member yet, wasn't that what baptism was for?

In his heart, Elder Daniels knew that wasn't right. As much as he wanted to see him baptized that day, he knew he wasn't ready if he still had a Word of Wisdom problem, especially not when he was hiding it from his wife and the missionaries.

"What does the "A" stand for," Elder Reyes asked, trying to get the middle name of Brother Nguyen's father.

"Aguinaldo."

With a long sigh, Elder Daniels turned from the open window and looked at his companion, still scribbling the information on the baptismal records for Brother Nguyen and his children. "Elder Reyes, can I talk to you a minute?"

"Ano, . . . uh, what?" his companion asked, remembering it was an English day.

Walking to the bamboo steps leading from the raised nipa hut, Elder Daniels didn't even wait for his companion, "I need to talk to you outside." Once there, separating themselves from the rambunctious children, Elder Daniels related what he'd just encountered.

After a couple of passes, both in English and Tagalog, Elder Daniels finally got the message across. Elder Reyes' shoulders drooped forward and his eyes fell to the ground. Elder Daniels had found no easy way of breaking the news to his companion.

"What we do?" he asked, looking to his senior companion for guidance.

"I don't know but we can't baptize him today. I guess we need to go talk to him and then break the news to Sister Nguyen."

Standing in the shade of a large coconut tree, Elder Daniels and his companion were sweating as if they'd spent the last twenty minutes on a hard bike ride. Neither of them wanted to proceed with the task at hand.

"C'mon," Elder Daniels finally said. "Let's get this over with. We can still baptize the children today, and hopefully Brother Nguyen next week."

Starting from the protection of the shady tree, the two missionaries stepped around the side of the house as Brother Nguyen came around back. Dripping wet in his cutoff shorts he'd just finished taking a bucket shower at the hand pump.

"Good morning, Elders," he called as they approached, extending his hand with an energetic smile.

"Good morning," both missionaries returned, although somewhat less enthusiastically.

"Brother," Elder Reyes had begun, confronting the man in the gentlest way he could think of. "How do you feel about your baptism today?"

"Good. Very excited."

"How have you been doing with the Word of Wisdom?"

"Good," he responded, still drying his hair with a small hand towel.

Realizing there was only one way to approach the situation, Elder Reyes continued, "Brother, have you had any more cigarettes since your interview with Elder Neil?"

Freezing in mid wipe, Brother Nguyen looked back and forth between the two missionaries and then dropped the towel over his shoulder. "Yes," he said, matter-of-factly, "I smoking again."

"Do you know what this means?" Elder Daniels asked, louder than he intended. "It means you can't be baptized today."

Shrugging his shoulders, the man replied, "It okay. I not do any more. I be baptize today."

Elder Reyes bit his lip, hoping the man would understand. "No, you don't understand brother, you can't be baptized until you have repented, and you can't do that until you've given up smoking."

In the seconds that followed, a change came over the man that actually scared Elder Daniels. The mood and demeanor of Juan Nguyen instantly became one of defiance and anger. Taking the towel in his hands and wringing it tightly he took a defensive stance and stared hard at Elder Daniels.

"Okay! I not want baptize today," he yelled, scaring the children who had gathered around. "I not baptize ever!"

"Brother, don't do this, . . ." Elder Reyes began, trying to reason with the incensed man. "We just need to wait a week or two, . . ."

Taking his arm, Elder Daniels took a step back, pulling his companion with him.

Pointing toward the nipa hut, Juan Nguyen commanded his children to get inside. Then swinging his arm forward, he pointed at the Elders and with spittle flying from his lips, he said, "Go! No come back! Go! No come back!"

\* \* \* \* \*

With more than half the sun peaking over the highest rooftop, Elder Daniels collapsed in a heap on his bedroom floor. There was no holding back his emotions as he remembered walking away from Brother Nguyen and hearing the sobs of his brokenhearted wife. Sister Nguyen had stood in the window witnessing the entire encounter.

"God?" Elder Daniels whispered, huddled on the floor with his face in his hands. "What did we do wrong?"

\* \* \* \* \*

Elder Daniels slid into the seat next to his companion, holding his bamboo pack on his lap. The minibus was cramped enough, but the fact that he had to hold his bag made the situation even worse. Every person who walked by bumped him as his broad torso and shoulders jutted out into the aisle. It was a Monday morning and people were anxious to get to the market for new produce.

Lucky to have even found an open seat, Elder Daniels laid his arm across his pack and leaned forward, resting his head on his forearm. As the bus lurched forward, he closed his eyes. He wished the entire experience with Brother Nguyen had been nothing more than a bad dream. Since sleep had eluded him the entire night, he hoped to get a few minutes of rest on the twenty-kilometer bus ride to San Juan.

For the next five minutes Elder Daniels didn't move. He didn't want to talk with anyone. He didn't want to read anything. The only thing he wanted to do was get to the district meeting and get it over with. He desperately wanted to get on with their P-Day and put missionary work out of his mind for a few hours.

Without warning, the minibus driver swerved hard to the left to avoid a trike that pulled out in front of it unexpectedly. Elder Daniels almost fell into the aisle but a woman standing there took the force of his weight as he slid off his seat into her. Holding onto the railing above her head, the older woman barely stayed on her feet as passengers and possessions flew about the cabin.

His own heart thumping in his chest, Elder Daniels regained his balance, and his seat, as the screams and murmuring diminished. A thunderous barrage of obscenities and horn blasts left a heart-pounding trike driver wondering just how close he'd come to death.

Looking around for the first time, Elder Daniels realized that the bus had made enough stops along the way that every seat and aisle space was filled to capacity. The woman at his side had been so careful not to disturb him that rather than risk waking him, she stood in the aisle holding a large paper bag in one arm and her other arm steadying herself with the railing. How she'd managed not to fall when the bus swerved, Elder Daniels would never know.

Without a word, he picked up his bag and stood, shuffling into the aisle. "Please sit down." he said in Tagalog. It was the least he could do to show his respect. Because of his upbringing, there was no way he could occupy a seat when a woman was left standing.

The woman thanked him and accepted his offer, finding herself in a conversation with Elder Reyes as soon as she sat down. Awake now and aware of his surroundings, Elder Daniels surveyed the bus.

In the seat to his left sat an older woman, advanced in years and looking quite frail. The enthusiasm in her voice told a different story as she cursed every driver in San Fernando they passed.

Two rows ahead stood another woman with a four-month old baby. Lovingly, she played with the babe, who was smiling and cooing as he laid in her arms in nothing more than a toddler sized T-shirt. Although he had no diaper or play toy, he was as happy as his mother. Elder Daniels couldn't help but hope he was already potty-trained.

Closer to the front of the bus sat a young boy, barely seven years old, holding a large bag of chicher'ron, a snack made by boiling chunks of pig skin in hot oil. Headed to the market, he would sell them on the corner, probably earning just enough money to help feed his family for a day.

Catching sight of his reflection in the window, Elder Daniels shook his head, chiding himself for wallowing in his own self-pity. In the midst of his own worries he'd forgotten just how blessed he was.

*C'mon man! How bad do you really have it?*

Throwing his shoulders back, he drew in a deep breath. Maybe things hadn't turned out as expected, but there was nothing he could do about that now. They would continue to fast and pray for Brother Nguyen and maybe his heart would change again.

\* \* \* \* \*

Alicia Decker sat at her desk behind a locked door. With a pen in hand and a piece of stationary in front of her, she stared at the lines on the paper in silence wondering how to begin. In over an hour she'd only gotten as far as "Dear Aaron."

This was the first letter she'd written in over a month and only the second since meeting David. She tried to tell herself she had been too busy but she knew she'd put off this letter for another reason—a reason she now had to explain to Aaron.

Her eyes were once again drawn to her left hand and she stared at the diamond ring that sparkled even under the faintest of lights. In the past twenty-four hours, she'd done little else. More than once she'd told herself it was a dream—that she'd wake up and find nothing there. Every time she held up her hand, moving it this way and that, the three-quarter-carat marquis diamond sparkled brilliantly. Flanked by three baguette diamonds on each side, it was the most beautiful ring she'd ever seen. As many times as she told herself the size of the ring wasn't important, the one-karat total-weight made her feel like a queen.

"I can't believe I'm engaged!" she shrieked aloud, flabbergasted at the very thought. "I can't believe I'm getting *married!*"

\* \* \* \* \*

Sister Adams sat on the front steps of the San Juan chapel watching her companion fill out the weekly report. Looking over Sister Jornacio's shoulder, she watched her companion's hand glide fluidly across the paper, making pen strokes with beautiful penmanship.

"You write beautifully."

"Thank you. My mother always felt writing was more important than almost any other skill. She often said 'the spoken word will be forgotten but the written word will last forever.'"

"Really?" Sister Adams asked. "Your mother must have been a good teacher."

"She was. In fact I studied under her for most of my childhood, each year I progressed through school, she somehow became my teacher."

"Is she the one who taught you to speak English so well?"

"Yes. She's always wanted me to go to the States and get an education, so Tagalog was very rarely spoken in our home. I've probably learned as much Tagalog in the mission as you have!"

Sister Adams sighed, "Do you ever think about what it will be like when we're released from our missions?"

"I do."

"I mean, leaving all this behind. It's just so easy on a mission. If you work hard—you enjoy the work. If you're obedient—you get the blessings. It's simple! Back home there's bills to pay, deadlines to meet, and not to mention, trying to find a righteous husband and raise a family. It's almost overwhelming to think about!"

Laying down the pen and putting the report with their seven baptismal records, Sister Jornacio smiled. "I don't think you'll have much difficulty finding a husband."

Hearing a high-pitched squeal, both sisters' heads turned as Elder Reyes pulled the front gate open.

"Good morning."

"Good morning," both sisters chimed in perfect melody.

"Uh, aren't you a little late?" Sister Jornacio teased as her companion unlocked the chapel door.

Watching Sister Adams struggle with the key, Elder Daniels relaxed for the first time all morning. Teasing back, he replied, "Well you could have at least had the doors unlocked."

"Oh be quiet!" Sister Adams said, shaking the door until the latch turned with the key. "Besides, the mission rules say that Sister missionaries can't be in the church without a priesthood member present."

"Really? They don't trust you, huh?"

"It's for our *protection*."

"I see." Elder Daniels admitted, feeling much more spirited than he had just a few moments before. "Then I guess we're here to protect you."

Shaking the Elders' hands, Sister Adams said, "I'm glad to see you're feeling a little better than at the baptism yesterday. Thank you, again for baptizing the Martinez family for us. Don't get too down about Brother Nguyen. His time will come."

"I know," Elder Daniels agreed. "I also remembered what President Hart said about depression—that it's a tool the adversary uses to drive the Spirit away."

Once inside, Elder Reyes began setting up chairs as Elder Daniels checked over the baptismal records. The two sisters unlocked a small closet next to the chapel and pulled out a small electronic keyboard used in place of an organ during their Sunday services. Flipping through a hymnbook, Sister Jornacio picked "When Upon Life's Billows," knowing the hymn would be especially meaningful that morning.

Elder Reyes was just about to ask how long they would wait for the Bacnotan Elders when the two Elders walked in grinning from ear to ear.

"Sorry we're late. We had to visit Sister Valdez this morning."

Surprised that they would have been out doing missionary work that early, Elder Daniels asked, "Do you mean the Valdez family I met a couple weeks ago?"

Elder Sullivan, normally half asleep at district meetings, could hardly sit still. Tapping his foot and shuffling through his weekly report, he pulled out a single baptismal record and handed it to Elder Daniels.

"What's this? I thought you didn't have any baptisms projected this week."

As Elder Daniels looked at the name on the record, Elder Sullivan and his companion waited impatiently.

"Ronaldo Valdez?"

Elder Daniels was puzzled, recalling an image of the old man with glaucoma and kidney disease, shriveling away on a mattress under a checkerboard tin roof. "You baptized Brother Valdez?"

Elder Sullivan jumped out of his chair. "You're never going to believe what happened! This is so awesome!" Slapping Elder Torres on the back, he said, "Comp, you tell 'em."

"No, you!"

"No, really, you tell 'em!"

Excited to see some life in these two missionaries, Elder Daniels jumped in, almost shouting, "Somebody just tell us what happened!"

Elder Sullivan walked to the front of the room, eyes wide and aglow.

"Man it was incredible! The zone leaders came to work with us on Saturday. But we didn't have much planned, right? So we figured we'd take them to the barangay where the Valdez family lives, trying to get some referrals from the members there and maybe make some intros."

"So I'm working with Elder Tolentino, and Elder Torres, here, he's working with Elder Neil…"

The other missionaries in the district sat in awe. None of them had ever seen Elder Sullivan carry on in such a way. He was talking almost too fast for the rest to understand, even the native English speaking missionaries.

Elder Torres, only half the size of his American companion was sitting on the edge of his chair, interjecting pieces of the story every chance he got. Between the two, they explained Brother Valdez's condition to the Sisters and how they'd met him several weeks before.

"…so just as we were about to leave the barangay, Elder Tolentino turns to me and asks, "Is there a part-member family in this area with a father that is bed-ridden?"

"I said, yeah, you must mean the Valdez family," Elder Sullivan exclaimed. "Since we'd never talked to the zone leaders about the Valdez family, I assumed you two had," looking at their district leaders.

Elder Daniels looked to his companion and shook his head. "I hadn't. Did you?"

After a brief translation by Elder Torres, Elder Reyes also shook his head, confirming he'd never mentioned the Valdez family either.

"So, I took him over to their place and before we even knocked on the door, Elder Tolentino says, 'I've been here before…but it was in a dream.'"

Elder Daniels sat on the edge of the table in astonishment. "In a dream?"

"That's what he said. And then he turned to me and asked, 'Why haven't you baptized this man?' I told him we didn't feel he was well enough to be baptized. And Elder Tolentino says, 'he needs to be baptized today.'"

"You mean, he told you to baptize him even though he hasn't been out of his bed in three years?"

"Yeah! He said he'd met this guy in a dream and he was convinced he needed to baptized."

"So what did you do?"

"Well, he interviewed him right there, and we waited for our companions who were going to meet us there when splits were over."

"How did you get him to the Church?" Elder Daniels asked.

"Oh man, you're not going to believe this! His wife got his stuff together—you know, his towel and underwear and… Anyway, I carried him to the highway where we got a trike."

"You're kidding me!" Elder Daniels protested, remembering how long it took him and Elder Torres to walk from the highway just a couple weeks earlier. "You mean you carried him two kilometers by yourself?"

Shrugging his shoulders, Elder Sullivan said, "Yeah. I mean the guy probably didn't weigh more than sixty pounds, so I just cradled him in my arms and started walking."

"But this was so cool," he continued, "while we're walking to the road, ya know—crossing bridges, cutting through fields, skirting fish ponds, the whole bit—I look over at Brother Valdez and he's crying. So I figure he must be in pain, right? But when I ask if there's any way I can make him more comfortable, he reaches this skinny, frail arm up and touches my cheek and says, 'I wish I could see your face.'"

Forgetting their district meeting and the awaiting P-Day, the five other missionaries in the room sat in perfect silence.

"Once we got to the highway we waited about two minutes before an empty trike came along and I stepped inside—still holding Brother Valdez while my comp sat on the back of the motorcycle with the driver. The zone leaders had to wait for another trike to come along so that we had two witnesses at the baptism."

"As we waited for them at the church, Elder Torres and I dressed Brother Valdez in the baptismal clothing. Once they got there and we carried him into the baptismal font."

Already thinking ahead, Elder Daniels asked, "How did you baptize him if he couldn't stand on his own?"

"Well, that was kind of hard," Elder Sullivan admitted. Holding both arms out in front of him, he demonstrated how he'd cradled the man in his arms—supporting the man's head as he knelt in the baptismal font. "The water was all the way to our necks."

"Seriously?" Sister Jornacio breathed, shaking her head in disbelief.

"My comp had to stand behind me, hold his arm to the square, and say the prayer."

"So who actually baptized him?" Sister Adams asked.

"Elder Torres did. I just helped get him get all the way under the water."

Elder Sullivan's companion jumped in, saying, "We do two times."

"That's right," Elder Sullivan acknowledged, "the first time his leg popped up because he had no muscle control. So Elder Torres had to raise one arm to the square and hold the man's legs underwater with the other."

"That's amazing!" Elder Daniels uttered, still trying to comprehend the entire thing. "I wonder why Elder Neil and Elder Tolentino didn't mention it to us last night?"

"Because we asked them not to." Elder Sullivan explained. After the baptism we made them promise not to say anything because we were so excited to tell you ourselves."

"That's unbelievable!" Sister Adams exclaimed. "I mean, it's awesome, but what an amazing story!"

"That's not even the end of it!" Elder Sullivan continued. "We got him dressed, and took him home so that his wife could be there for the confirmation and then we had to leave to get to our next appointment. Then, yesterday, we're at church and his daughter approaches us. You'll never guess what she tells us."

"What?"

"Brother Valdez died Saturday night!"

The room was completely silent for several moments while the words Elder Sullivan said sunk in.

Elder Reyes was the first to break the silence. "What you say?"

Not a soul in the room believed what they'd just heard.

Elder Sullivan repeated himself. "Brother Valdez died Saturday night."

Voicing the question that was on everyone else's mind, Elder Daniels asked, "We didn't kill him did we?"

Elder Sullivan smiled. "No, but that thought crossed my mind too. I could hardly believe it so my comp and I got on the first jeepney to their barangay to talk with Sister Valdez. The whole way I was scared to death she might blame us—because we baptized him when he was so weak. And who knew what the non-members would say when they heard this man died the day we baptized him?"

"What did she say?"

"Well, we walked into her house and there's Brother Valdez lying in a coffin in the middle of the room. You know how they have 'a wake' before the funeral for people to pay their respects. I still couldn't believe it," he continued. "Not even when I saw him lying there looking so peaceful."

"What did you say to Sister Valdez?"

"Well that's what I'm getting to," Elder Sullivan replied. "She told us that she'd never seen her husband as happy as he was after his baptism. She said for the rest of the day, he'd just laid there with a smile on his face humming church hymns."

If there was a hush in the room before, what Elder Sullivan said next magnified it a thousand times. "Ya know, I've never really understood how important baptism is to our converts, . . . until now."

"Do you know what I think," Elder Sullivan continued, "I think Brother Valdez prolonged his life until he could be baptized. I think he didn't want to wait until his work was done in the temple. I think he'd waited long enough and wasn't crossing through the veil until he was a member of the Church."

A bird chirped outside—the only other voice to break the silence.

"It kind of makes you wonder," he concluded, "how many others are waiting for us to bring them the Gospel in this life. I think this work is more important than any of us realize."

# CHAPTER 16

*But behold, faith cometh not by signs, but signs follow those that believe. Yea, signs come by faith, not by the will of men, nor as they please, but by the will of God. Yea, signs come by faith, unto mighty works, for without faith no man pleaseth God; and with whom God is angry he is not well pleased; wherefore, unto such he showeth no signs, only in wrath unto their condemnation.*

*—D&C 63:9–11*

Elder Daniels turned the page of his missionary journal, looking for a passage he'd written four months earlier. It had been his last journal entry in San Fernando and marked the eight-month mark of his mission.

Turning through the pages brought back many memories. He vividly recalled how his mission had changed when he became a district leader. A word or two jumped out at him on each page, bringing distinct images and feelings to mind. Every few pages he'd read the entire entry, reliving the event—sometimes in exhilaration—other times in despair.

On a page he'd dated early September, he remembered meeting Elder Reyes for the first time and finding that he didn't speak a word of English. A few pages later he'd written a very depressing account about how he felt his teaching was inadequate and how his greatest desire was to learn to teach like Sister Adams—a dynamic missionary assigned to his district.

He had written in depth about the Spirit testifying when she taught. On the next page he wrote about the agonizing trip to San Juan where he had to relay to the same Sister missionary that her mother had been killed in a tragic car accident. In that entry, he had also written of his own misgivings of whether or not he would have stayed in the mission field if he had been the recipient of such devastating news.

Looking back now, seven months after expressing his misgivings, he was surprised to see how much his faith had increased since writing that entry.

Given the same situation now, he knew he would stay in the mission field, giving the Lord every minute of the two years he'd promised.

Another page told of his irritation with two Elders assigned to Bacnotan—Elders as lazy as his first companion. Shaking his head, Elder Daniels chuckled, remembering that he'd later written a two-page entry about the same two Elders who'd taught twenty-one discussions in a single week.

The last full entry Elder Daniels read was the one he sought and had been written the night before being transferred. It was dated December 25th—Christmas Day. Although he could've recited the passage from memory—having returned to it many times—there was still an element of incredulity about that last day he was assigned to Lingsat.

\* \* \* \* \*

Christmas morning brought with it a mix of emotions for me this year. It is a day of celebration, commemorating the birth of our Savior, but it also marks my last day in Lingsat. Tomorrow I will be transferred to Candon.

Waking up on Christmas morning in the Philippines was very different from any other Christmas I have experienced. As I awoke, I immediately thought of my family at home, probably just sitting down to a Christmas Eve dinner with turkey, stuffing, pie, and all the other traditional food of the Western world. Last night I ate Maggi noodles—the Filipino equivalent of Top Ramen.

Although we didn't have a Christmas tree, I did receive a package from my family. There were a few wrapped presents for my companion and I, but the best gifts I received were letters from each family member.

P-Day is usually held on Monday, but our entire mission worked this past Monday and held our Preparation-Day in conjunction with Christmas. Christmas fell on a Tuesday this year. Instead of having district meetings, we met as a zone here at the Church in San Fernando and celebrated together. It was especially nice seeing some of my best friends one last time before being transferred.

It looks like Elder Hastings is staying one more month in Bauang, and Sister Adams is headed home. I can't imagine how I would feel if this was my last area, I'm starting to see why she is having such a difficult time leaving the mission. I am sad that she is leaving, but she has been an extraordinary missionary and a very good friend.

At the end of our P-Day, which was pretty much spent at the Church playing basketball and shopping at the market, we changed into our missionary attire and went proselyting. After following up on a few contacts, and teaching a new member discussion to the sister we baptized two weeks ago, there was one last stop I felt I had to make before being transferred. We went to see Brother Nguyen.

I can hardly put into words the thoughts that were going through my mind as we walked through the barangay to their home. It reminded me of that day back in Rosales when Elder Flores and I went back to the Baribal's after being told we couldn't teach them anymore. Part of me wanted to turn around and run, but this time, I was the one pulling my companion, where before Elder Flores was pulling me.

I wish I could say that we had a similar experience as before—that Brother Nguyen asked to be baptized. But he didn't. He wasn't even home. Although my intentions were to speak with him one last time, I was actually quite relieved. We were told he was out drinking with his friends and we didn't want that kind of encounter with him anyway. Needless to say, we didn't stay too long.

Sister Nguyen was nervous when she saw us. She hasn't been to church in nearly a month. I know she wants to go, but right now there is still too much anger in Brother Nguyen for her to even discuss it with him. It hurts me to see her this way.

After visiting with her a few minutes, I got the impression she'd hoped we would have visited her sooner. She is in such a difficult situation!

To tell the truth, I'm not sure whether we did the right thing in waiting this long. Every day since the incident I have wanted to return, I've wanted to knock on their door and hear that everything's okay. Something inside—either the Holy Ghost or my fears—tells me it's not the right time.

What did transpire in those brief moments is something I will never forget. I've put off writing about it until now because I'm still trying to comprehend how it happened. I don't know how many people, missionaries included, can say they have ever experienced the Gift of Tongues. I don't imagine there are many, and for that reason I don't know exactly how to explain it. Because of how personal that experience was, I don't know how much to say.

Let me suffice in saying that over the past two months I have worked harder at learning Tagalog than anything I've ever done. I've stayed up late at night studying. I've forced myself to speak Tagalog in situations when English would have been much easier. I've stumbled over words, forgotten complete sentences and embarrassed myself so many times it no longer matters.

Looking back now, I've even made it a part of every prayer, every fast, and nearly every waking thought. In the end, after barely being able to understand, let alone speak the most basic of words just two months ago, I can now say that I am fluent in Tagalog.

As Elder Reyes and I were leaving Sister Nguyen's home last evening, saying a final good-bye to her and her lovely children, I had the distinct impression that she wanted a Priesthood blessing. I think that she was too afraid of her husband coming home to ask for it. So there in the flickering light of a single candle, with no more than a sheet of tin over our heads, we pulled up a rusty old chair and set it in the middle of the hard-packed, dirt floor. I asked Sister Nguyen to sit down and she instantly knew that I understood what she needed. As her children gathered around, kneeling in reverent prayer, we administered to Sister Nguyen as Elders of Israel.

In that humble home—amidst the sniffles and the tears—I felt the Spirit very strongly as I laid my hands on her head. As I began the blessing, I heard these words: "Trust in the Lord with all thine heart and lean not unto thine own understanding. In all thy ways acknowledge him and he shall direct thy paths."

The words that came out of my mouth in that blessing were words I had never before spoken. Many of the words I don't even know if I've heard before. But one thing I know for sure is that I am an instrument in the Lord's hands—a voice through which He blesses his children—hands through which he comforts the anguished.

I will forever be grateful for the three months I spent in this area. I will greatly miss my companion, my zone leaders, and the Saints in the Lingsat Ward. Having had many faith-promoting—and many faith-testing experiences—I have learned more about faith than I ever thought possible.

I am beginning to see that faith truly is a Principle of Power!

On a jeepney, traveling south through the lowlands of Ilocos Sur, Elder Daniels sat in silence, contemplating the emotions that accompanied leaving another area. In the company of eight other missionaries—heading for the transfer point at which he would get on another jeepney—Elder Daniels had much on his mind.

Closing his journal, he sat back in his seat, letting the hum of the diesel engine drown out the conversations around him. Moments of rest were rare in the mission field, so closing his eyes he took advantage of the few hours of relaxation he would have on the jeepney ride. With the erratic weaving through traffic, sleep was out of the question. This rare time provided him an opportunity to ponder some of the things he had experienced in the past four months in Candon.

*Four months! How could four months have passed so quickly?*

\* \* \* \* \*

Candon is a growing seaside town near in the second-most northwestern province of the Philippines. Known as the "tobacco capitol of the Philippines," the low-lying farmlands produce a vibrant, agricultural-based commerce for nearly 100,000 Filipinos. For Elder Daniels, it was an area that produced a different entity, though one of great importance to a missionary—faith.

Without having to read a single word in his journal, he remembered having dozens of faith-promoting experiences that served to help him understand the importance of faith—and that faith truly is a *Principle of Power*. There had been tests and there had been trials—but more than anything else—there had been blessings and baptisms. It had all started with a companion who had more charity than any other person he'd ever met—Miguel Bautista.

Elder Bautista had already been in Candon four months when his new companion arrived. Unlike many missionaries whose efforts taper off over time, Elder Bautista knew this would be his last month in the area and promised himself, his companion and the Lord, that it would be his best.

At well over six-feet tall, he could have played in the Philippine Basketball Association, or PBA, but even with his height he was well-grounded in his love for missionary work. Together with Elder Daniels, neither one entering a room without ducking, the duo stood out in a crowd and never lacked for attention in the small barrios of Candon.

Perhaps the most vivid memory Elder Daniels had of Elder Bautista was seeing him standing in water up to his waist, baptizing a former minister of the Iglesia Ni Cristo Church—more commonly known in the Western world as The Church of Christ. Everything about that memory left Elder Daniels with a testimony of faith.

Elder Bautista had made an intro to the man right after running his bicycle into the door of the car the minister was driving. The minister had stopped in the road to recover a scrap of paper that had blown out the passenger-side window and opened the driver-side door unexpectedly.

The tall Filipino Elder flew over his handlebars when he came alongside and crashed into the door. Brushing the dust off his pants and shirt and holding a handkerchief over a nasty cut on his elbow, Elder Bautista had introduced himself as a missionary of The Church of Jesus Christ of Latter-day Saints. Illustrating his depth of faith and charity, his first comment was from a scripture in the Doctrine and Covenants that said, "doors that once were closed would be opened to them."

That experience alone had taught Elder Daniels a great deal about his new companion—and about his faith. Elder Daniels had been very reluctant at first to sit down with the minister to talk about the gospel, expecting a Bible bash, but Elder Bautista had convinced him that the Spirit would guide them. Never once did his companion say a negative word about the accident, or the cuts and bruises he received. For Elder Bautista, the entire incident was an answer to prayers, even if it required a trip to the hospital for x-rays.

It seemed that everywhere the Filipino went he was greeted with as much curiosity and interest as was Elder Daniels. In the remote barrios of Candon, a cry went out as soon as the Elders were seen coming down the lane. In the blink of an eye, streets filled with small children hoping to get a high-five from either Elder. In most cases, the attention soon turned to Elder Bautista, who drew a crowd as soon as he brought out a candy wrapper attached to a metal washer. It was a game similar to Hacky-Sack, and laughter rang through the barrios everywhere he went.

Elder Daniels' second companion in the area, and the Elder he was leaving now, was none other than Elder Rivera, the companion with whom Elder Hastings had spent two months in Bauang. Having spent many a P-day playing basketball with Elder Rivera, it had taken Elder Daniels no time at all to feel comfortable in his new companionship.

If there was a single word to describe Elder Rivera, it was "inspired." On more than one occasion, the two Elders had set off on their bicycles—the awkward, fixed-gear type with springs on the seats—without a single destination in mind. Each time, Elder Rivera had taken the lead, guiding them through the winding streets of Candon, listening for promptings from the Sprit. Without a moment's hesitation, he would stop on the side of the road and get off, waiting for Elder Daniels to catch up. With a smile, he would say, "I think we should teach at this house today."

In an area in which members gave few referrals, more baptisms had resulted from cold-calling, or "intros," than Elder Daniels had witnessed ever before in his mission. But then Elder Daniels had learned that was the sort of thing that happened when a missionary's morning prayer is '*Father, lead us this day to a family who is ready to hear the gospel, that we may testify of your love and bring them to the waters of baptism.*' Seeing such a prayer answered again and again, Elder Daniels soon noticed a craving within himself to become proficient at discerning the whisperings of the Spirit. That desire had become his goal for the two months he was companions with Elder Rivera.

Visualizing the 3 x 5 cards he'd had taped to his mirror, Elder Daniels retraced the steps he'd taken in learning to recognize the promptings of the Holy Ghost. He'd read and reread that card so many times the words were still never far from his mind

---

### My Resolves

1. Earnestly listen for the promptings of the Spirit.
2. I will not rationalize promptings away faithlessly, mistaking my own thoughts for the Spirit.
3. Act upon promptings without hesitation, following Joseph Smith's advice: "When the Lord commands, do it!"

---

---

### My Commitments

1. I will obey every commandment and mission rule with diligence.
2. I will purify myself by ensuring that my desires are in line with His will.
3. I will be constantly aware of my own thoughts, making certain that nothing in my control will inhibit my responsiveness to the Spirit.

---

### Help I Will Need from the Lord

1. Reveal His will through promptings of the Holy Ghost.
2. Trust in me that I will not ignore or disobey those promptings.
3. Infinite patience—understanding that I have weaknesses but desire to turn my weaknesses into strengths.

---

Although it had been difficult to know exactly when he would achieve his goal, Elder Daniels knew it was important to set a specific date in which he wanted to see his desire fulfilled. He'd seen the fruits of their labors increase a hundredfold over his past areas and had no doubt this success was a result of Elder Riviera's mastery of recognizing the promptings of the Holy Ghost. Therefore, he'd set his goal date as March 31st, marking the end of his third month in the area, and giving him two full months with Elder Rivera. His only concern was that one of them would be transferred before the goal date. As if in confirmation that the Lord wanted him to achieve his goal, neither of them was moved at the next transfer of missionaries.

As Elder Daniels reflected on the events that transpired in those eight weeks, his mind raced in astonishment. With the work progressing so rapidly, he had not been allowed much time to ponder the entire course of his progress. Looking back now, there was no mistaking that Elder Rivera taught him well.

In the first week he'd struggled, often feeling bewildered and uninspired. For most of his life he'd persuaded himself that promptings only came to certain men and women—people like his parents, Church leaders, and, generally, anyone he considered more spiritual than himself. For Elder Rivera, who worked with Elder Daniels in setting his goal, that was a misconception he worked hard to overcome.

The first step in doing so was convincing Elder Daniels that the Lord desires to communicate with everyone—that he didn't pick and choose based on authority, leadership position, or even one's personal spirituality. He had to convince him that God is in a constant state of readiness to offer guidance, to answer prayers, and to bless his children. The next few weeks provided much growth for Elder Daniels as he experimented with, and tested, that idea.

In his third week in Candon, he'd been asked to speak in Sacrament meeting on a subject of his choice. As a test, rather than sitting down and writing out a talk as he normally did, he resorted to much fasting and prayer, not even deciding upon a topic until he was standing at the pulpit.

In those, initial moments, as he looked over a crowded room filled with members and investigators, his mind drew a complete blank. He stood silent at the pulpit for what seemed like an eternity. After a few uncomfortable moments, distinct thoughts began to flow into his mind—almost as if someone were standing next to him speaking directly into his ear.

After the meeting, many members thanked him for the powerful talk he'd delivered on fellowshipping new members. Many of them stated that they'd been concerned with their duty but didn't know how to go about it.

The crowning event, however, happened only three days before transfers. In the early morning hours of March 28th, he and his companion were awakened by a knock on the front door. Dragging himself wearily to the door, he opened it to find the zone leaders waiting patiently under a shared umbrella in the pouring rain.

"Did we wake you?" Elder Farnsworth asked jokingly, looking at his watch, which read 6:13 A.M.

Elder Daniel's yawn sufficed as a response.

"We need you to get a message to Elder Aquino and Elder Garcia about transfers."

"Both of them?" Elder Daniels asked in a deep, morning voice.

"Yup. President Hart has to close Santa Maria. Not enough missionaries to keep it open. It looks like the Elders in Narvacan will have to work both areas until we can get missionaries back there."

Elder Daniels sighed, The Elders would be disappointed the area was being closed and the Branch President and Branch Mission Leader would be crushed. The two missionaries had worked diligently and were just about to see some great baptisms. Shaking his head, Elder Daniels wondered if he should have expressed that information earlier, perhaps informing President Hart of the consequences of pulling them out.

Elder Farnsworth was looking at his notebook, making sure he got the transfers right. "Yeah, Elder Aquino is going to Narvacan with Elder Borja; Elder Garcia is going to Burnham with Elder Canton."

Rubbing the sleep out of his eyes, Elder Daniels asked, "Burnham? Isn't that up in Baguio?"

"Sure is. Tell him to get a sweater, it's very cold up there during the rainy season," his Filipino companion added.

"All right, . . . is that it?" Elder Daniels asked, hoping he could get ten more minutes sleep before his alarm sounded.

Elder Farnsworth flipped through some pages in his notebook hastily, "Yeah, that looks like all of them."

Only when his companion elbowed him in the side did Elder Farnsworth smile and add, "Oh that's right. I almost forgot. And you're going to Lingayen with Elder Zamora."

Pausing, Elder Daniels asked, "Elder Zamora? Isn't he one of the zone leaders down there?"

The smiles on the faces of his own zone leaders answered that question and sent Elder Daniels running into the next room to tell his companion. There was no longer any chance of falling back asleep.

Later that morning, still reeling from the thought of being called as a zone leader, Elder Daniels stepped off the minibus in Santa Maria, a small provincial town twenty kilometers north of Candon. Wanting to catch the Santa Maria Elders at home, he and his companion had showered and dressed immediately, catching the first minibus that came along. If they got back to their area soon enough, they wouldn't have to cancel any of their own appointments. At the Elder's apartment, the news about transfers was taken with mixed emotions.

Both Elders were going to good areas, especially Elder Garcia who would be finishing his mission in Baguio, the vacation capital of the Philippines. However, as anticipated, neither was happy to see Santa Maria close. Many potential converts might slip through the cracks if the Narvacan Elders had to split their time between the two areas. And what would happen to the new members who needed extra fellowship?

Elder Garcia and Elder Borja were well acquainted with Santa Maria. Knowing how long it had taken to get a branch here, they hoped it wouldn't be long before it opened again. The Santa Maria branch was still very small—there wasn't even a plan to build a chapel yet. The members met in a small, one-room warehouse behind a local gas station.

In addition, many of the smaller branches didn't have a very strong support system for fellowshipping. If the missionaries didn't teach the new member discussions or ensure worthy, prospective priesthood members were ordained in the first week or two after baptism and received callings, the still maturing leadership, all too often, forgot about them entirely. Even the branch president had only been a member three years.

"Well, Comp, we'd better get back to our area, we've got a teaching appointment at 9 A.M. with the Velasquez brothers."

Elder Rivera nodded in agreement, picking up his bag and wishing farewell to the Elders. It was never certain how long it would be until they saw each other again. For friendships made in the mission, saying 'goodbye' often meant, 'It's been great working with you, but I may never see you again.'

As Elder Daniels walked alongside his companion back toward the bus stop, he couldn't help but feel some of the pains he knew his companion was experiencing. For many Filipinos, once they returned to their home provinces, there was little chance of seeing old mission friends again. Scattered throughout the 7,000 Philippine islands it was difficult to imagine getting together for a mission reunion.

With the cement pavilion in sight marking the center of town, Elder Rivera quickened his step. A bright, neon-green minibus had its engine running and was loading passengers. Across its side was written the name 'Eddy's Express'—the name of the owner and driver.

"Let's catch that minibus!"

Lengthening his stride, Elder Daniels tried to keep up with his smaller, but quicker, companion. A slim, sweaty man was hanging out the doorway waving a handkerchief and motioning them to hurry for the last two spots on the bus. The driver was honking the horn frantically, anxious to get on with his route and collect the fare.

Just then, Elder Daniels stopped dead in his tracks about ten meters short of the bus.

"Hold on, Comp, we've got to go back."

"What?" Elder Rivera retorted, motioning for the impatient driver to wait.

"Uh, . . . we need to go back to the Santa Maria Elders' apartment."

"Why?" Elder Rivera, asked, pointing toward a wall that lined a small empty field. "Just go behind that wall. We'll still be able to catch this minibus."

Shaking his head, Elder Daniels didn't budge. "No, let's go back to the Elders apartment. I don't feel comfortable here."

Remembering at least a half-dozen times when they had both ducked behind a tree or a building to relieve themselves, Elder Rivera shot back, "Well, that's never stopped you before."

Unusually adamant, Elder Daniels held his ground, "Comp, I just feel that we need to go back."

Without further argument, Elder Rivera waved off the annoyed minibus driver and followed his companion back to the missionary apartment. Elder Rivera didn't say a word during the five-minute trike ride back to the apartment. In fact, he was unusually quiet until they were back to the cement pavilion, after reminding the Santa Maria Elders to notify the apartment manager that they would be terminating the lease.

"Sorry, Comp, I shouldn't have been so obstinate back there."

Elder Daniels laughed, having forgotten the entire incident. "Obstinate? Where the heck did you learn that word?"

"Elder Neil used to say it all the time when we were companions together."

"I didn't know you were comps with Elder Neil! When was that?"

"In Aguilar. He was my trainer. We had a good companionship but he always said I was 'obstinate' when I first arrived in the mission."

"Well, you are pretty stubborn sometimes."

At first, Elder Rivera was taken aback by his companion's comment until he saw him barely holding back a smile. Stepping up to the minibus, Elder Daniels put his arm around his companion, "I'm going to miss you comp!"

"Me too."

With a twenty to thirty-minute ride ahead of them, both Elders opened their scriptures, trying to get in some of the personal study they'd missed that morning. Just outside of town, as the road opened up with less congestion, Elder Daniels was surprised to feel the minibus slow rapidly.

As the bus came to a stop, a chorus of gasps erupted from many of the passengers toward the front of the bus. Elder Daniels stood to get a better look through the large Plexiglas window. What he saw sent a shiver through his entire body.

On the side of the highway the 'Eddy's Express' was wrapped around a 60-foot tall oak tree. Large pieces of wood and shards of glass littered the roadside area. The head-on collision with the stout oak tree left a grisly scene.

As Elder Daniels moved forward and peered out the front window, he saw the chaos and panicked state of those inside the crippled bus. A few people were trying frantically to sort out the wounded from the dead. Others lay in shock with blank stares on their faces. Still others screamed hysterically as the pain of their injuries set in.

At the very front of the bus, nearly the entire tree trunk engulfed the engine compartment. The deceased driver lay slumped over in his seat with the steering wheel post projecting from between his shoulder blades.

Elder Daniels felt his stomach do a somersault as he surveyed the wreckage. Remembering the prompting he'd received to return to the Elder's apartment, his first thought was *"we could have been on that bus."*

That thought sent another chill down his spine. But seconds later he felt a peace wash over him like an ocean wave, easing his heart and mind. That feeling confirmed to him that he'd obeyed the promptings of the Holy Ghost.

Pushing the thought aside momentarily, Elder Daniels took out his handkerchief and rushed toward the gruesome scene. Four bodies had already been pulled from the wreckage and were lying lifelessly under the tall expanse of the giant tree.

"C'mon, Comp," he yelled over his shoulder as he exited the minibus. "We're here to work miracles, aren't we?"

\* \* \* \* \*

Elder Daniel woke up sweating. The sound of heavy traffic passing in the other direction stirred him from the recesses of sleep. Lifting his head, a sharp pain exploded in his neck. It was his body's way of protesting the position in which he'd drifted off to sleep. Looking out the jeepney window across from him, Elder Daniels immediately began recognizing landmarks.

The streets of San Fernando brought back as many memories for him as the pages in his journal. As their rented jeepney passed through the provincial capital on its way to transfers, Elder Daniel's eyes darted from store to store, street corner to street corner, recalling experiences he'd had at nearly every one.

Passing La Farmacia, he remembered buying an over-the-counter cold medicine that would have required a prescription back home. The yellow and orange sign of Jollybee's reminded him of soybean burgers and milkshakes.

The Bazaar, a clothing store where he'd bought a pair of dress shoes still had the same advertisements in the window as it had months before. It seemed as if nothing had changed in the past four months, except himself.

Even the display window was the same. The shoes in the front window were identical to the ones on his feet and he remembered digging deep into his monthly allotment to buy them. Admittedly, he reminded himself that external factors had also played a large role in making that purchase.

The letter had come with much anticipation, not having heard from Alicia but once over the previous eight weeks. Excitedly, he'd ripped open the envelope and pulled out a two-page letter that brought intense emotional pain and frustration. Even now, almost four months since he'd torn the letter to shreds, he could still remember the first few lines.

*Dear Aaron,*

*So much has happened in the last two months that I don't know where to begin. For the past few weeks I've been trying to figure out how to tell you what I need to say without hurting you. After a great deal of thought, I've realized that's probably not possible. I guess the best thing for me to do it is to come right out and tell you that I'm engaged...*

At first he'd felt angry and hurt, followed shortly by disappointment and discouragement. An overwhelming feeling of shame swept over him as guilt crept into his conscious. He'd allowed his self-pity to justify his unrighteousness. There was only one reason he'd bought that pair of shoes in that store—his physical attraction to the young sales clerk that made him forget Alicia.

* * * * *

Her name was Josie and she was the most beautiful Filipina he'd ever seen. He'd often gazed upon her for long moments as he pretended to search the tie racks for a new design each P-Day. She had naturally tan skin and silky black hair that fell to her waist. Her eyes a dark brown—nearly black—were almond-shaped and mesmerizing against her pale Asian skin. Her knee-length skirt and fitted blouse left little to the imagination about her petite figure.

With each passing visit he'd gained more confidence to talk with her and, with his companion out of range of hearing, had begun to flirt with her, asking about a boyfriend and other seemingly harmless questions. He'd also allowed himself to think about her during the week, oftentimes interrupting his personal study or during a lesson while his companion was teaching. He hadn't thought much of it at the time, but from what he'd recently learned about listening to the promptings of the Spirit, he knew he'd been unworthy.

Nothing ever happened between him and Josie, but he'd entertained thoughts he shouldn't have allowed himself to have. They were carnal thoughts—completely inappropriate and non-conducive to maintaining the Spirit or drawing on the Powers of Heaven.

And he'd paid a horrible price for it.

Elder Daniels closed his eyes and wept once again. He recalled that dark night when he'd knelt at his bedside weeping over the loss of a potential baptism. As the guilt pricked his soul, he knew he could only blame himself for the way things ended with Brother Nguyen.

His thoughts and actions had disqualified him from the companionship of the Holy Ghost. Although he'd repented of his transgressions a hundred times over, he couldn't help but feeling responsible for losing the opportunity to baptize Juan Nguyen and turn a part-member family into an eternal family.

\* \* \* \* \*

Arriving at transfers twenty minutes later, Elder Daniels sat up in his seat. He picked up the journal from his lap and tried to clear his mind. As he reached for the bamboo backpack at his feet, a single sheet of paper fell out of his journal and landed face up on the jeepney floor.

He recognized the writing immediately and retrieved it. On the sheet of paper was a quote given him months before by Sister Hart. She'd specifically sought him out and told him she'd written it down just for him. She'd also asked him to do something for her.

"What is that? Elder Daniels had asked.

"I want you to memorize it," she'd said. "I mean *really* commit it to memory. These words will bring you strength when you need it most."

As Elder Daniels stepped out of the jeepney, he was already reciting the words as if he were reading them.

*"Be anxiously engaged. You can't afford to waste time. This is the one season of your life when you can devote all of your effort and all of your time to the work of the Lord.*

*The day that is passing can never be recalled or lived again. It will be gone with the sunset. Thank the Lord that there will be a new day tomorrow with new opportunities, but do not waste that which is today.*

*These are days long to be remembered—days when, with singleness of purpose, you served the God of heaven and His Beloved Son, worthy of His commendation— 'Well done, thou good and faithful servant.'"*

—*Gordon B. Hinckley*

There was no measuring how valuable those words had become in what had been the most trying months of his mission. Little did he know that far

170

greater trials ahead would test his faith even more.

# CHAPTER 17

*And it shall come to pass, that inasmuch as they are faithful, and exercise faith in me, I will pour out my Spirit upon them in the day that they assemble themselves together.*

*And it shall come to pass that they shall go forth into the regions round about, and preach repentance unto the people.*

*—D&C 44:2 & 3*

The missionaries gathered in a circle beneath the tallest tree in the chapel courtyard waited quietly for the meeting to begin. Elder Daniels stretched himself out to his full, six-foot, two-inch height, and surveyed his fellow zone leaders in the Philippines, Baguio Mission. All of them were seasoned missionaries.

Elder Zamora stood at his side, quiet and expressionless. Elder Daniels didn't know what to think of him yet. He'd only met him a few minutes beforehand. All he knew was that he had a chiseled jaw and a serious voice. He'd been assigned to Lingayen for two months, and even though one zone leader was not considered senior to the other, he was more familiar with the area and with the Lingayen zone. Elder Daniels knew he would learn a great deal from him if he remained teachable.

Across the circle stood President Hart—a man whose very presence commanded respect. He reminded Elder Daniels of a large battleship, tested by storms and hardened by combat. His words and demeanor characterized his values—duty, honor, righteousness.

The mission president was flanked on both sides by his two assistants. Their title was just that—Assistants to the Mission President—and they knew the place they held in the leadership chain. Elder Daniels couldn't help but think of it that way—akin to a military chain-of-command. Perhaps that was the reason he had always felt a little uneasy around them and often shied away from them at zone conferences and transfers. He had to admit that he was a bit intimidated by them and somewhat jealous of the close relationship they had with President Hart. He also knew they were highly favored and trusted by the mission president.

Making up the rest of the circle were 18 other missionaries, all leaders in their own right and pillars of faith in their respective zones. As President Hart welcomed them and began issuing instructions, each of them listened intently. He scanned their faces and recognized many of them—some he knew personally, others by reputation. There were a few he didn't recognize at all. But even then, he knew they were leaders in the mission and men who motivated others by their words and actions.

On the other side of Elder Zamora stood his former zone leader—Elder Jones. This was one of his first zone leaders and the missionary who acted on the promptings of the Holy Ghost to bring him news of a transfer only moments before he was to mail a letter sealing his decision to leave the mission early.

Next to him was Elder Neil, his zone leader in San Fernando who'd taught him how to exercise his faith to draw upon the Powers of Heaven. Across the circle was Elder Flores, his second companion who'd taught him about the pure blessing zone. Turning back to President Hart, Elder Daniels wondered how he would fit in with this elite group of missionaries.

*Why* did *President Hart pick me to be a zone leader?*

The second the question entered his mind, he consciously pushed it aside. He replaced the question with a positive thought. His training was working and the thought he chose had been committed to memory months before.

> *"Be anxiously engaged. You can't afford to waste time. This is the one season of your lives when you can devote all of your effort and all of your time to the work of the Lord."*

With that thought, Elder Daniels closed his eyes and basked in the warmth of the sun peeking through branches of the banyan tree. His thoughts drifted to times he'd devoted all his heart, might, mind and strength to the work of the Lord.

He saw himself sweating in the hot Rosales sun, physically weak after twenty-eight hours of fasting. He saw himself studying Tagalog at his desk in San Fernando long after his companion and zone leaders had fallen asleep. He saw himself sitting on the side of the road in Candon with his companion, praying for guidance about where to go next.

Elder Daniels opened his eyes and looked straight ahead. As he listened to the inspiring words of his mission president, he pulled his shoulders back an inch or two further, and stood even taller.

*I am ready to be a zone leader or else I wouldn't have called! "Whom the Lord calls— the Lord qualifies!" (Thomas S. Monson).*

"The success of this mission depends upon you," President Hart continued. "If you are personally worthy and you work diligently, you will see your zones flourish. If you work with an eye single to the glory of God you will find there is no missionary too challenging; no investigator too difficult; no baptismal goal too high. Let the spirit of missionary work permeate your every thought, for there is no other purpose that you are here. Draw near to the Lord and he will draw near unto you."

"Now remember," he continued, pausing momentarily. "The message you carry is true. There is no other cause worthy of your attention in the mission field. I testify, in the name of Jesus Christ, that He will abide you—He will send his angels to carry you forth—if you place your trust in him."

"Know that Sister Hart and I love you. Know that we pray for you by name every single day."

With that, President Hart bowed his head and prayed over them. He mentioned specific zones, and missionaries. He asked that the Lord bless him as a new zone leader. He pleaded for those who were struggling with their testimonies—members, investigators, and missionaries alike. He invoked the Spirit upon each one of them—promising that blessings—even miracles— would be showered upon the faithful.

After closing the prayer, he dismissed the group. "Now go forth to your assigned areas and continue the work of the Lord."

\* \* \* \* \*

The first thing Elder Daniels noticed about Lingayen was how much it reminded him of his first area. It had the same small town feel and the people were friendly and affable. Not that he hadn't found friendly people in his other areas, but the people in Lingayen were more willing to open their doors to strangers—even missionaries. There was no secret—the southern portion of the mission brought the most conversions. Much of that had to do with the economic demographics of Provincial Pangasinan. Most people were less affluent and humble—and that correlated with a readiness to hear the Gospel of Jesus Christ.

The sights, sounds and smells were so familiar that he halfway expected to see Elder Juarez seated next to him. Every once in a while he would catch the scent of smoke and see an elderly woman burning a pile of leaves she'd swept from her yard. He'd hear the distinct ring of hammer on iron and know that they were approaching a vulcanizing shop. He'd see a lazy caribou grazing in a field, relaxing after a hard day of plowing. It was all reminiscent of his first few months in the mission when he'd learned to love the Filipino people.

As the two missionaries stepped out of the jeepney in the center of town, a trike pulled up next to them. "Good afternoon, Elders!"

"Good afternoon, Bishop Soriano. I'd like you to meet my new companion, Elder Daniels."

Extending his arm, the man shook hands with the Elders and gestured to the empty sidecar, "Get in. I'll take you to your apartment."

"Thanks!" Elder Zamora answered, stepping in after Elder Daniels.

Looking at his polished shoes, Bishop Soriano asked, "How long have you been in the mission field Elder Daniels?"

Elder Daniels knew what he was asking and chuckled, "Just over a year," he said in Tagalog. "This is my third pair of shoes."

"Oh, you speak good Tagalog,"

"Thank you," he replied, pleased with the compliment.

The inside of the trike lacked many of the prominent decorations he normally found in the privately-owned, yet public transportation vehicles, in the Philippines. There were no rosary beads or pictures of the Virgin Mary. Instead, a single picture of the Manila Temple hung just above the front Plexiglas window.

"How long have you been a bishop?"

"Almost two years," he replied in a gentle, soft-spoken voice that was barely heard over the high-pitched whine of the 125-cubic-centimeter engine.

"How long have you been a member?"

"Almost five years."

Elder Daniels admired the man already. This was a good bishop. He could tell just from the way he spoke. Traveling down just two short streets and a long road lined with coconut trees and they were in front of the missionaries' apartment. Elder Zamora stepped out first, stretching from the cramped space of the small sidecar. Elder Daniels reached in his pocket for his coin purse, pulling out six pesos with which to pay the bishop.

"No, Elder. I can't take the Lord's money."

Surprised, Elder Daniels looked at his companion. "Bishop Soriano never lets us pay."

Elder Daniels shook the man's hand once more and watched him drive away. He was impressed with this bishop and felt very good about his new assignment in Lingayen.

* * * * *

"What's the matter, Comp?" Elder Zamora asked as the two walked side-by-side from the Elder's apartment in Binmaley.

"I don't know," Elder Daniels shrugged, "I guess I never realized how hard it is being a zone leader."

"What do you mean?"

"Well, you know, being in charge of twenty missionaries and responsible for everything that goes on in the zone? It's a bit stressful!"

"Are you talking about the Binmaley Elders?"

"Well, that's part of it. I mean, look at those guys, all they do is argue. They couldn't even agree on how to divide the area for splits today. And when we ran into each other at the ward mission leader's home, I thought they were going to tear into each other right there. I guess I'm just a little worried about the morale of the zone."

"Morale? What do you mean?"

"You know—the mood of the zone. When morale is bad, people aren't happy. When it's good, people like the way things are going."

"Oh," Elder Zamora replied, still learning some of the English words his American companions used.

Offering his observations from the past two weeks, Elder Daniels said, "I just see a lot of these guys going through the motions."

"Like what?"

"Well, take these Elders for example. What's their goal this month?"

Elder Zamora pulled a notebook from his shirt pocket. "Ten baptisms."

"Ten baptisms," Elder Daniels repeated, "but there's only six days left in the month and how many baptisms have they had so far?"

Flipping back a few pages, Elder Zamora counted the figures in his head. "Four."

"And what was their goal and how many baptisms did they have last month?"

Searching further back, Elder Zamora said "A goal of ten but only three baptisms."

"That's what I mean," Elder Daniels explained. "They're saying they want to be successful, but they're not putting in the effort to achieve it. I mean what were their stats last week? Twelve contacts, six discussions and two church investigators? And it's like that all over the zone."

Elder Zamora nodded his head. "So what do you think we should do?"

Having given it some thought, Elder Daniels explained, "We need to help our zone catch the vision of missionary work."

Passing a waiting shade, Elder Daniels took off his backpack and set it down, ducking under the cement covering to escape the blistering sun. "First we have to unite this zone. There's too much discontent and back-biting going on to get any work done."

It was apparent Elder Zamora was having a hard time following the conversation by the upward shift of his eyebrows so Elder Daniels put it in terms he would understand. "We need to get the Spirit of missionary work back in our zone."

"Oh, I see," his companion agreed, remembering the bickering he'd seen in more than a few companionships. "So how do we do that?"

Elder Daniels scratched his head, having asked himself that same question a dozen times. "I think it has to do with living a higher law. I think that if we can get this zone on a higher spiritual plane then the rest will work itself out."

"Are you saying our missionaries aren't keeping the mission rules?"

"No, I'm just saying we can do better than the mission rules. The mission rules just give us the minimum standards—you know, basically the things we have to do so that we don't offend the Spirit. But just not offending the Spirit is not the same as seeking the Spirit."

"I don't understand."

"Well, the mission rules are like the Law of Moses. We're expected to follow them. And don't get me wrong, most missionaries do, but a few of them only follow the letter of the law."

"Oh, you mean like Sister Hart was saying last month about living the letter of the law' versus living the spirit of the law."

"Exactly!" Elder Daniels replied. "That's what gave me the idea. Look at the Binmaley Elders—they're working until 9:00 P.M. every night because the mission rules say we're supposed to stay out until then. But, are they really working? From what I've heard they sure spend a lot of time at the ward mission leader's home just hanging out."

"How do you know that?"

"Brother Castillo mentioned it to me on Sunday."

"Really?"

"Yup, I guess when they don't have anything to do they just hang out there until it's time to go home."

Seeing his point, Elder Zamora said, "and that's what you mean by living the letter of the law rather than the spirit of the law."

"Right! The only reason they're not home by 7 P.M. is because the mission rules say we're supposed to work until 9 P.M.—that's living the letter of the law—you know, just reading the mission rules and obeying the words. Living the spirit of the law would mean they would be staying out until 9 P.M. doing every bit of missionary work they could find—that's the intent, or spirit, of the rule."

"So what kind of law are you talking about?"

"I don't know, . . . maybe we can call it the Celestial Law."

Elder Zamora smiled. "I like the way that sounds."

"Me too," Elder Daniels agreed. "I figure if we could get every missionary in this zone to be more obedient, more faithful, more worthy, then the Lord would have to bless us in a greater abundance."

"He would *have* to bless us?"

Elder Daniels smiled, thinking back a few months to a similar conversation with Elder Flores. "We'll talk about that tomorrow in our companionship study."

"But this is what I've been thinking. Next Monday, instead of having the districts hold separate district meetings, let's get everyone together for a zone meeting. Then you and I can present our ideas to them all at once and commit every missionary to living the Celestial Law."

"But I still don't understand what the Celestial Law is," Elder Zamora admitted.

Pulling out his Bible, Elder Daniels began flipping pages. "Do you remember the Sermon on the Mount?"

"Sure."

"Well, some of the people there, including the Pharisees, thought that Jesus had come to destroy the Law of Moses. They had great respect for Moses and were offended by Jesus's teachings."

Finding the page he was searching for in the Book of Matthew, Elder Daniels began reading. "Think not that I am come to destroy the law, or the prophets: I am not come to destroy, but to fulfill."

"In other words, Jesus was saying, 'Look, I'm not here to put down Moses or the law he introduced, I'm here to fulfill that law.' Jesus taught them that the Law of Moses was the preparatory law, the law that would prepare them for the higher law; the Gospel he introduced. Remember, Moses gave them the Ten Commandments, but Jesus made it clear in his sermon that they were expected to live on a higher spiritual plan than just those basic commandments."

Returning to the open page Elder Daniels continued, "Ye have heard that it was said by them of old time, Thou shalt not kill; and whosoever shall kill shall be in danger of the judgment. But I say unto you, that whosoever is angry with his brother without a cause shall be in danger of the judgment."

Skipping to a later verse, he read, "Ye have heard that it was said by them of old time, Thou shalt not commit adultery. But I say unto you, that whosoever looketh on a woman to lust after her hath committed adultery with her already in his heart."

"That's what I'm talking about," Elder Daniels explained. "Holding ourselves accountable to a higher law."

Elder Zamora was quiet.

"Think of the mission rule about not reading newspapers. Most missionaries know we can't go out and buy a morning paper, but how many have you seen glance at the headlines as they walk past the magazine racks?"

"Or the rule about not listening to worldly music. How often have we sat in a jeepney listening to the radio as it plays, thinking we're not doing anything wrong?"

"Yeah," Elder Zamora agreed. "I see what you mean."

His mind racing, Elder Daniels went on. "Or how about this one. You see a pretty girl walking down the street and turn away from her only to glance back a few moments later to get another look."

"But nobody's perfect," Elder Zamora protested.

Nodding quickly, Elder Daniels agreed. "You're right, and I have as much to work on as anyone. Just imagine how much stronger we would be—how much more spiritual we could be—if after we made a mistake like that we immediately repented. I mean instantly asking for forgiveness and trying harder to do better, even with the smallest of sins. How many times do we let a bad thought or memory sit in our minds and do nothing about it? Those are the things we need to be aware of. They're the things we need to repent of, immediately."

Letting out a deep breath, Elder Zamora whispered, "Wow! That is a celestial law! But do you think our zone is ready for it?"

"Oh yeah! They are so ready for it! I can see it in their eyes. Every one of them knows we can do better. They want to do better. We just have to commit them to do it. Think about how much better the companionships would be if we forgave each other immediately if our companion said something critical or hurt our feelings. Think about how many more contacts we could teach if we worked every minute as if it were the last. Think about how many converts we would have if they felt the Spirit every time we walked into a room. Comp, if we can get our zone to that level, our baptismal goals will take care of themselves and we will enjoy the work so much more."

Feeling the blood pumping through his veins, Elder Zamora picked up his bag. "Then let's do it! Let's you and I start right now, and we can tell them on Monday how good it feels to live the Celestial Law"

Elder Daniels smiled. "I like the way you think!"

\* \* \* \* \*

Bishop Soriano sat at his kitchen table with two books in front of him. The one—his single-most prized possession—was a leather-bound copy of the Bible, Book of Mormon, Doctrine and Covenants, and Pearl of Great Price, comprising the Standard Works of the Church of Jesus Christ of Latter-Day Saints. This one had been a gift from Elder Stevens, one of the missionaries who had taught him the gospel and baptized him five years before. Turning the pages carefully, he treated the book as if the pages were made of gold.

The other book, actually a binder, was something else he'd spent a great deal of time poring over. Providing much needed insight as it contained the policies and instructions pertinent to the calling of a bishop, the pages were marked and underlined, highlighted, and creased—each page as personalized as the scriptures from which he read daily. Appropriately titled *The General Handbook of Instructions*, this manual was specifically written for bishops and stake presidents. He'd read and reread it so many times that many of the paragraphs between its cover were as ingrained into Bishop Soriano's memory as his favorite scripture verses.

He looked at his watch as if it were a source of annoyance. The precious hour he dedicated to gospel study was nearly over. He'd only covered two pages of the handbook and felt short-changed. Closing the book, he reminded himself that much of that hour had been referencing specific instructions to the Standard Works. Rarely did he read a paragraph or verse without looking up every footnote, endnote and cross-reference available.

Pushing the chair back from the table, he closed his study with prayer. Just as he said "Amen," the front door opened and the muffled thumping of bare feet echoed through the house.

"Daddy?," a young child's voice called as he brought himself to his feet. "Are you done yet?"

"Yes child," he responded lovingly. "Did you enjoy your walk?"

"Yes!" she screamed, running in the room and jumping into his arms. " Did you know the ocean tastes like salt?"

"It does?" he asked, "How do you know that?"

"Cause Momma let us go swimming."

"Swimming?" he said with playful enthusiasm. "You know how to swim?"

"Well, no, but Momma let me wade out with Vanessa. But, I couldn't go past here," she said, touching her finger to her knee.

"Then how did you find out the ocean tastes like salt?"

"I licked it!"

"She sure did," Sister Soriano conceded, walking into the room to hear the last part of the story. " And she was told not to do it again, weren't you young lady?"

"Yes, Momma," she admitted, scrunching her cheeks, "Because the ocean is dirty."

Setting his daughter back on the ground, Bishop Soriano agreed, "You're right sweetie, the ocean is dirty."

"I need to tell Grandpa,"

"Okay, Desiree, but don't stay more than an hour," her mother yelled. "The missionaries are coming for dinner tonight."

"All right Momma," a little voice promised as she closed the front door.

Bishop Soriano gathered his books and cleared off the table. "I'd almost forgotten they were coming over."

"Well, I got some fish at the market and rice. I don't think the missionaries eat much fish, so I thought this would be a nice change. Maybe you could help me set the table?"

"Okay."

"Are you going to work with the missionaries tonight after dinner?" Sister Soriano asked, sorting out the few pieces of matching silverware they owned.

"Yes, I told them I had a referral for them."

"Oh, really, who is that?"

A slight pause in his voice foreshadowed the significance of what he was about to say. "My father."

Sister Soriano's heart skipped a beat as the words reached her ears. Her hold on the pieces of silverware in her hand faltered as she reached for the countertop to steady herself.

"Rolando! Are you serious?"

Bishop Soriano closed his eyes, trying to regain the assurance he'd received a few nights before. He'd nearly talked himself out of it a dozen times but the promptings that night had convinced him it was time to try to get his father to meet the missionaries again.

"I think these are the Elders that will be able to get him to listen."

Bending over to pick up the forks and spoons, Sister Soriano recalled the harsh words he'd endured from her father-in-law. It had taken three years to get back on speaking terms with him after their baptisms. But even now, he seldom withheld criticizing remarks about the Mormon Church. The only thing that had kept the old man in their lives was his complete adoration for his youngest granddaughter, Desiree. The bond between the two was stronger than any father-son relationship her husband had ever known.

"Does he know you're coming?"

"No."

"What makes you think he'll listen?"

"I don't know," he replied, setting the last of the dishes on the table and walking to her. "There's just something different about these missionaries. I don't know what it is, but I believe if anyone can get through to him, these two Elders can."

"They don't seem different to me. Why them?"

"I just feel something different about them. The way Elder Stevens made us feel when we met him."

Putting her arms around him, she said. "I hope they don't get offended easily."

\* \* \* \* \*

Elder Daniels looked at the fish on his plate and swallowed hard. "I love fish."

It wasn't a lie—but then, what lay on his plate wasn't what he had in mind when he said it.

"Thank you. Now don't be shy Elder," Sister Soriano said, seeing he'd taken the smallest fish on the serving platter. "There's plenty here for everyone."

The chill that raced down his spine made him light in the head as he looked at his plate one more time. For the past few minutes he'd been trying to figure out how he was going to eat this meal without gagging. He'd had some interesting food in the Philippines but this was too much. On his plate, next to a large scoop of white rice, lay a nine-inch silver fish staring up at him with lifeless eyes.

It wasn't the eyes that bothered him, nor was it the tail. He'd eaten many fish in the Philippines with their heads and tails still attached. What set his stomach into convulsions was the fact that this fish had been caught, boiled and served. No part of this fish had felt the slightest prick of a knife, let alone been gutted or cleaned.

Elder Daniels already knew what would happen when he cut into the fish. He'd caught and eaten many fish on camping trips with this brother and father. But even those fish had been fried over the fire—these fish were boiled!

He swallowed hard again as he pictured the organs and fluids draining out of the fish's belly onto his plate. He could already feel the acid in his stomach crawling up his throat. No matter how much rice he ate, every bite was going to be a struggle.

Only one thing prevented Elder Daniels from declining the meal entirely. As unsavory as it may be, it was still a sacrifice for this family to invite two more people to their dinner table. The possibility that he would offend them if he didn't eat it was far too great.

Staring at the plump, white belly, Elder Daniels reached for his fork and knife and cut into the fish, thinking back to his seventh grade biology class and the awful smell of formaldehyde that had greeted him then. Already he could see the bloated intestines being held back by nothing more than the tines of his fork and a silent prayer.

He remembered the first time he'd eaten 'balut' in the Philippines and how he'd survived that experience. The nearly developed duck embryo was days within hatching when it was boiled and served to him in his first area. The smell and crunching bones had almost been enough to make him vomit.

He also remembered the first time he'd been served 'black dog'—a delicacy in the Philippines often served at birthdays, weddings and other celebrations. When he'd asked why it was a 'black dog,' his companion had explained that all dogs turn black when roasted over a fire pit. Surprisingly, dog wasn't the worst meat he'd ever tasted and he realized right then and there that 'pets' were a luxury in first-world countries—none of the chickens, goats, pigs or dogs he saw in the Philippines were there to entertain people.

"Remember, Elder, there's enough for you to have two if you want another."

"Oh, thank you," he answered, "but this will probably be fine. I know my companion's got more of an appetite than he lets on about. I may have to let him have that other fish."

"Okay," Sister Soriano replied. "But I don't want anyone going away hungry."

*Don't worry*, Elder Daniels thought as he took his first bite. *There's no way I'll be hungry after this!*

\* \* \* \* \*

The old man sat in the rocking chair in total darkness. The old cinderblock house was musty and a bit smoky as the embers from his cooking fire faded into the night. The full moon that crept into a cloudless sky provided no illumination through the covered window at his back. He didn't want to be disturbed. He liked being alone—with nothing but his own thoughts to keep him company.

*Why did she have to die?*

His wrinkled, gnarled fingers gripped the armrest of his chair mercilessly as he slowly rocked late into the evening.

*Why did she have to die?*

They had been young—practically children in many people's eyes. They had also been young and in love. She was the perfect woman—bright, benevolent, and beautiful and she had stolen his heart the very moment he set eyes on her. With shoulder-length hair pulled back and secured with a bow, her wire-rimmed glasses gave her an intellectual look. Behind those glasses was a tender young woman whose heart was filled with compassion—a heart that was soon betrothed to him.

They'd met during their last year of college and most people told them to wait until they graduated before getting married. But after only three months of courting, it had made perfect sense to them to get married right away, for they spent nearly every free moment at one another's side. From the library to the public market, other than the few hours of class, they were hardly ever apart.

They were more than husband and wife—they were soul mates and complemented one another perfectly. What one-person thought, the other acted upon. What one person needed, the other provided.

Starting out so young, their life together was simple but filled with dreams. It was those dreams with which they filled the empty spaces in their home. Together they looked forward to a bright future—he with a job offer in marketing and she with a nursing degree. With eyes that saw nothing but opportunities, there was no end to what they could accomplish together.

Just a year into their marriage, and three months out of school, their plans took a turn that would change their lives forever. She was pregnant..

Already pinching every peso to get by, the young couple realized the 400 pesos they paid each month in rent would be too much with the added expense of a baby. Even with a dual income, the school loans took more than a little of the incoming money and the prospect of her having to take three or four months off work to deliver and care for a newborn baby cemented the fact that they would have to find cheaper housing.

With his wife into her second term of pregnancy, he moved what belongings they owned, into a small rented shed he was able to secure with 200 pesos a month. Nothing more than 3/4-inch plywood separated the young couple from the elements, but it was a roof over their heads and that was all that mattered.

Even then, though their possessions were few and their living conditions modest, the love they shared made up for the amenities they lacked. Even the once worrisome thought of a son being born to them became something of great anticipation as it, if humanly possible, pulled them closer together as the last few months drew to a close.

Early in the morning of August 7th their son was born. What they'd previously known as a completely satisfying life was multiplied a hundred-fold. There was no way to describe the absolute exhilaration she felt as she took that tiny babe in her arms. He marveled at the strong beat of his son's heart next to his own chest. Together, their dreams morphed to include this infant son with whom they would share the joys of mortality.

But those dreams never materialized. Only a single month passed before that devastating night. September 10, 1969 would be a day, and a night, he would never forget.

The rainy season had been mild that year, predictable to say the least. Each afternoon started with a light rain, steadily increasing into late afternoon showers before the sun reappeared and burned off the lingering clouds. Farmers rejoiced. Fishermen pulled in full nets. Children laughed and played in the soggy streets. The three short blasts from the public loudspeaker couldn't have contrasted more with the joyous setting. It had been seventeen years since a typhoon warning sounded in this part of the county.

Mothers scurried about the markets buying candles, rice, and other last-minute supplies. Fathers boarded up their windows for protection and threw additional ropes over their roofs to secure the bamboo. Children tried to stay out of the way.

With no money to buy anything and nothing to secure his home, he gathered his young wife and one-month old son in his arms and huddled between a mattress and the back wall of the wooden shed. Their best hope was that the typhoon would lose intensity before hitting land. For many hours the young family waited as the rain poured down. They listened to the tin roof amplify every drop of rain and every gust of wind as the storm intensified.

The small stream-lets of water that started under one wall and ran through the middle of their house soon became faster currents of water, eroding away the firm-packed, dirt-floor on which they sat. As the minutes passed, the heart-wrenching howling of their infant son faded away as the torrential winds and rain drowned out his interminable crying. Even the incessant wailing of the typhoon warning signal gave way to the almost deafening howl as the brunt force of the typhoon arrived.

The Japanese scale on which tropical storms in Southeast Asia are measured classifies sustained winds between 130 and 156 miles per hour as a Category 4 typhoon. While buildings in Manila and other large cities may survive a "Cat 4," few structures, if any in the provincial lowlands stand a chance.

Having grown up in a Catholic home, he mind-numbingly recited Hail Mary after Hail Mary, each one increasing in intensity to match the raging tempest outside. When his growing anxiety reached its peak, the typhoon was upon them, tearing off the roof of the tiny shed and carrying it away.

That was the last thing he remembered of that night. He lay in the hospital unconscious for the next four days.

He wasn't awake when they found the small family still clinging together under the waterlogged mattress. He wasn't awake when looters pilfered every possession of value from the scraps of wood they once called a 'home.' He wasn't awake when they pulled his wife's lifeless body from his arms. He wasn't awake when they released his uninjured son from the hospital to a relative to make room for more patients. He wasn't even awake when they buried his wife in a mass grave he would never have the strength to visit.

*Why did she have to die?*

For 45 years he'd asked that question every single night. He sat in the same rocking chair watching the shadows grow. The only thing that changed from one night to another was what he was drinking and how much moonlight filtered through the single-paned window behind him.

He didn't speak the question aloud. He didn't need to. No one had answered that question for him in 45 years. No one was going to answer it for him now.

People had tried telling him that it was god's will for her to die. He didn't believe any of it!

God *willed* for people to suffer?

He wanted nothing to do with a god like that—a god others described as merciful and just who would take the mother of his infant child?

After 45 years of silence he was certain of only one thing—there simply was no god.

During those many years he'd sat in that same chair as many other typhoons ravished the land. He wanted that roof to topple in on him! He'd begged for it to happen! He'd cursed everyone and everything, begging to be spared from his miserable existence!

But each time, though sirens screamed overhead, he came away from the storm unscathed. How could god be the author of such injustice?

*That* fact, more than any other, reinforced in him that there could be no god in heaven.

\* \* \* \* \*

The three figures walked side-by-side down the dimly lit street. Very few street lights were lit up in this part of town—not with neighborhood children and slingshots around. Nevertheless, a full moon cast enough light onto the pothole-strewn road that they didn't need the overhead lights.

In a way, Bishop Soriano didn't mind the poor lighting. It gave him the freedom to wear his emotions on his face rather than hide them within as he'd been doing all evening. If the Elders could have seen his wrinkled brow or tight-lipped smile, they may have hesitated, or even talked him out of visiting his father altogether. As it was, there were already enough voices in his head telling him to turn around and go back home. He didn't need anyone else trying to sway his decision.

"I have to warn you Elders that my father may not be happy to see us. We had somewhat of a falling out a few years ago when we told him we were taking the missionary discussions."

"I'll bet that was difficult for you," Elder Daniels replied, sensing the hurt and frustration in the bishop's voice.

"It was," he sighed, pausing in reflection of what had transpired after that. "I haven't been allowed to step foot in his house since the day we were baptized."

Elder Zamora remarked in astonishment. "Why is he so bitter toward you joining the Church?"

"He's had a really hard life. He sees religion as foolishness. I guess you would call him an atheist."

"But didn't your daughter come from his house just after we got to your home this evening?"

"Yes she did," he nodded, though in the dark shadows they couldn't see his movements. "There's a bond between those two that is very strong. From what I've heard, no one but my mother ever had as strong a relationship with him. In fact," he added with emphasis, "she's much closer to him than I've ever been."

"Is that why you wouldn't let her come along with us tonight? You're afraid of what he'll say in front of her?"

Bishop Soriano nodded, "She doesn't need to see that side of her grandfather."

For the next few minutes they walked in silence—the Elders putting some of the pieces together from earlier conversations—the bishop once again shaking aside the doubts he'd been wrestling with the past three days.

\* \* \* \* \*

He'd sat in the rocking chair for two hours before he heard the knock on the door. *Who could that be?* Very few visitors came to see him anymore—none after dark. He didn't know what time it was but he knew he didn't want visitors.

With bones that creaked and muscles that had long ago lost their strength, he pulled his weary frame out of the chair and walked to the corner table he knew more by touch than by sight. In the darkness his hands found a small candle he'd used the previous night and from his shirt pocket, along with a pack of menthol cigarettes, he withdrew a book of matches. Lighting a cigarette, and then the candle, he walked to the front door.

"Who's there?" he asked in a deep, throaty voice.

"It's me, Rolando."

"Rolando? What do you want? Don't you know what time it is?" he asked through the closed door.

"Yes, Father. I was hoping we could talk with you for a few minutes."

"*We?* Who's *we?*"

Bishop Soriano stumbled for the right words. "Some friends I invited to come with me. Can you just open the door and let us talk to you for a minute?"

Opening the door a few inches, the old man peered out into the darkness seeing little more than his son and two figures standing behind him. "What do you want?"

Stepping forward he said, "Father…please! Can you just open the door and let us in?"

Feeling too old and tired to argue at this time of night, the old man opened the door a few more inches, letting the light from his candle drift out into the darkness. It took his eyes a moment to adjust but there was no mistaking the white shirts and ties he saw on the two figures standing behind his son.

In a matter of seconds, his blood was boiling, coursing through his veins like a steaming locomotive. If there was one thing he'd promised himself a long time ago, it was that he would never let a Mormon missionary in his home.

"Get out of here!" he yelled as he slammed the door. "Get away from my house."

"Father, just hear me out," Bishop Soriano pleaded, knowing his window of opportunity may have closed as quickly as the door.

"There's nothing you can say that will change my mind! Go back to your *wives* and your *churches* and leave me alone!"

Shaking his head, Bishop Soriano stood his ground. "I'm not leaving until I've said what I came here to say. If I have to do it with this door between us— then so be it."

Taking a deep breath to calm himself, his whole body sighed as if he were about to unload a heavy burden from his shoulders.

"I know how difficult this is for you," he began. I've seen how life has treated you—how cruel it's been at times. I know that a part of you died with Mother, and that it took more than I'll ever understand for you to raise me alone."

"I also know how much you despise the fact that we've been baptized into the Mormon Church—even when you begged us not to."

"But Dad, it's been difficult for me too," he said, taking a step closer to the closed door. "All those nights watching you drink yourself sick, then laying in my bed hearing you cry yourself to sleep. All those years watching you throw your life away. Well…it took some of my life away too!"

Leaning his head against the weather-beaten door, he continued more softly. "I wanted my mother there just as much as you did. I wanted to know who she was. I wanted to love her and be loved by her. I wanted you to tell me stories about her. Help me know her—but you didn't—you kept all that locked up in your heart. And that wasn't fair to me either.

Wiping a tear that traced the outline of his nose, he sobbed. "I wanted to know her so I could know you and what it would have been like to have a family. I feel like I lost a father the same day I lost a mother."

Elder Daniels and his companion stood a few steps back, hearing more than they felt they should. Their hearts grieved to see one of the most righteous and loving men they knew pour his heart like this.

Elder Daniels thought of his own father and cherished moments from his childhood—youthful years of love and laughter—years he'd taken for granted. He would have given anything at that moment to sit down with his father and tell him how much he loved him—but he couldn't. And for that very reason, he empathized with Bishop Soriano, who felt no less distant from his father than the ocean that separated Elder Daniels from his.

Straightening himself with another deep breath, Bishop Soriano lifted his head. "Dad, I have to tell you something that I've wanted to tell you for years. I am going to see Mother again. It won't be in this lifetime, but I will see her again and live with her for eternity. I'm going to know her and love her just like you did. And, Dad, . . . *you* can too! God has made it possible for us to be together as eternal families. I know it! I know it's true! God lives and He wants us to live with Him again!

There was no sound from within the small house.

"Our Father in Heaven knows how much you hurt inside. He knows that you feel it was your fault Mom died because you moved into that tiny shack. But, Dad, all of this was part of God's plan—and that's what these missionaries want to tell you about. Just give them a chance. I promise—you too can know the peace of having a personal relationship with Jesus Christ and know that you can be with Mother again in the next life."

Letting his voice trail off into a whisper he said quietly, "That's all I wanted to say. But it's something I know for a fact and I leave my testimony with you. . . in the name of Jesus Christ, Amen."

Turning from the door, he walked away, not knowing whether a single word had been heard inside. For an instant he paused, hoping the door would swing open, his father standing in the doorway with arms open wide. But the door didn't open.

Slowly, he started back toward home, the Elders falling in step behind him. He'd said what he'd come to say.

About halfway home he departed company with the Elders, leaving him to his own thoughts. Summoning strength from his testimony, he quickened his pace, hurrying back to his own family who would be waiting for him. It would take time, he knew, but his father's heart would be softened. Someday. Somehow.

# CHAPTER 18

*Wherefore, my beloved brethren, have miracles ceased because Christ hath ascended into heaven? . . . Behold I say unto you, Nay; neither have angels ceased to minister unto the children of men.*

*And Christ hath said: If ye will have faith in me ye shall have power to do whatsoever thing is expedient in me.*

*—Moroni 7:29 & 33*

Elder Daniels and his companion sat at the kitchen table looking at their list of contacts. Their appointment sheets told a great deal about the success they were having in Lingayen.

"I don't know," Elder Daniels said. "Maybe we can follow up on the Ramirez family after we teach the third discussion to Brother Gabot."

Shaking his head, Elder Zamora didn't sound too convinced, "Uh, . . . what about on our way to the Samson's? I think we told Brother Rizal we would stop in and see how he's doing with his Word of Wisdom problem after we teach that third discussion."

"Oh, that's right! Maybe we could stop by a sari-sari store and buy a bag of candy for him, you know, for a substitute instead of cigarettes."

"That's a good idea," Elder Zamora replied, writing their plan in the small space provided on his appointment calendar. "Let's just wait and see if we get punted from any of our other appointments to visit the Ramirez family. As it is, I don't think we will have any other time to see them.

"Yeah," Elder Daniels agreed, "It's going to be another busy day tomorrow. There never seems to be enough time to get everything done.

That thought lingered in their minds as the two missionaries knelt on the floor with their appointment calendars open in front of them. Folding his arms, Elder Daniel led them in companionship prayer. He thanked his Heavenly

Father for the four discussions they'd taught in their own area and the work they did with the sisters in the Lingayen 3rd Ward.

It was easy to see that the Lord was blessing them exceedingly. The morale in the Lingayen zone was much higher after only three weeks of living the Celestial Law. The Aguilar Elders had baptized seven people that past Sunday and even the Binmaley Elders were projecting to have five baptisms the next. They'd been able to get all twenty-one of their investigators to church the previous Sunday. Missionary morale and baptisms weren't the only things on the rise. More than half the wards and branches had increased their church attendance in each of the last three weeks.

In fact, the only area that was struggling in the zone was Bayambang—a newer area that had opened only four months earlier and should have been ripe for success. But Bayambang wasn't producing as it had before. Each week the Elders averaged twenty contacts, fifteen discussions, and upwards of ten investigators at church, yet week after week they had no projections and no baptisms. A great deal of Elder Daniels' prayer was directed in their behalf.

As for the zone leader's area, they were barely able to keep up with the work. They were punted from appointments occasionally, but in almost every case, they were able to follow-up with other contacts and find new contacts to add to their teaching pool. Trying to balance the work between proselyting in their own area and working with each set of missionaries in their zone was difficult. Elder Daniels and his companion came in every night completely exhausted.

Halfway through his prayer, Elder Daniels asked for a special blessing for Bishop Soriano. "And, Father, . . . please send thy Spirit to comfort him, that he might be strengthened. Bless him with peace and assurance that what he did tonight was your will. We know that he is one of your chosen leaders and we love him. Please help us to assist him in his missionary efforts."

Remembering the rage in the eyes of the man who answered the door that evening, Elder Daniels paused to discern what he should ask. "And Father, please bless Bishop Soriano's father. Help him to put aside the pain and anger he's harbored all these years so that he might open his heart to the gospel of Jesus Christ. Let us be instruments in thy hand in bringing the truth to him that he might accept the gospel and partake of the sweet assurance of the resurrection and eternal life."

Elder Daniels also prayed for their own assurance that the activities they had planned for the next day were in accordance with the Lord's will. He had learned a long time ago that unless they took their plans before the Lord for approval, they often found themselves standing on the side of the road the next day, arguing about where they should go.

As the two Elders got off their knees, Elder Daniels said, "I think we should attend the district meeting in Binmaley this Monday. Maybe we can find out how we can help the Bayambang Elders if we talk to them ourselves."

"Okay," Elder Zamora replied, "we'll have to leave here about sunrise."

Retiring to their room and turning out the lights, neither of them fell asleep quickly. The encounter they'd witnessed that night left a strong impression on their minds. Words and phrases replayed themselves repeatedly, pushing away the sleep for which they both longed.

For the first time in a great while, Elder Daniels didn't know how to proceed. This situation was one he had not yet encountered. Somehow, he knew, the Lord would provide a way for them to share the gospel with the old man. Similarly to Bishop Soriano, he didn't know how or when.

When sleep did overtake him, he dreamt of camping with his own father. Ironically, in his dream he forgot to tell his father how much he meant to him. When morning found him, he reprimanded himself for his thoughtlessness. Even if it were only a dream, it woke him up to the fact that he'd taken for granted a father he revered above any other earthly man. If only he could pick up a phone and call home or sit down and write a letter. Even the latter would have to wait until P-day but he promised himself he would write his father individually and share things with him he'd never told him before.

* * * * *

"C'mon, Comp, we'd better get going."

"I just need to find a pair of shorts," Elder Zamora yelled from the bedroom. "We're playing basketball after the district meeting, right?"

"You'd better believe it!" Elder Daniels replied, looking forward to a "relaxing" P-day afternoon after attending the Binmaley District meeting. P-days always had a way of rejuvenating his mind and body, even though their basketball games were quite physical. It was a nice break no matter what they did, even the trips to the market were highly anticipated and gave them a change of pace and scenery.

Appearing moments later with his bamboo pack so full the lid wouldn't fit, Elder Zamora bounded toward the front door. "Okay, I'm ready." He was just as excited as Elder Daniels for a day-off.

After a quick prayer, both missionaries headed out the door, waving down the first trike they could find to take them to the bus stop near the central market. Elder Daniels looked at his watch. It was 7:05 A.M.

*Pretty close,* he thought. *It's an hour bus ride to Bayambang if we can catch a Philippine Rabbit. Otherwise, a minibus will take us closer to an hour and a half.*

Arriving at the town plaza, the Elders found an almost full minibus trying desperately to get a few last passengers to fill the remaining empty seats before heading west toward Binmaley.

"Let's wait a few minutes," Elder Zamora suggested, also hoping a larger bus would come along soon.

"Okay, but if one doesn't come quick, and we miss this minibus, it could be another fifteen minutes before we see anything else."

"Trust me."

Sure enough, a few moments later, a large, red Philippine Rabbit appeared down the distant highway, barreling toward them at an enormous rate. Having to slow quickly as it merged with jeepneys and trikes, the large, drum brakes let out a loud screech as the bus stopped just in time to avoid making a brightly colored trike its new hood ornament.

Elder Daniels looked at his companion warily. "You sure you want to take this one?"

Nodding, although hesitantly, Elder Zamora stepped inside. Elder Daniels felt a wave of cool, dry air hit him in the face. It was a welcome change to the sultry steam bath outside.

Having the luxury of air-conditioning along with high-backed, reclining seats, the buses were definitely worth the risks they posed by traveling at dangerously high speeds. Besides that, many of them had a television mounted just above the driver's head on which they played movies brought over from the States. Without even looking at the screen as he walked by, Elder Daniels could hear the distinctive voice of Arnold Swartzenegger saying, "Get to the choppa," a line from one of his favorite movies.

Taking a seat next to his companion, he immediately took out his Book of Mormon. It wasn't just that the movie was "Rated R," there were specific mission rules that prohibited watching any television whatsoever. For Elder Daniels and his companion, living the Celestial Law meant even stealing a glance at the screen was out of the question.

Sadly enough, Elder Daniels knew, not all missionaries felt that way. At the beginning of his mission he'd also rationalized things like that away. He hadn't yet been taught that his obedience—or disobedience—to the mission rules directly affected their success as missionaries.

Sitting near the front, and a head taller than every Filipino on the bus, Elder Daniels took a few minutes to reflect on his personal growth. He stared out the front window as they drove along the lowland highway.

As he stared out the window, his mind was diverted from its thoughts as another large bus passed them at an amazing speed. Elder Daniels jumped when the other drive honked its horn as a warning to the other bus. Looking around, he realized that he was the only one startled and showed any particular interest in the bus as no one else took their eyes of the TV or awoke from their slumber.

As Elder Daniels watched the speeding bus shrink into the distance, his eyes caught movement on the left side of the road ahead of it. Half a kilometer down the road, a large black dog darted into the road like a frightened deer, disappearing in front of the speeding bus. He held his breath for a split second, almost willing the dog to appear on the other side. He initially thought the dog had made it as all but its hind-legs came into view. But at that exact moment the right-front wheel snatched the dog up under it, tossing it high into the air. To Elder Daniels' disappointment, it landed on the side of the road in a twisted heap.

For a brief moment, he wondered if his mind was playing tricks on him. *Did that really just happen?* As if not shocking enough, the rest of the act that unfolded before him left him speechless.

192

The moment the dog's limp body hit the dirt, an elderly man crouching on the side of the road just a few meters away stood up with considerable effort and picked up the dog's broken body. As the bus passed by, he saw the man look to heaven and close his eyes. Elder Daniels could only imagine the sadness and grief he must have felt.

For the remainder of the trip to Binmaley, Elder Daniels had no problem tuning out the television overhead. When the bus stopped in front of the chapel where the Elders met for district meeting, Elder Daniels was still thinking about what he'd witnessed nearly twenty minutes earlier.

\* \* \* \* \*

*"For behold the field is white already to harvest; an lo, he that thrusteth in his sickle with all his might, the same layeth up in store that he perisheth not, but bringeth salvation to his soul. And faith, hope, charity and love, with an eye single to the glory of God, qualify him for the work."*

*"Remember faith, virtue knowledge, temperance, patience, brotherly kindness, godliness, charity, humility, diligence. Ask and ye shall receive; knock and it shall be opened unto you. Amen."*

As the last of the eight voices trailed off, Elder Culebra, stood and led his district in a fast-paced rendition of "Called to Serve." Elder Daniels watched the district leader carefully as they sang. With admiration he saw a young missionary who had only been in the mission field five months—charitable, bright, and good-spirited by nature. But Elder Culebra's most distinctive quality was his humility. He was simply a man without guile.

After the song, Elder Santos, a missionary assigned to Bayambang, gave the opening prayer. In broken English, the new missionary, baffled and dazed by an unproductive two months in the mission, prayed for guidance and strength in a seemingly impossible area. His voice was faint and tired and Elder Daniels was touched by the sincerity of the disheartened missionary's prayer. Elder Santos would need some encouragement and Elder Daniels was anxious to see how the district leader would respond.

"Thank you," Elder Culebra said, as Elder Santos took his seat. "Let's get the reports for last week. How about starting with our area first."

Elder Tandoc began reading off their statistics as his companion wrote them down in his notebook. "Proselyting hours: seventy-nine. Contacts: twenty-seven. Discussions: seventeen. Church investigators: eleven. Home teaching: eight. Comebacks: three. Convert baptisms: five. Projected baptisms: three ."

Elder Daniels smiled as he listened to the report. Their work was exemplary. Looking back a week in his own notebook, he saw that the Binmaley Elders had projected five convert baptisms and were halfway to their goal for the month.

"Thank you, Comp," Elder Culebra said as he looked over the report, "and how do you feel about our work?"

Elder Tandoc couldn't help but smile from ear to ear. "Very good," he said, his expression doing most of the speaking. "We have good baptisms and still get more to church. I know we get three more baptisms this week."

"And where do you think we need the most improvement?"

Looking over their stats once again, Elder Tandoc said, somewhat disappointedly, "We only get three comebacks to church."

The district leader nodded, "Yes, we need to concentrate on more of our members who have become inactive. How about setting a goal of twelve hours of home teaching this week instead of eight?"

"Yes. We do twelve hours and get more comebacks!"

Elder Daniels listened intently from the back of the room. He liked the way Elder Culebra set an example for his zone quietly rather than boasting about their success. He shared their report and let his district draw their own conclusions about their work. He also admired the way he looked for the things they could improve.

"How about Aguilar?" Elder Culebra asked.

"Proselyting hours: seventy-two. Contacts: twenty. Discussions: fourteen. Church investigators: six. Home teaching: seven. Comebacks: eight. Convert baptisms: two. Projected baptisms: two."

"Excellent," Elder Culebra remarked, more excited with their success than his own area. Did the Ramirez family come back to Church?

"Yes, they did!"

"Congratulations! That story you shared about your older brother coming back to the Church really inspired them. Keep fellowshipping them and introduce them to as many members as you can."

"Our ward mission leader invited them over for Family Home Evening."

That's wonderful! That also gives you nine baptisms this month and you've still got two more projections. What area of your work do you feel you could improve?"

Explaining that most of their contacts were single investigators, both Elders felt they were having a difficult time finding families. After a short discussion, they set a goal to find two new families to add to their teaching pool.

"Okay, and how about Bayambang?"

Slumping in his chair, and with the same tired voice Elder Daniels heard during the opening prayer, Elder Santos began to read their report. "Proselyting hours: seventy-nine. Contacts: twenty-eight. Discussions: twenty-one. Church investigators: thirteen . . ."

Elder Daniels sat in shock! Their report was even better than the district leaders!

". . . Convert baptisms: zero. Projections: zero."

Elder Daniels heart sank. This was the eighth straight week the Bayambang Elders hadn't had a convert baptism—neither did they have a single projection for the next week. Holding back the urge to ask questions, he sat quietly in his chair waiting to see what Elder Culebra would say.

"Wow! You guys are doing awesome! You had twenty-eight contacts, twenty-one discussions, and almost half of them came to church!" Not knowing how to address the issue of no baptisms or projections he asked, "How is Brother Escobia doing?"

Barely lifting his eyes, Elder Santos said, "He still has word of wisdom problems."

"And the Arrubio family?"

"They have concerns about The Book of Mormon."

"How about Brother and Sister Hernandez?"

Almost in tears Elder Santos replied, "Brother Hernandez asked us not to come back."

Elder Culebra closed his notebook. "Well, I'm sure things will start picking up, just keep working and the Lord will bless you."

After a brief silence, Elder Daniels raised his hand. "Elder Culebra, can I say something?"

"Yes, please."

"I want to share with you something that happened on our way here this morning. My comp and I arrived at the town square in Lingayen just as a minibus was headed out. Knowing we were already a few minutes behind schedule, I wanted to take the minibus. Looking over at his companion he continued, "But Elder Zamora assured me that a larger bus would come along if we just waited a few more minutes."

"Now anyone who knows me very well knows that I hate being late. It took a lot of faith for me to let that minibus pull away with nothing else in sight. But sure enough," he said, "after waiting just a couple of minutes, a Philippine Rabbit came around the corner and I can't tell you how glad I am that we caught that bus."

"An air-conditioned bus?" Elder Culebra joked. "That's better than a minibus any day."

Shaking his head, Elder Daniels chuckled, "Well that's not why I was grateful. You see, I saw something happen on that bus that might help a few of us here."

Relaying the incident about the dog, the speeding bus and the old man, Elder Daniels explained how he'd pondered over it for quite some time.

"At first," he said, "I felt terrible for the old man—thinking he'd lost his dog. But as I've had time to think about it, a particular thought keeps coming into my mind."

Standing up from his chair in the back of the room, he walked to the small desk in front of the chalkboard and sat down. He looked like a schoolteacher getting ready to instruct his class.

"What if that wasn't his dog at all?"

His question was met with blank stares.

"What I mean is, what if that dog was put there for another reason?"

"What are you saying?" Elder Zamora asked, unsure where his companion was going with this story.

Seizing the opportunity he'd been waiting for, Elder Daniels continued, "Sometimes we ask the Lord for things we really don't expect to receive. Think about it, how many times have we prayed that he will help a particular investigator and then walk out the door and never give it another thought until we're on our knees again?"

Seeing a nod from nearly every missionary in the room he explained, "When I was ten years old there was nothing in the world I wanted more than to learn to play the guitar. I remember begging my parents for almost an entire year to buy me one. I asked, and asked, until I had them convinced a guitar was something I didn't just want—but something I couldn't live without. And of course," he added, "I promised them I would practice every day."

"Well, by the time my birthday came around, all my begging and pleading had paid off. I got my guitar. You should have seen me those first few days. I played for hours, trying to learn the basic chords and strum patterns so I could play, what I thought was, music. I remember my fingers were so sore I could barely touch the strings."

"That first week or so I took that guitar everywhere I went. I took it to the dinner table. I took it to the bathroom. I would have taken it to bed with me if my parents would have let me. I told everyone at school how I was going to start a band. At night I dreamed of writing music and making videos."

"Well, after a couple weeks I started to lose interest in the guitar realizing how much work was involved. So, my mother set up some guitar lessons for me where I could get some real instruction. But that only lasted a couple of months until I stopped practicing all together. About the only time I touched it was the hour I spent with my guitar instructor who finally persuaded my mom to take me out of the lessons entirely. After that, my guitar sat under my bed collecting dust for several years."

"You know what I remember the very most about that time in my life?" Elder Daniels asked. "I never stopped wanting to play the guitar. Even though I didn't want to practice, I still would have given anything to play the guitar. Well," he confessed, "anything but the time and patience it took to practice."

Pausing a moment to make sure he had everyone's attention, he said, "Sometimes we do that same thing in missionary work. We say, 'Heavenly Father, I would give anything to baptize,' but we fail to do the one thing that is required above all else."

Unusually quiet for the moments preceding a P-day, the entire room waited for him to continue.

"I wonder what that old man was doing five minutes before that bus came along. What if he had been kneeling in prayer in the quiet of his nipa hut, saying something like, 'Father, I know you hear and answer prayers. Right now my family is starving. I'll do whatever you ask. Just tell me what to do."

The thought of the old man pleading for food put things in a different light.

"What if the Spirt had told that old man to go outside and sit on the side of the road and wait. What if the old man had walked outside, not knowing how, or what, but having perfect faith that the Lord would provide for him."

"Projecting baptisms is just like walking out to the roadside with an expectation of fulfillment. It would have taken a lot of faith for that man to step out of his nipa hut and walk to the side of the road, not being able to see how the Lord would answer his prayers. For you and me, it takes a lot of faith to project people for baptism that we are unsure of."

"But that's the key!" Elder Daniels exclaimed. "The Lord requires us to exercise our faith! If we have someone who is begging to be baptized and can hardly wait until the next Sunday rolls around, it's doesn't take a lot of faith to include them in our projections. But when we get someone who's fulfilled all the requirements for baptism but is struggling with a Word of Wisdom problem or has concerns with The Book of Mormon—well that's the type of projection that takes a great deal of faith to make."

Speaking up from the second row, Elder Santos said, "But I thought projections were the people we expected to baptize the next week. Are you saying that we should project everyone we are teaching?"

"No, of course not," Elder Daniels said, shaking his head. "If someone hasn't heard all the discussions or been to church the required number of times then we shouldn't project them because we can't baptize them. But those we can," he explained, "maybe we *should* project."

Elder Culebra stirred in his seat, noticeably uncomfortable with that idea.

"But if we project all those who *could* be baptized, what's going to happen when we project five and only baptize one or two of them? People going to ask why we projected them."

Elder Daniels paused a moment. He knew the other missionaries were thinking the same thing. As much as he hated to admit it, he knew that there was pressure in the mission to baptize. It didn't come from the Mission President or Church leadership, but it was there—an expectation that good missionaries baptized. While some zone leaders and district leaders pushed their missionaries to baptize, the majority was self-imposed. He did not want that to affect his zone. His goal was to increase their faith—and thereby increase their success as missionaries.

He also knew that many missionaries believed projections had to be "sure baptisms," and he knew that in some districts and zones, if a companionship missed a projection, they were told that they should never have projected them in the first place.

"Let me ask you this," Elder Daniels said in response to the district leader's question. "How do we use projections in the mission?"

Thinking it over a moment, Elder Culebra replied, "I don't know, I guess to get an idea of how many baptisms we're going to have the next week."

"So if we were to add up all those numbers, what good does it do us?"

Elder Culebra shrugged.

"Most of the numbers we give in our reports are nothing more than a way to compare ourselves against the standards the Lord has set for this mission. I mean think about it, since the standard for proselyting hours is seventy per week, if a companionship comes in with only sixty-five hours, we want to know how they spent their time. If they come in with ninety, we want to make sure they are not ignoring their personal and companionship study. If we only have fifteen people in our teaching pool and the standard is to have thirty, we want to know what efforts the companionship is taking to find more contacts, right?"

"Yeah."

"Okay, so what is the standard for projections?"

"There isn't one." Elder Culebra replied.

"Exactly!" Elder Daniels shouted, "So if you project five people in your area and only get two, can anyone fault you for trying to exercise faith?"

"No, I guess not."

"And if the entire mission projects to baptize 100 souls and only baptizes 50—is there anything wrong with that?"

"No."

"Elders, the Lord wants to help us convert and baptize our brothers and sisters. He wants us to bring His children unto Him. But sometimes," he explained, "we need the Lord's help to touch the hearts of our investigators."

"I mean think about it. It's not an easy thing for someone to give up smoking, or to believe in the Law of Tithing, or to leave behind the traditions they've practiced all their lives. The Lord understands this and is more than willing to help us in this work. But, here's the thing...we have to do our part first."

Opening his scriptures, Elder Daniels read from Ether 12:18. "And neither at any time hath any wrought miracles until *after* their faith."

"My point is that sometimes we have to step out of the light—out into the darkness—to a place where we can't see exactly how things are going to come about. We have to say 'Heavenly Father, we've taught this family as well as we can. They've attended church, they're reading The Book of Mormon, and they've done everything else required of them for baptism, that is everything but commit to being baptized.'"

"We say, 'They're a good family, Father, and we believe that if we exercise our faith, they will accept our challenge and enter the gate through the waters of baptism. We're going to project them for baptism. We ask that you help them accept the Gospel in their hearts and commit themselves to baptism.'"

In the same soft voice, Elder Daniels turned to the discouraged missionary and said, "Elder Santos—in the name of Jesus Christ—I promise you that if you will exercise every ounce of faith you have, the Lord will help Brother Escobia overcome his Word of Wisdom problem. He will tell you what to say to the Arrubio family to inspire them to read The Book of Mormon and find out for themselves that it's true. I promise that Brother and Sister Hernandez will have a change of heart and beg you to come back and teach them the rest of the discussions."

"Elders, the Lord *wants* to bless us! He *desperately* wants to bless us! But He can only do so according to our faith.

Elder Daniels walked back to his chair while the rest of the room sat in perfect silence. It was a good long time before anyone spoke.

Turning to his companion, Elder Santos whispered something to his companion and then turned back to the district leader. "Elder Culebra, can we be excused for a moment. We need to talk about our projections for next week."

# CHAPTER 19

*And it came to pass that after I had prayed and labored with all diligence, the Lord said unto me; I will grant unto thee according to thy desires, because of thy faith.*

*Whatsoever thing ye shall ask in faith, believing that ye shall receive in the name of Christ, ye shall receive it.*

*—Enos 1:12 & 15*

"Grandpa, why do you like that chair so much?"

"I don't know," the old man said, rocking back and forth, as he'd been doing for the past hour. "I guess I've finally broken it in the way I want it."

"Like your flip-flops?" she asked, pointing to the holes in the heel where he'd worn them through.

"Yes, just like my flip-flops. This is the way I like them."

"Why don't you get new ones?"

"I don't need new ones," he said. "I don't have no place to go."

Perfectly content with that explanation, Desiree turned back to her doll. She brushed a few stands of blonde hair off its face as if they were bothering the sleeping baby.

A few meters away, her grandfather watched with admiration. He loved it when she played at his house. Especially when she forgot he was there and acted on the impulses of a little child. He especially enjoyed listening to her talk to herself. Ironically, that was when he felt closest to her.

Watching her care for the doll, he was reminded of his own attempts at parenthood. He'd been left alone to care for an infant son only a few weeks old when his wife died. It had been difficult—more like *impossible*. He'd moved back in with his parents after the typhoon. His own mother became as close to a mother his son would ever have.

*What else could I have done? I had to put food on the table.*

Looking down at the glass of whiskey in his hand, he scolded himself silently.

*You could have been there for him! That's what you could have done! You could have given up the bottle and acted like a man!*

There in the almost silent house, with his beloved granddaughter playing only a few meters away, the old man berated himself once again, kicking himself for failing as a parent.

*You didn't do a thing to raise your own son!*

As much as he hated to admit it, he knew the things his son had said were true. He did blame himself for his wife's death. He'd blamed himself every day. After all, he had been the one who persuaded her to move into the less expensive home to save money.

*Why shouldn't I blame myself? It wasn't her idea! It was mine!*

He'd decided on the tin-roofed shack and it didn't matter how much she wanted to stay in the cinder-block home on Rizal Street. She'd even promised she'd take another job to pay to make ends meet.

*Why did you have to be so hardheaded?*

In his grief, he'd locked everyone, including God, out of his life. Not only did he stop believing in God—he hated anyone who did.

*"How can anyone pray to a god who let's these things happen?"*

His life had gone nowhere but downhill from there. Turning to alcohol, he'd buried his problems as far from his consciousness as the intoxicating liquor would allow. Maybe his son was right—he'd wasted his entire adult life. He had nothing to show for himself but the run-down house he'd inherited from his parents. Everything else was gone.

*You're pathetic!* He screamed at himself. *What would she say if she saw you now?*

"Grandpa, are you okay?"

"What?" he asked, shaking himself.

"You dropped your glass," his granddaughter said with a frightened look on her face.

Looking down, he saw a puddle of whiskey next to his chair. A couple meters away, his glass lay tipped over on its side.

Embarrassed, he reached for the glass. As his hand extended in front of him he saw it shaking. Really shaking!

"What's wrong, grandpa?" Desiree asked, standing up and taking a step back.

He pulled his hand back quickly. "I'm fine. I just fell asleep!"

"I'd better get home."

"No, child, it's okay. Please don't leave."

Desiree picked up her doll. "Mommy will be worried. I'd better go now."

Rushing past him, Desiree turned as she shut the door. "Bye grandpa. Hope you feel better soon."

The old man erupted into a fit of rage.

"Now look what you've done!" He screamed. "You scared off the only good thing left in your life!"

He kicked at the glass in front of his chair, sending it crashing into the far wall. Falling forward out of his chair he stumbled toward the broken glass, completely engulfed in anger. As much intoxicated by rage as the whisky he'd been drinking, he fell to the floor.

He hated his life!

He hated everything!

For a long time he didn't move. When he did, he held a piece of broken glass in his hand.

*Why not?* He'd thought to himself, just as he'd done almost every day for fifty years. *What do I have worth living for?*

\* \* \* \* \*

"It's a humid one today," Elder Daniels said as he wiped his forehead with his handkerchief.

"Yeah, that cloud layer locks in the moisture and it saturates the air." his companion remarked, pointing at the overcast sky.

Each afternoon for the past week they had been soaked with showers, catching them off guard the first day as neither of them had thought to bring an umbrella. The next couple of days they'd huddled together under his companion's small umbrella since he didn't have one.

Their investigators asked why he didn't just buy an umbrella and didn't understand when he told them he had to wait until their P-Day, on Monday. There were umbrellas to buy in Lingayen but he wanted to save his money and buy a quality umbrella in Dagupan. He'd had a good one in San Fernando but had left it with an elderly woman he'd met in a jeepney that needed it more than he.

Walking down a crooked road near the ocean, the two missionaries gazed quietly over the massive expanse of water ahead. Ominously dark clouds rolled in off the ocean toward them.

"I hope Brother and Sister Ramirez are home," Elder Zamora said as they neared a small group of nipa huts about a hundred meters up the shoreline. In front of them, the beach stretched down the coast as far as the eye could see.

"We really need to commit them to baptism in this discussion."

Elder Daniels nodded again, remembering the two-hour long discussion they'd had with him and his wife the morning before. The man, a humble but intelligent fisherman, had been adamant that his baptism as an infant was sufficient and that to be baptized again would be a sin.

"That was a rough discussion we had yesterday," Elder Daniels remarked, remembering the growing sense of frustration he'd encountered as the man continually rebutted their arguments. "We've really got to try harder at bringing in the Spirit when we testify. He came at us with so many questions we didn't even get to say an opening prayer."

They'd spent a great deal of time flipping through scriptures to answer the man's questions. On another occasion he'd brought up concerns about polygamy—a concern neither Elder had much experience addressing.

"I can't believe we got into a debate with him. I've never felt anything like that before. It was like an evil spirit entered the room."

Elder Daniels had felt it too. This man had ripped apart everything they said. He was obviously one who had spent much time in the Bible. Not much to look at on the outside—with leathery, sun-weathered skin—he'd proven himself well-versed in his knowledge of The Church of Jesus Christ of Latter-Day Saints—at least in the falsehoods surrounding the Mormon doctrine.

The Elders walked between the first two nipa huts and saw a lone figure squatting in the sand near the water's edge.

"Good afternoon," Elder Zamora called as they neared Brother Ramirez, "What are you doing?"

Crouching over a large, rectangular net spread out over the moist sand, the man looked up as the Elders approached, returning the greeting with a toothless smile.

"Repairing my nets," he replied, sticking his entire hand through a large hole near his bare foot.

"Any luck today?"

"Not much," the old man shrugged, pointing to a tall bucket at his side. "But it should pick up with this rain coming in."

Elder Daniels walked toward the bucket expecting to see fish in the bottom. Instead, he saw a half-dozen large crabs clawing at the sides of the bucket.

"Crabs? That's cool!"

Elder Zamora, amused at his companion's excitement joined him at the side of the bucket. He picked up a small stick from the ground and gently poked one of the larger crabs with it. The crab, much less amused than his observers, snapped at the stick with a large claw, holding it fast in a vice-like grip.

As his companion withdrew the stick with the perturbed crab dangling from the other end, Elder Daniels pulled his camera out of his backpack and said, "Hey, can you take a picture with me and that crab?"

Taking the stick from Elder Zamora, Elder Daniels held the large crab out in front of him. Elder Zamora was trying to figure out where the shutter release was on the camera. Just as he found it and was about to snap the picture, the annoyed crap loosened its grip on the stick and dropped to the ground. Before either missionary had a chance to react, the crab scurried off into the surf.

Brother Ramirez burst out laughing when he got a look at the picture Elder Zamora had taken. Elder Daniels was standing in the picture with a stick in his hand, but no crab.

"I'm sorry," Elder Daniels apologized. "I didn't mean to lose your crab."

"That's okay. There'll be plenty more once I get this net in the water."

Careful not to tangle the lines, Brother Ramirez scooped up the net and walked towards the water. He waded in until the incoming waves broke at waist-level and, with a half-turn of his upper-body, he tossed the net toward the open sea. The net unfolded while still airborne and landed gently on the water's surface. With small weights lining its edges, the net sunk to the bottom, covering ten square meters of the ocean floor.

The precision with which he cast the net reminded Elder Daniels of his father. He'd often admired his dad's perfect technique of casting a fly with his fly-rod on the Little Cottonwood River back home. A feeling of homesickness enveloped him as he watched Brother Ramirez work.

Paying out a length of rope attached to the edge of the net, Brother Ramirez walked back toward shore. He tied the rope around a large piece of driftwood stranded on the beach.

"Is that how you pull in the net?" Elder Daniels asked.

Taking him over to another net that lay in a heap upon the shore, Brother Ramirez explained how to crab.

"This rope goes all the way around the net and attaches to this large ring." Holding up the metal ring, which was about the size of a key ring, Brother Ramirez showed the young missionary how to thread the loose end of the rope through the ring. With one good pull the edges of the net were gathered inward toward the center of the net, trapping the crabs in the middle.

Looking up at the sky, Brother Ramirez felt the first sprinkle of rain, "Let me get this last net in the water and then we'll go inside and get started."

A few minutes later, all three of them were running for shelter as fast as their legs would carry them. Large drops of water splashed on the sandy beach making small craters of water that slowly seeped into the sand below. Overhead, the darkening sky crackled to life with a heavy burst of lightning which lit up the horizon, appearing not more than a few hundred meters off shore.

"Come inside," the man said over his shoulder as he climbed the small ladder up to his nipa hut. Following him in, Elder Daniels gingerly stepped where he could see the wooden supports lining the floor below, careful not to stray where his weight might prove too much for the thin strips of bamboo underfoot.

Elder Daniels had noticed long ago that all the nipa huts close to the water were built on stilts. Essentially, this served as 'flood insurance.' This hut in particular was a good meter off the ground, indicative of the hazards associated with coastal living.

The "Ramirez family" consisted of Brother Carlos Ramirez—a lean, gray-haired man in his late-fifties—his wife, Loretta—a quiet, and somewhat withdrawn woman in her forties—and anyone else that happened to show up for the discussions. At any one discussion, there was always between three and seven people—most of them aunts, uncles and cousins of varying degrees.

From what the Elders had gathered, Brother and Sister Ramirez had no children of their own. They'd lived a quiet, secluded life together, occupying the smallest nipa hut at the distant end of the small barrio. Yet, they seemed to be the center of attention whenever the missionaries showed up.

Elder Daniels knew much of it was curiosity about the American who spoke fluent Tagalog and even some of the provincial dialect of Pangasinan. He also suspected that Brother Ramirez was a figure of authority, being the eldest of the men in the village and one of influence. For that reason the Elders were very persistent in teaching him. If their hunch was correct, the Elders saw an opportunity for great success in the barrio if Brother Ramirez led the way. Besides that, in the young branches and wards in the Philippines, there was always a need for leaders.

Taking a seat on the bamboo floor next to his companion, Elder Daniels asked, "Where's Sister Ramirez?"

"She went to Dagupan this morning to visit her sister, who is sick. She will stay there tonight and return tomorrow."

Looking at his companion, Elder Daniels asked, "Should we wait until she gets back?"

Overhearing the question, Brother Ramirez shook his head, "No. We will have our talk about Joseph Smith and I will tell her what we talk about. But first," he added, "I have some questions I want to ask you."

Feeling his hopes for a smooth discussion fleeting away, Elder Daniels looked back at his companion, hoping he would agree that they should just wait. "Have faith, Comp," Elder Zamora whispered as he took out his scriptures.

"Why isn't Joseph Smith's name in the Bible?" Brother Ramirez began, talking as fast as his mouth would let him. And I hear that Mormon's pray to him? And what . . ."

As tactfully as he could, Elder Zamora cut him off in mid-sentence, putting up a hand in protest, "Brother, we're happy that you have questions and we'll be happy to answer them, but on two conditions."

Caught off guard, the older man paused. "Conditions?"

Elder Zamora set his scriptures aside and looked deeply in the old man's eyes. "Well, first," he said, speaking in a slow, quiet voice, "we want to invite the Holy Spirit into our discussion so that we can better understand the things of God. To do that," he explained, "we'd like to start with a prayer."

Shrugging his shoulders, the man said, "Okay," and shut his eyes. "Our Father which art in heaven, hallowed be thy name. Thy kingdom come. Thy will be done, on Earth as it is in Heaven."

Elder Zamora looked at his companion and rolled his eyes. That wasn't what he'd had in mind. When the man finished, Elder Zamora smiled, saying, "Thank you Brother Ramirez, but with your permission we'd like to say another prayer. Perhaps one where we can ask for the Spirit to help in our discussion."

Confused, the old man shrugged again, hoping to get back to the many questions he wanted to ask.

"In the Sermon on the Mount," Elder Zamora began, opening his scriptures to the sixth chapter of Matthew, 'the Lord said, But when thou prayest, enter into thy closet, and when thou hast shut thy door, pray to thy

Father which is in secret. And thy Father which seeth in secret shall reward thee openly. But when ye pray, use not vain repetitions.'"

"In other words," Elder Zamora explained, "Jesus told us to pray to the Father in secret, or in a personal, private way. You see the Pharisees of his day loved to go out in the street and yell out their prayers so that everyone around them could hear. They did this so that they may be seen of men. But Jesus instructed them not to just repeat memorized words but to talk to our Heavenly Father from our hearts, saying, 'After this manner therefore pray ye.' He was saying, this is an example of how to talk with my Father."

"First we address our Heavenly Father. Second, we thank him for the things for which we are grateful. Next, we ask him for the things we need. Finally, we close in the name of Jesus Christ, because he is our advocate with the Father. This was what Jesus was trying to teach us when he said, 'After this manner therefore pray ye.' You see, when we talk to our Father in Heaven, it should be a dialogue with Him rather than a memorized prayer."

Brother Ramirez remained quiet. Sensing his hesitation, Elder Zamora asked, "Brother, since this is your home, which of us would you like to give the opening prayer?"

Without saying a word, he looked at Elder Daniels, who nodded and bowed his head. Elder Daniels closed his eyes partway, just enough to see the old man do the same.

His voice, barely audible over the pouring rain outside, rang with sincerity. "Our Father in Heaven, we're so grateful to be here with Brother Ramirez this afternoon. He has opened his door to us that we might share with him your message. We thank you for your great love for us and for giving us strong, healthy bodies. We thank you for giving us families that love us, and, most of all, we thank you for giving us your Son."

"We ask, Father, that you allow the Holy Ghost, or the Holy Spirit, to be with us this afternoon. We know that only through the Holy Ghost can we understand your will and the truths concerning your plan for us."

"We know we are your children and that Jesus Christ is our Savior. Please bless Brother Ramirez that he might know that we are your servants, carrying the gospel message that will bring him peace, happiness, and eternal life."

Brother Ramirez rubbed at his arms, feeling warmth come over him. Although the rain was coming steadily now it was still very hot and humid. In amazement Brother Ramirez opened his eyes enough to see goose bumps on his arms and legs.

Elder Daniels continued. "We pray that you would bless Sister Ramirez as she visits her sister in Dagupan. Please comfort her and protect her. Please bless her sister that her health may return. Father, we love you with all of our hearts and ask these things in the name of Jesus Christ, Amen."

When the prayer ended, the inquisitive man sat silent. He'd never heard such a prayer in all his life. Elder Zamora picked up on his bewilderment and said, "Brother Ramirez, our prayers don't have to be formal—they just need to be sincere—from our hearts."

The old man nodded humbly, astonished by the personal relationships these two young men seemed to have with God.

Elder Daniels asked, "Brother Ramirez, how do you feel right now?"

Usually quick to respond, Brother Ramirez paused, taking a moment to survey his feelings more deeply. He knew that he had felt warmth, but that warmth was contradicted by the goose bumps that made his hair stand on end.

"I feel peaceful."

"What do you mean by, peaceful?" Elder Daniels asked.

"I don't know. I just feel happy inside."

"Where do you think those feelings come from?"

"I don't know," he replied again.

Opening his scriptures to a verse marked with red pencil. "You're probably more familiar with this scripture than I am, Brother Ramirez, but would you mind reading this verse in Galatians?"

Handing his Bible to the old man, he said, "In this verse, Paul is writing to the Saints in Galacia, telling them that if they follow the Holy Spirit, they won't be led astray.

Brother Ramirez took the book slowly, "But the fruit of the Spirit is love, joy, peace, long-suffering, gentleness, goodness, faith, meekness, temperance; against such there is no law."

"When the Spirit speaks to us," Elder Daniels explained, "it is usually through feelings. When we feel the joy, peace, or goodness that Paul spoke of, we can know that what we are doing is right—or that what we hear is true."

Rereading the verse to himself, the man continued pondering his emotions. In an unmistakably meek voice he asked, "And what is the second condition?"

"The only other thing we ask," Elder Zamora answered, "is that we agree not to get caught up in a debate. Like we said," he continued, "we'll be happy to answer any questions you have but we're here to share a message about our Heavenly Father's plan for His children. If you'll allow us to share our message, we will do our best to answer those questions."

With one more nod from the man, Elder Daniels began teaching about the restoration of the priesthood. For most investigators, discussing the Great Apostasy, or the period of time after the death of Christ's Apostles when the priesthood authority was lost, challenged their traditional beliefs. To hear that it had been restored through Joseph Smith was even more challenging to accept.

Having been raised in a devoutly Roman Catholic home, Brother Ramirez's meekness faded as he listened to the twenty-year-old missionaries tell him that his church had no authority to act in Christ's name.

"Do you mean to tell me that John the Baptist—the same John who baptized Jesus—appeared to Joseph Smith 1,800 years later?"

"That's exactly what we're saying," Elder Daniels replied wearily, having heard nothing but comments of disbelief and unanswerable questions in the last half-hour. "And a short time later the apostles Peter, James, and John, whom Jesus had called to lead his Church, restored to Joseph Smith the higher priesthood authority. This is called the Melchizedek Priesthood. Through this higher power and authority, the Church is directed and rich blessings are brought into the lives of its members."

Brother Ramirez was completely taken back by what he'd just heard. Taking advantage of his investigator's rare loss for words, Elder Daniels continued, trying to get in as much as he could before being bombarded with more questions. In almost one entire breath he explained that the through the power of the Aaronic and Melchizedek Priesthood, righteous men can perform sacred Gospel ordinances and that the Lord commanded Joseph to reestablish the Church of Jesus Christ on April 6, 1830.

In closing he added, "The Lord testified that this is the only true and living church upon the face of the whole earth' when he said in the first section of the Doctrine and Covenants:"

*"And also those to whom these commandments were given, might have power to lay the foundation of this church, and to bring it forth out of obscurity and out of darkness, the only true and living church upon the face of the whole earth, with which I, the Lord, am well pleased, speaking unto the church collectively and not individually."*

"Now wait a minute," Brother Ramirez protested, "are you trying to tell me that you believe your church is the *only* true church just because you have this book that says so? You're saying my church, and every other church on the face of the Earth, is *wrong*?"

The questions split the air with sharpness. Elder Daniels, weary of the constant struggle the man put up, didn't say a word. He just slowly closed his scriptures, knowing the Holy Spirit had withdrawn and that he could not teach without it. By his side, Elder Zamora shifted uncomfortably, wondering whether he should say something and not sure what his companion was planning to do next.

The man sat across from the Elders with his arms folded waiting for an answer. As the seconds passed, his impatience grew. When neither said anything more he rose to his feet and started for the door, saying, "How dare you come in my home and say such a thing?"

"We didn't say it," Elder Daniels responded. "This is what the Lord said."

Turning around abruptly, Brother Ramirez shot back, "You mean that's what your Joseph Smith said."

Elder Zamora gathered his belongings and started to rise to his feet but a quick glance at his companion told him they weren't yet through. Elder Daniels didn't move.

When he got to the door, the old man pushed it open, letting the wind and rain welcome his unwelcome guests. A sharp crack of lightning over the water charged the already electrifying atmosphere within the tiny hut. As he turned around, he realized the two missionaries were still sitting right where he'd left them.

"I think you should leave," he demanded, holding the door open. "I don't think I want to hear any more."

"We can't do that, Brother Ramirez," Elder Daniels explained. "We agreed to answer your questions if you allowed us to share our message. That," he explained, "you haven't let us do."

Astounded by the missionary's boldness, the man stood speechless in the open doorway, his silhouette becoming a dark figure every time the lightning cracked outside.

Pausing for a moment, Elder Daniels uttered a quick prayer in his heart, hoping to find the right words.

"Brother Ramirez, you asked us to share our message with you, and when we did, you ridiculed us. We asked that you not turn this into a debate, but you've done that too. You felt the workings of the Spirit when we started earlier with a prayer, but you've driven that Spirit away by closing your mind and challenging everything we've shared with you."

Taking his black nametag from his shirt pocket, he held it out for the man to read. "We are Elders of The Church of Jesus Christ of Latter-day Saints, holders of the same Melchizedek Priesthood passed down to us by our Lord and Savior, Jesus Christ. We have been sent out into the world by Him, bearing His sacred name, and witnessing before all mankind that He lives, that He loves His children, and that this is His only true and living church."

"We explained to you the first time we met that you don't have to take our word for any of this. The Lord has promised that if you will read, ponder, and pray, He will manifest the truth of these things unto you by the power of the Holy Ghost."

"You know what that power feels like, don't you? You told us today how you felt when the Spirit touched your heart, Brother Ramirez, if you will humbly and sincerely ask our Heavenly Father whether or not this is His true church, you can expect those same feelings of peace, joy, and goodness. If you don't, you will never know."

As his voice trailed off, Elder Daniels gathered his scriptures and set them in his backpack, allowing the silence that filled the room to carry his words to the heart of their investigator. Standing next to his companion, Elder Daniels replaced his nametag on his white shirt and stood taller than he ever stood before.

"In the name of Jesus Christ, I testify that these things are true. It is up to you now to decide what to do. You can do as we've asked and gain your own testimony that what we've shared is true, or you can turn your back, risking nothing more than your eternal salvation. Either way, the decision is yours."

Swinging his backpack over his shoulder, Elder Daniels stepped toward the door, extending his hand as he approached. With a firm handshake, he locked onto the man's steady gaze.

"Brother Ramirez, thank you for letting us come into your home today. We appreciate the time you've given us. But know this—if you choose to turn your back on our message, in a coming day, Elder Zamora and I will stand as witnesses against you. We will testify that you had the opportunity to accept the true Gospel of Jesus Christ and yet even after the Holy Ghost touched your heart, you chose to close your mind and your heart—unwilling to humble yourself before the Lord and ask for His divine answer. I testify of this as an Elder in the Melchizedek Priesthood and in the sacred name of Jesus Christ, Amen."

# CHAPTER 20

*Verily, verily, I say unto you, even as you desire of me so it shall be done unto you; and, if you desire, you shall be the means of doing much good in this generation.*

*Behold, thou hast a gift, or thou shalt have a gift if thou wilt desire of me in faith, with an honest heart, believing in the powers of Jesus Christ.*

*Seek not to declare my word, but first seek to obtain my word, and then shall your tongue be loosed; then, if you desire, you shall have my Spirit and my word, yea, the power of God unto the convincing of men.*

*—D&C 11:8, 10 & 21*

Like a fish swimming against the current, Elder Daniels wrestled his way through the crowded market streets of Dagupan, trying to stay within a step of his companion. Slowly and painstakingly, they fought their way past stands of kalamansi, mangoes, and watermelons, toward the rice vendors. With his bamboo backpack held high over his head, it was no easy task getting through the bustling walkways—neither was it a pleasant one.

Doing his best to skirt the "meat market," Elder Daniels held his nose as they walked past the chunks of meat hanging in the hot sun. There was always a nasty smell in this part of the market with the discarded cabbage, tomatoes, and other items rotting in the gutter, but the stench that filled his nostrils on this particular Monday nearly made him gag. Averting his eyes from a skinned caribou's head that hung amidst a swarm of black flies, he stayed close to his companion to guide him through the bustling mob and away from the pungent odor.

"I'm getting six kilos," Elder Zamora said over his shoulder as they approached a vendor standing behind a large cart of white rice. "You never know when we're going to get stuck in Lingayen during a typhoon and not be able to get to the market on P-day."

"Okay! Just hurry!" Elder Daniels said in a nasally voice. In the last five minutes, he'd felt his stomach lurch three times, making it a top priority to find fresh air as soon as he could.

"Elder Daniels!"

Hearing his name, the tall American turned, searching the crowd behind him.

"Elder Daniels!" A voice called again.

A good six or seven inches taller than every other person around him, Elder Daniels still had trouble seeing the short Filipino scurrying toward him through the busy horde.

When the young missionary finally got within shouting distance, Elder Daniels asked, "Hey, Elder Santos! Where's Elder Bordellos?"

"He's right behind me," he said, turning to find his companion nowhere in sight. "Well, he was right behind me."

A few seconds later, another missionary appeared as Elder Bordellos pried his way through the throng of shoppers.

"My goodness!" He exclaimed, looking down at his shoes. Each one bore the scuff marks of a hundred people who'd walked on them in the short distance he'd just traveled. "Someone could get killed in there!"

"Let's move over here," Elder Daniels suggested, seeing an empty patch of pavement next to a boarded-up alleyway.

"Hello," Elder Zamora shouted as he made his way back to his companion. "What are you guys doing here?"

"Same as you," Elder Santos replied, holding up a small bag of groceries. "There's some lanzanoes over there. Thirty pesos a kilo."

Elder Daniels' mouth watered as he thought of the bittersweet fruit he'd eaten many times. "That's cheap! We'll have to get some of those."

"Here, try one. They're really juicy."

Taking the walnut sized fruit in his hand, Elder Daniels began peeling back the soft, white covering when his companion grabbed it from him. "Comp, don't you think you should wash that first? You know what Sister Hart would say if she saw you eat that!"

Ignoring him, Elder Daniels snatched it back, tearing off the last of the peel and popping the whole thing in his mouth. "I've been in the Philippines so long, I'm half-Filipino."

"Okay, but don't come whining to me when you get sick tonight!"

Turning back to the other Elders, he asked, "How was your week?"

"That's what we wanted to tell you about. You'll never believe what happened!"

"What's that?" Elder Daniels asked, wiping at a stream of lanzanoes juice that dripped from his chin.

"Do you remember Brother and Sister Escobia that we told you about last Monday?"

"You mean the couple who stopped taking the discussions?"

"Yes! The one's we had given up on until you told us about projections."

"What happened?" Elder Zamora asked.

"Well, after we projected them this last week, like you said we should, Elder Bordellos and I made them our highest priority. I'll tell you," he explained, shaking his head, "I wasn't all that convinced we could get them to listen but we decided to do everything we could to be able to teach them again."

Elder Bordellos, speaking up for the first time, tugged at his companion's shirtsleeve. "Tell them about the note!"

"I will." he said, turning back to the zone leaders. "The first thing we did on Tuesday morning was show up at the Escobia's house. I think we surprised them a bit, but we got an appointment anyway."

"You mean you taught them that morning?" Elder Zamora asked, sounding more shocked than he wanted to.

"No, not exactly. They said they had to get out and drain a field that's flooding with all the rain, so we said we'd come back that evening."

"That sounds like it would have been a good service project." Elder Zamora pointed out, always looking for service opportunities.

"We thought that too, but when we suggested it, they kind of just changed the subject, telling us it would be better if we came back later."

"That's too bad."

"Tell them about the note!" Elder Bordellos pleaded again.

"I will! I will!" he said diving back into his story. "Brother and Sister Escobia live pretty far out of town. It was about a forty-five minute bike ride from our last appointment. So we got out there for our appointment that evening, and were pretty disappointed when we found a note on their door telling us again that they were too busy to take the discussions."

"Really?"

"They said their crops are dying because of all the rain and flooding. They also said that their caribou was sick and that the lightning the other night split a tree in half and knocked down their fence. They said they were sorry but they wouldn't be able to spend time with us right now."

"But you know what?" he asked in the same breath, "that didn't stop us."

"What do you mean?" Elder Daniels asked.

Elder Santos looked at his companion, giving him a little wink. "Well, we were about to get back on our bikes and head home but Elder Bordellos convinced me that we shouldn't give up so easily. He said that's where our faith had to come in after we projected them for baptism"

"So we locked up our bikes and just started walking, you know, trying to figure out where their field might be. Since neither of us had worked in their barangay before, and we couldn't find anyone around to ask, we just started walking down the road until we found them."

"I bet they were surprised to see you!"

"Yeah, you could say that," he chuckled. "For a minute I didn't know if Sister Escobia was going to run or have a heart-attack. When she saw us coming, she looked at us, looked at the trees, looked back at us, you know, like she was checking the distance and seeing if she could hide before we saw her. I guess she figured we'd seen her cause she just froze there, up to her knees in muddy water."

"What did you do?"

Elder Santos shook his head, almost as if he couldn't believe what he was about to say. "We waded into the rice field to help them."

"Seriously?"

"Yeah," he said, looking at his companion who was nodding with him. "We took their shovels, drained the field, and fixed their fence all in about an hour."

"In your missionary clothes and everything?"

"Yup!"

Trying to imagine the two Elders standing in a rice field in their white shirts, ties, and slacks, Elder Zamora asked, "What did you do about their sick caribou?"

"Well, as much as we wanted to lay our hands on its head and administer a blessing, we decided that might have been too much for them. So we told them we should go back to their home and pray for it."

"Pray for the caribou?"

"Of course!" Elder Santos replied, "This family lives so far out of town, some days Brother Escobia has to ride that caribou into town just to get supplies."

"Wow!" Elder Daniels exclaimed. "That's a cool story for your journal."

"That's not the end! Brother and Sister Escobia were so touched that they invited us in for the most awesome lesson we've ever had."

"I wish you could have been there," he said. "The Spirit was so strong it was like you could have reached out and touched it. We taught them for two hours, committed them to baptism and asked if we could come back again, but they begged us to stay and teach them more!"

"We went back on Thursday night, read The Book of Mormon with them, and then taught the last lesson on Saturday."

"What about getting them to Church?" Elder Zamora asked.

"Hold on," he said, "I'll get to that in a minute. That last lesson was incredible. They'd lost their only son to pneumonia a few years back and have never really recovered from it. When we told them about the temple and sealing families for eternity, they just held each other, sobbing like children. It took us twenty minutes to teach that principle alone because neither of us could speak without breaking down."

"But you know what?" Elder Santos said, with a frown. "We were so busy teaching them that we forgot to arrange for them to be interviewed by the district leader. We were in our apartment Saturday night when we realized we weren't going to be able to baptize them on Sunday."

Looking at his companion, he said, "You should have heard us pray that night. We couldn't believe what we'd done. We'd promised them they would be baptized the next day and couldn't bear the thought of having to tell them we couldn't do it."

"What about getting the district leader on Sunday morning?" Elder Daniels asked, speaking the very question his companion was about to ask.

"Our church starts at 8:00 A.M. We knew we'd never be able to fetch them, find the district leader and get our other investigators to Church before Sacrament Meeting. And the trikes and jeepneys to Binmaley shut down at night. For a minute we almost gave up hope."

"But, Elder Daniels," he said, looking his zone leader straight in the eye. "Last Monday in our district meeting you promised us that if we projected Brother and Sister Escobia that the Lord would make it possible to baptize them. Our faith in that promise was the only thing that kept us going."

"On Sunday morning we showed up at the Church very weary after a long night on our knees. The hardest thing was not letting doubt creep into our mind and overpower our faith."

Elder Daniels stood speechless at the young missionary's insight about faith.

"When we got to the Church at 7:30 A.M. with our first investigators, President and Sister Hart's car was in the parking lot. It was such a beautiful sight because we knew President Hart could interview them. As we walked up to the chapel gates, President and Sister Hart walked out and greeted us. They said they'd both woke up at 3:30 A.M. with the feeling that they needed to attend Church in Bayambang that morning."

Elder Daniels felt shivers all over his body. "That is the most amazing thing I think I've ever heard!"

"There's more!," Elder Santos replied, grabbing his zone leader's arm. "Brother and Sister Escobia were sitting on the lawn reading their Books of Mormon when we got to the Church. When we asked them how long they'd been there, Brother Escobia said, 'about two hours.' Pointing to his caribou grazing on the chapel lawn, he told us they'd left their house at 4:00 A.M.—just in case their caribou got sick again and they had to walk the rest of the way."

\* \* \* \* \*

Raising his head slowly, Elder Daniels wondered if he was hearing things. When he didn't see his companion stir, he closed his eyes and went back to sleep.

"Tat-tat-tat." He heard it again. This time he jumped out of bed, feeling for his flip-flops. "Comp, I think someone's knocking on the front door!"

"What? It can't be!" Elder Zamora said, lifting his head enough to see his watch on the desk. "It's not even 6:00 A.M.!"

"I know, but I heard someone knock twice already," Elder Daniels mumbled, trying to find his other flip-flop.

"It could just be a rat in the kitchen." Elder Zamora mumbled, turning on his side and closing his eyes. "Or a bird outside, or . . ."

"Or it could be a missionary with an emergency." Elder Daniels replied sharply.

Moving as quickly as he could, the small Filipino zone leader was out of bed and no more than a step behind Elder Daniels when they reached the front door. Yanking the door open, both Elders expected the worst. A ward member in trouble? A missionary's apartment broken into? One of the sisters sick?

When they saw the old man standing in their doorway, eyes red and tearstained, neither of them knew what to say.

"Brother Ramirez?" Elder Daniels whispered, trying not to sound like he'd just woke up. "What are you doing here?"

Dressed in little more than a pair of ragged shorts and flip-flops, the man whose sun-dried skin made him look twenty years older stood with his head bowed in humility.

"Are you sick, brother?" Elder Zamora asked, seeing large drops of sweat on the man's shiny forehead.

The man shook his head, trying unsuccessfully to swallow. It had been almost forty-eight hours since he'd ate or drank anything—much longer since he'd slept.

His body sagged forward from the hip, as if he bore a terrible weight upon his shoulders. Elder Daniels watched him carefully, half-expecting him to topple over. It wasn't even until the man started to speak that he noticed the book in his hand.

"Teach me. Please, . . ." he whispered, barely lifting his head.

In unison, the two missionaries looked at each other.

Putting his arm around him, Elder Daniels said gently, "we will teach you everything we can."

With eyes that brimmed with tears, the man looked up at the Elder's faces for the first time. His lower-lip trembling, he said, "Thank you."

Realizing for the first time that he was wearing an old T-shirt and cut-off sweats as pajamas, Elder Daniels asked, "Could we come over this afternoon? Maybe about 4:00 P.M.?"

The look of disappointment on the old man's face nearly made Elder Daniels cry. "Or, we could teach you now," he said quickly, looking to his companion for reassurance.

Nodding, Elder Zamora said, "Yes, give us ten minutes to get changed and we'll be right out. We can teach you right here. Right now!"

Sighing as if he'd just been relieved of a great burden, Brother Ramirez sat down on the steps to the missionary's apartment, content to wait while the Elders got dressed. He was not, however, about to wait even an hour longer to hear more about the Prophet Joseph Smith.

Opening the book, he turned to the place he'd marked in 3 Nephi. Over 442 pages into the book, Brother Ramirez continued reading as he'd done for almost three straight days. While still exhausted, his spirit soared, knowing he would be given a second chance—a second chance at accepting the true Gospel of Jesus Christ.

\* \* \* \* \*

As she walked past the large piece of cork-board hanging in her kitchen, Ann Daniels stopped when she noticed the piece of paper tacked to the upper-right corner with tiny colored circles across the page. The circles were stacked in rows and increasing in height toward the center of the page then decreasing like a flat pyramid.

The calendar was a visual reminder of everyday her son spent in the mission field. From the very first day he'd entered the MTC, she'd colored in the tiny circles. Each circle contained a number in ascending order from 1 to 365. On the opposite side the numbers decreased from 365 back to 1. Aaron Daniels had been in the mission field twenty months and was almost within double-digit days of returning home.

"What's today?" she asked.

"Tuesday,," her husband replied without taking his eyes from his newspaper.

"No. I mean the date!"

"The twenty-first."

With a disappointed sigh, she said, "I can't believe it."

"Can't believe what?"

"I can't believe I went a whole week without filling in any circles on Aaron's calendar!"

Taking a magenta colored marker from a drawer, she filled in seven circles on the declining side of the pyramid.

"Did you hear me?" she asked, recapping the pen and turning to her husband.

"What's that, Dear?" he mumbled, from behind the sports page.

"We missed a whole week of filling in Aaron's missionary calendar."

"That's nice, dear."

Dropping her shoulders in exasperation, she walked to the kitchen table where her husband sat. She was frustrated and pulled the paper out of his hands."

"Hey! Why'd you do that?"

"Would you listen to me for a minute?"

"I'm sorry, dear," he said as he stood up and put his arms around her. "I'm listening now. What were you saying?"

Wiping at a tear, Sister Daniels buried her head in her husband's shoulder, "Sometimes I feel like I'm the only one who misses him."

"Aaron? Are you kidding? We all miss him!"

"Then why is it so easy for you to talk about him? Whenever I think about him I almost start crying."

Pulling her a little closer, Steven Daniels said, "I know, Sweetheart. We all miss him, . . . it's just that your feelings are a little closer to the surface than ours. Just the other day I was at my desk and pulled out that old photo album I took for the company picnic last year."

"You mean the one with the green cover?"

"Yeah. The one from when we lived in Manti. Remember when Aaron was about four years old and tried to fly off the fence?"

"He broke his arm." His wife remembered, revealing a bit of a smile.

"Right. I can still see him climbing up on that old picket fence and waving to us in the window. He looked like he was as free as a bird that day, and he probably felt like one too—right up until he jumped and his pant leg caught on the fence.

"Ohhh." His wife groaned, "I remember. He went straight to the ground. He had a cast on that arm the rest of that summer. It was the same summer we'd promised him we'd put him in swimming lessons."

"Until this day," he said, "I still get a sick feeling in my stomach when I think about how helpless I felt watching him from the window as he fell. I remember how much pain was in his eyes when I picked him up."

"I know," Sister Daniels said.

Pushing her back so that he could look in her eyes, he said, "Ann, that's how I felt when he first went out on his mission. I felt like there wasn't a thing I could do to help him. I remember reading his letters from his first area, knowing that he was hurting. I knew he was homesick and wanted to come home. But just like that day in Manti, there was nothing I could do but trust Heavenly Father and know that he would be taken care of."

Blinking away the tears that came freely now, Sister Daniels looked up at her husband, "So are you saying that's what I need to do? Put more trust in Heavenly Father?"

Nodding gently, her husband said, "Aaron's a man now. He's going to be a different person when we see him again. A better person." Pointing to the calendar, he said, "Everyday he's out there he's growing. You've heard it, right? When he called at Christmas and again on Mother's day? He's not the same boy we dropped off at the MTC."

"Can't I still miss him a little?"

Pulling her head to his chest, her loving husband said, "Yes. You can miss him. You can think about him. And you can love him. You can do all those things as long as you remember that our Heavenly Father knows what Aaron is going through and is watching over him."

"Sometimes" he continued, "when I think I've got it pretty bad or I'm going through a difficult time, I think to myself '*what does our Heavenly Father want me to learn from this?*'

"You know," he continued, "as hard as it is being separated from our son for two years, that's nothing to how hard it must have been for Heavenly Father to send His Son to Earth. He knew exactly what Jesus would have to do"

"Pulling her head back to see his face, she asked, "Do you think God wants us to know how much He hurt?"

"No," her husband reassured her. "I think he wants us to know how much he *loves* us!"

"Oh," she said, relaxing again.

"I can't imagine how much He must love us to have allowed His son to come into this world and be crucified. Sometimes I try to compare that with the thought of how painful it was watching Aaron fall from that fence, or leave on his mission, and I realize there's no comparison at all.

Ann Daniels closed her eyes. "I guess I should be thankful he's where he's at, shouldn't I?

Wiping the last of the tears, she gathered herself and breathed in deeply. "But can we try to talk about him more?" she asked, still feeling guilty for missing a week on the calendar.

"We *will* talk about him more," her husband said. "And we'll continue to pray for him every day."

* * * * *

"So if I come to church this Sunday," Brother Ramirez asked, "I can be baptized the next?"

"That's right!" Elder Zamora replied, grateful to see that the gleam had returned to the old man's eyes. "We'll finish the last couple lessons next week. On Sunday we will introduce you to the bishop and as many of the other ward members as we can."

"And when can I get the priesthood?"

Elder Zamora smiled at the old man's enthusiasm. "Well if you're baptized in two Sundays, . . . I guess we can do that in about, . . . a year."

"Oh," the old man replied, "a year?"

"I'm just kidding. How would you feel about being ordained to the office of a Priest in the Aaronic Priesthood on the Sunday after your baptism?"

"A Priest?" the man asked with eyes as large as silver dollars. "You mean I'll be a priest in the Mormon Church?"

"You sure will. Bishop Soriano will sit down with you and discuss the duties and responsibilities of the Aaronic Priesthood and then that Sunday you will be ordained a Priest."

"And what about my wife?"

"Well, . . ." Elder Zamora explained, "women don't hold the priesthood in our Church, . . ."

Breaking out into laughter, Brother Ramirez said, "I mean, when can she be baptized?"

"Well, we could finish the rest of the discussions with her and baptize her with you, or, . . ." he said, excited about the prospect, "since she's two discussions behind you, we could wait and let you baptize her the same Sunday you receive the priesthood."

The old man's wrinkled skin softened under the rising sun as a joyful smile appeared on his face. Though he had no more money in his pocket than he'd had an hour before and he still had on the same tattered shorts and flip-flops he'd worn the last time they'd seen him, the Gospel of Jesus Christ had changed this man. His toothless smile was one of pure joy.

"I would like that," he said humbly. "I think my wife would like that too."

Julio Ramirez had felt the Spirit. In less than four days of reading, pondering, and praying about The Book of Mormon, he'd discovered that all his questions, all his concerns and all his fears were no match against the testimony of a young man who had not been afraid to proclaim the truthfulness of his beliefs.

"Good, it's settled then!" Elder Daniels exclaimed. "You'll be baptized on the 15th and you will baptize your wife on the 22nd!"

After making a return appointment, but this one at the home of Brother and Sister Ramirez, Elder Daniels wrapped things up. "Comp, we'd better get going if we're going to work with the sisters this morning."

"Oh, that's right!" Elder Zamora exclaimed, "I'd forgotten all about that."

Brother Ramirez hopped up from the step and gathered his Book of Mormon. "I'm sorry. I didn't mean to keep you so long."

"No, it's our pleasure." Elder Daniels explained. "You have no idea how happy we are that you came to see us this morning."

"Well, I'll see you on Saturday," he said, extending his hand.

"Great! We'll see you then."

Back inside their apartment, Elder Daniels looked at his companion. "Can you believe that?" he asked, still wondering if he was dreaming.

"The Lord works in mysterious ways, my friend,"

"Let's grab something quick for breakfast and get going. You know the sisters in Binmaley. If we're five minutes late they'll leave without us."

"I think there's some rice in that pot on the stove," Elder Zamora said, looking in the refrigerator for something to go with it. "I don't think we have time for anything else."

Lifting the lid of the small kettle sitting on the stove, Elder Daniels looked inside, hoping to find a portion large enough for them to share. Although he hadn't eaten plain rice on his mission for a long time, the growling noises coming from his stomach told him he wasn't above the simple meal— especially when there was sugar in the house, and perhaps even a little cinnamon he could sprinkle on top.

"Ouch!" he yelled, dropping the lid back down on the pot.

"What's wrong?"

"Ants!" he yelled, brushing the last of the pesky critters off his hand. "That things swarming with ants!"

Finding a trail of tiny red ants making their way across the counter, Elder Zamora traced the line to a small crack between the kitchen window and the frame where the molding had become brittle and cracked away. "They're coming in here," he said, grabbing a can of insect killer from under the sink.

"Forget it," Elder Daniels replied. "This rice is gone. I guess we'll have to grab something at a sari-sari store along the way."

"Tat-tat-tat."

Another knock on the door caught both Elders by surprise.

"What now?" Elder Zamora asked.

"Probably Brother Ramirez," his companion replied. "He must have forgot something or thought of another question."

Walking to the door, Elder Daniels swung it open, expecting to see their newest baptismal candidate waiting outside.

"Vanessa?"

Aside from the tears, the first thing Elder Daniels noticed about the bishop's fourteen-year-old daughter was that she was out of breath and shaking so much he thought she might collapse.

"C-C-Come quick! Daddy needs you at the hospital!

"What's the matter?" Elder Daniels asked. "What happened?"

"It's Desiree!" she said, referring to her four-year-old sister. "There's been an accident!"

"Desiree? What kind of accident?"

Blinking back the tears that filled her dark brown eyes, she said, "S-S-She was w-walking to school and got hit by a jeepney!"

Grabbing Elder Daniels by the arm, she tugged at him as her voice trembled. "Hurry! Please! The doctor doesn't think she's going to make it!"

# CHAPTER 21

*Therefore, they must needs be chastened and tried, even as Abraham, who was commanded to offer up his only son.*

*For all those who will not endure chastening, but deny me, cannot be sanctified.*
—*D&C 101:4, 5*

*Be patient in afflictions, for thou shalt have many; but endure them, for, lo, I am with thee, even unto the end of thy days.*
—*D&C 24:8*

If the gathering outside the four-room "hospital" in Lingayen was any indication as to the extent of injuries to Desiree Soriano, Elder Daniels should have known immediately there was little chance of the young girl surviving. More than forty people, including family members, neighbors and people from the ward, waited nervously outside the front doors for any word of her condition. Only the immediate family was allowed inside the hospital doors and even then, only the bishop and his wife were allowed in the patient's room where the young girl lay unconscious.

"Excuse me. Pardon us," Elder Daniels said, as they slipped through the crowd toward the entrance. Amidst the sobbing of those who lingered in the mid-morning sun, he heard a myriad of whispering—speculations about the small child's chance of surviving. Each negative word tore at his already broken heart.

When the three finally arrived, they found an armed police officer standing between them and the door turning away anyone who approached. Elder Daniels' heart sunk even lower.

"I'm her sister," Vanessa explained to the man in the faded blue uniform. "My father sent for these two Elders."

"Wait here," the rigid officer said sternly, opening the door slightly to whisper something to the nurse standing inside. After a brief exchange, the young nurse disappeared down the hallway, only to return a few minutes later, giving the guard a nervous nod.

"You go in now, already," the officer said in broken English, holding the door open just enough to let the three pass by.

Once inside, it became truly apparent just how dire the situation was. He hadn't seen Desiree or even talked with a single person, other than Vanessa, but one look at the condition of the primitive hospital told him just how little anyone could do for her here.

As soon as he stepped inside, the smell of stale air nearly over-powered him. Images of an old Army tent he'd once spent the night in on a camping trip with the Explorer Scouts flashed through his mind. It wasn't mildew that he smelled now, but it smelled old and archaic—like nothing had changed since McArthur's return to the beaches of Lingayen in 1945. It wouldn't have surprised Elder Daniels if this hospital had been built during World War II— his impression was that more dying had taken place within these walls than he cared to know about.

Instead of a reception desk, a small table was set up with a folding chair that sat empty. The walls were bare, cracked with the passing of years and the shifting of a foundation composed primarily of sand. The hallway was dark, having only two of four light bulbs actually in place.

At the end of the hall was a closed door. Besides their footsteps, they heard no other sounds.

The nurse, guiding them toward the last door, closed two other doors as she passed. A step behind, Elder Daniels caught a glimpse in one of the rooms before she got the door closed.

Leaning against the examining table was a dirty mop and a broom. On the floor, an array of cleaning supplies, some of which looked like they'd never been opened. In the corner, a pile of bloody linens, waiting to be laundered. Elder Daniels shook his head in disbelief.

*Was that Desiree's blood?*

As they reached the end of the hall, both missionaries looked at one another—neither of them knowing what to expect to see on the other side. The nurse turned the doorknob quietly and pushed the door open a few inches. "You go inside," she said, assuming that the tall American spoke only English. "No touch anything."

Although Elder Daniels had had plenty of time to brace himself for what he was about to see, the scene before him nearly took his breathe away. It wasn't what was there, but rather, what was missing from the room that shocked and appalled him at the same time.

There were no life-support machines, no blood pressure cuffs, no x-ray charts or clipboards, no lights or beeps to let anyone know if she was dead or alive. The only thing that resembled a hospital room was the IV running under a sheet and a small assortment of bandages, needles, and surgical knives lying in the open air.

There wasn't even a doctor or a nurse—only two lone figures standing bedside, holding one another for support. They hadn't heard the door open behind them or the footsteps of the Elders as they entered.

"Bishop?" Elder Daniels whispered. "We came as fast as we could."

It took Bishop Soriano a few moments to gather himself before turning around. Wiping the tears that fell from his eyes, he cleared his throat, trying to find his voice among his emotions. His hands, trembling, did little good as the tears continued to fall. "Elders, . . ." he choked, his voice faltering as great sobs racked his chest.

"Why did I let her go?" Sister Soriano sobbed. "Why didn't I go with her?"

Pulling a chair from the corner, Elder Zamora guided the distraught woman into the seat, trying his best to comfort her. "You need to sit down," he whispered. "It's not your fault."

Elder Daniels approached Bishop Soriano and got his first up-close look at Desiree Soriano. It wasn't the fresh blood seeping through the bandages around her head that disturbed him most, nor the bruised skin on her delicate chest. The thing that gave him a hollow feeling in the pit of his stomach was the color of the young girl's face—she was ashen-gray and did not move.

"How is she?" he asked

Summoning every bit of composure he had left, Bishop Soriano stood up straight, trying to be the pillar of strength he'd always been for his family. "They think she has internal bleeding. The doctor is talking to the hospital in Dagupan to see if they should send her there or to Manila. There isn't anything they can do for her here."

"How bad is her head injury?" Elder Zamora asked, barely holding back his own tears.

"Just some bumps and bruises," he said, "The jeepney hit her here," pointing to her midsection where the swelling was already visible under the hospital sheet. "They don't know if any internal organs ruptured or how many bones may be broken. All they can do right now is try to stabilize her and figure out what to do next."

Elder Daniels looked at Sister Soriano, her face in her hands. Her breathing was rapid and shallow and Elder Zamora was trying to calm her down.

"Elders, . . ." Bishop Soriano said, "I need your help."

"What can we do?"

"Help me give her a blessing."

Without a word, Elder Daniels reached into his pocket, pulling out a small silver vial. Elder Soriano made sure Sister Soriano was alright and then joined his companion and the Bishop at the head of the bed

"Who would you like to anoint?"

"Will you?" he asked, looking at Elder Zamora.

Handing the vial to his companion, Elder Daniels and the bishop watched as Elder Zamora placed a single drop of the consecrated oil on the crown of Desiree's head. Then, bowing his head, he placed his hands delicately on her head, careful not to touch any of the bandages.

"Desiree Lucia Soriano," he began, "by the authority of the Melchizedek Priesthood which I hold, I anoint your head with this consecrated oil, which has been set apart for the healing of the sick and the afflicted, that you may be made whole. This I do in the name of Jesus Christ, Amen."

As Elder Daniels opened his eyes, he saw the bishop standing across the bed, unable to lift his head as his hands trembled at his side. After a long moment, Elder Daniels asked, "Bishop, did you want to consecrate the blessing?"

Surprising both missionaries, Bishop Soriano looked up into Elder Daniels' eyes, shaking his head. "Will you do it? I-I just don't know if I have the faith to do it right now."

In the time it took him to realize what he was being asked to do, a dozen questions flooded his mind about his worthiness, his preparation and his faith. After that, a dozen more.

Was he really ready for this? Would he be able to hear the promptings of the Spirit? Would he understand God's will concerning the life of this child? Would he just say the things he and her parents wanted to hear? Would his faith be strong enough to call down the Powers of Heaven?

Elder Daniels stood speechless, trying to calm himself. At twenty years old, he felt young and inadequate. As he processed the task in his mind, he realized that Bishop Soriano wasn't just asking him to seal the anointing—he was asking Elder Daniels to *heal* her!

As much as Elder Daniels wanted to say, 'I'll try' or 'I'll do my best,' he knew those answers would never suffice.

"Of course I will!"

As Elder Daniels placed his hands on the crown of the unconscious child's head, it was if everything in the world stopped for that moment.

"Desiree Lucia Soriano. By the authority of the Melchizedek Priesthood, we lay our hands upon your head to seal this anointing and to give you a blessing."

Pausing, Elder Daniels listened for the promptings of the Spirit—the still small voice through which the Lord would speak to him.

"Desiree, you are a choice daughter of your Father in Heaven and He loves you very much. You were taught in the pre-mortal life the Gospel plan and you accepted it and rejoiced in the opportunity to come to earth and receive a body, . . ."

Knowing that he was stalling, Elder Daniels paused again, listening more intently for the promptings of the Holy Ghost.

"The Lord has reserved you to come forth in the last dispensation of time when the Gospel has been restored. You have also been blessed with righteous parents and a family who loves you very much. Now you are here, . . ."

Again he stopped, trying to discern his own thoughts from those of the

Spirit. For what seemed an eternity he waited, determined not to proceed further until he knew exactly what he was supposed to say.

He'd given too many blessings in his life where he'd said only the words that he wanted to say. He'd promised healing and no healing followed. He had promised blessings and no blessings came. Why? Because each and every time he had failed to seek the Lord's will. He had failed to listen to the Spirit.

But this time he listened. And as he listened for the promptings of the Spirit he never even heard the door open behind him. Because at that very moment, the Lord spoke to him.

*"Ask and ye shall receive. Knock and it shall be opened unto you."*

In a firm voice—a voice filled with confidence and certainty—he said, "Desiree, as holders of the Melchizedek Priesthood and by the authority Jesus Christ, we bless you that your life will be spared. You have not yet fulfilled all that you have come to earth to do. Through you, your family will be reunited and live in peace and harmony. In order to complete this task, we bless you that your body will heal quickly and that you will rise up from this bed and walk. You will have no long-term effects of these injuries and you will stand as a testament of our Heavenly Father's power and love for His children. This blessing we seal upon your head in the name of Jesus Christ, Amen."

As Elder Daniels took his hands off Desiree's head, he opened his eyes and waited. Desiree's chest continued to rise and fall, but nothing else moved. Her eyes did not open, neither did she rise from her bed and walk.

Elder Daniels immediately felt afraid and ashamed. Had he really heard the prompting of the Holy Ghost? Or did he just hear what he wanted to hear?

For many moments, no one in the room said a word. No one knew what to say. Finally, Bishop Soriano moved to the foot of the bed. Pulling up the linen sheet at her feet, he tucked it around the young girl's shoulders.

"Thank you for coming, Elders," he said, as he shook their hands and then walked over to his wife who still sat hunched over in her chair. Gently, he knelt by her side, putting his arm around her. "There's nothing more we can do now."

Turning shamefully, Elder Daniels took one step toward the door and stopped. He turned back toward the bed, hoping again that she would open her eyes. When she didn't, he whispered, "I'm sorry," dropping his eyes to the floor and walking from the room.

Not once did his eyes leave the floor as he walked toward to hospital entrance. Elder Zamora was the one who spotted the man standing in the hallway.

"Brother Soriano?" Elder Zamora exclaimed, recognizing the man as the bishop's father. Elder Daniels looked up to see the man they had visited a few weeks earlier. The stream of tears that flowed down the old man's face gave only a glimpse of the heartache he felt inside.

"She's all I have," he whimpered as they approached. "She's all I have!"

Drawing closer to the old man, Elder Zamora tried to console him. "It's going to be all right."

"No! You've got to help her!" he pleaded, turning to Elder Daniels with bloodshot eyes. "I heard what you said in there. Your prayer."

Glancing at his companion for an answer, Elder Daniels asked, "What do you mean you heard my prayer?"

The old man looked in his eyes, trying to steady his gaze as tears blurred his vision. "I heard you pray for her, telling her that she would be healed. You said that she would rise from her bed and walk."

Realizing he must have walked in while they were administering, Elder Daniels explained. "We are Elders in The Church of Jesus Christ of Latter-day Saints. We hold the priesthood authority to lay our hands on those who are sick and or hurt and bless them with strength."

"Do you really believe that?"

"Yes," he said in barely a whisper. "I do believe it."

"I hope so," the old man whispered back as he turned and started to leave. "If she dies, I die too."

\* \* \* \* \*

Sitting on the floor in the middle of a pile of laundry, Ann Daniels folded clothes while she tried to figure out how to bring the subject up to her husband. It had been an especially hard day at school and parent-teacher conferences were approaching. The fact that her thoughts had continually strayed to her son in the Philippines hadn't helped her concentration.

In addition to that, her youngest daughter had a piano lesson that evening and would need rides to and from—not to mention her visiting teaching that she'd put off for weeks. The end of the month loomed just two days away and there were four women she still needed to visit. Much like the clothes piled all around her, Ann Daniels felt buried .

"Hi," a familiar voice sounded behind her. "What's for dinner?"

"I don't know. I haven't had a chance to get anything started yet."

After twenty-four years of marriage, Steven Daniels could tell when his wife was frustrated. Although she always tried to hide it—always tried to put on a good face and pretend nothing was wrong—he could tell when something was bothering her.

"That's okay. I can just throw some hamburgers on the grill."

When she didn't answer, he knew it was time to be concerned.

"Is everything all right, dear?" With her back toward him, he couldn't see her tears or the way she bit her lip trying to hold them back.

"I'm fine," she lied, hoping he would leave and give her a few moments to gather herself.

Since she didn't even hear him approach, the warmth of his hand on her shoulder and the creaking of his knees as he knelt down by her side gave her a start. Too late to stop the tears, she covered her face with her hands.

"What's the matter dear? Did something happen today at school?"

Burying her face in his shoulder, she shook her head. She was already having a difficult time putting thoughts into words. The added pressure of her husband confronting her when her emotions had the best of her didn't help.

"Are the kids okay?"

She answered with a nod.

For a few minutes, the two just held each other. With his support, she finally felt strong enough to speak. "I think we need to hold a special fast for Aaron."

"Is something wrong?" he asked, never having known his wife to be thrilled about fasting.

"No," she said, embarrassed for suggesting it. "It's probably nothing. Just forget about it."

"Forget about what?"

Starting to rise, she tried to change the subject, "Let's get dinner started. You're probably starving."

Placing a hand on her shoulder, he persuaded her to stop, knowing she would never have brought it up if it hadn't been something she'd given a lot of thought.

"Talk to me, dear," he pleaded, searching her eyes for the cause of her distress.

"I can't get Aaron off my mind today. It's like every time I turn around something reminds me of him. It's weird. I keep getting this feeling that he's struggling with something."

When it came to her children's lives, Ann Daniels' had always had a keen mother's intuition. Whenever one of them was at school and got hurt, she'd know it even before the phone rang. If one of them was trying to hide something from her, she was never fooled. She could detect even the slightest lie if she got a good look in their eyes.

Her husband, knowing well his wife's knack for sensing trouble, didn't take her concerns lightly. Although thousands of miles away, she could tell how he was doing in the mission, even with the snail-like pace of overseas mail. Once, a half-world away, she had felt he was in danger at the exact moment a drunken man pulled a gun on him and his companion while they were walking back to their apartment late at night. That feeling had left her vulnerable.

"Struggling with what?"

"I don't know. I just felt like there's something he's having a difficult time with. All day I wanted to pick up the phone and talk to him. You know? Just to hear his voice and know he's okay."

"Do you want me to get in touch with his mission president?"

Shaking her head, she tried to ease her husband's growing concern. "It wasn't that kind of feeling. Not like before."

Relieved but now curious, he asked, "So you think we should hold a special fast for him?"

Nodding, Sister Daniels hoped her husband didn't think she was overreacting.

"Then that's what we'll do! We'll start right now if you want. Skip dinner and the whole bit."

"Could we? You don't think I'm crazy?"

"No, dear, of course not. It's been a long time since we dedicated a fast to Aaron. I think it's an excellent idea!"

"But you're probably starving."

Taking her in his arms, he gave her a big hug, silently thanking the Lord for such a wonderful wife and mother to his children. "I guess that'll make it even more worthwhile," he replied. "There'll be no doubt in Heavenly Father's mind how important this is to us."

\* \* \* \* \*

Elder Daniels pushed the front door open, nearly collapsing in the entryway of their apartment. The heavy wooden door resisted but finally gave way to the big shoulder he put against it. The effort took every bit of strength he had left and he barely had enough in reserve to get to the nearest chair and topple into it. As the fluffy cushion exhaled a thick cloud of dust, he let out a long sigh. For the first time since awakened by Brother Ramirez's knock, Elder Daniels finally relaxed.

The sun had long since slipped beneath the shimmering, golden horizon, melting into the ocean like a stick of hot butter. They'd taught Brother Ramirez on their front porch shortly after 6:00 A.M., and he and Elder Zamora experienced a sunrise and sunset in the fifteen hours they'd spent proselyting. Those fifteen hours included a brief twenty minutes in the Lingayen hospital that would change Elder Daniels' life forever.

They never did make it to the Binmaley sister's apartment as they'd planned. The trip to the hospital had cut their morning short and appointments that afternoon had kept them from even dropping by and leaving a note of explanation. Although standing up the sisters bothered him, Elder Daniels had little time to think about it. The only thing he'd been able to focus on the entire day was his concern for Desiree Soriano and the blessing he'd given her.

"Are you okay?" Elder Zamora asked, dropping into the sofa across from him.

"Yeah. But I feel as worn out as these shoes," he said, pointing to the dusty pair of wing-tips he'd purchased in San Fernando. After seven months, the heel on his right shoe flapped with every step and the sole of his left was worn down to the leather.

"You really should eat something. I think the Lord would understand."

Elder Daniels shook his head, trying to get the thought of food out of his mind as quickly as he could. They'd rushed out of the house that morning without breakfast and both agreed that a special fast was in order after leaving the hospital. Even though twenty-three hours had already passed since their last meal, Elder Daniels knew too much was riding on the outcome of the priesthood blessing he'd given to cut things short.

"Me neither," Elder Zamora said. "I'm going straight to bed."

Elder Daniels nodded but his mind was elsewhere. It had been a constant struggle all day to stay in the moment. His mind continually drifted to the bedside of Desiree Soriano.

Twice they'd returned to the hospital, only to be turned away at the door. The doctor was examining her while her parents gathered a few belongings from home. There was still a good chance they would need to transport her to Manila—of course, that was if she made it through the night. On their next visit, they were told that visiting hours were over and that they could return the next morning.

Even more of a struggle was the thought of the blessing he'd pronounced on her head promising her a full and speedy recovery. In the moment he'd given the blessing he'd been completely sure—he'd spoken the exact words that came to his mind. After twelve hours of contemplation, things weren't so simple—or so clear.

As he'd done all afternoon, he replayed the words of the blessing in his mind.

*". . . your life will be spared . . . your body will heal quickly . . . you will rise up from this bed and walk . . ."*

How could he have felt so certain? How could he have promised a miracle like that? Her father, Bishop Soriano, didn't even have the faith to ask such a thing and there were few men Elder Daniels respected as much.

Shaking his head, he tried to clear his mind and push the doubts and fears aside

"Well I'm going to bed," Elder Zamora said, rising to his feet. He was almost to the stairs when he heard his name.

"Yeah?"

"Would you give me a blessing?"

"A blessing? You mean a priesthood blessing?"

"Yeah. I feel really weak right now."

Elder Zamora looked at his watch. "Well, . . . it's a little before ten-thirty but we can probably get Brother Gomez over here, or do you feel well enough to go to his house?"

"No, no," Elder Daniels replied, "I'm not sick. I just feel like I need a blessing—you know—a blessing of comfort. To be honest," he said, his eyes falling to the floor, "I feel like my faith isn't what it should be right now."

Walking back toward the couch, Elder Zamora looked at his companion. "You? Weak in faith?"

"Well, . . .yeah. I just keep having doubts run through my mind."

"That was a pretty miraculous blessing you gave that little girl," Elder Zamora replied as he sat back down.

"But it wasn't me!"

"I know. I didn't mean it like that. You were just saying what the Spirit told you to say."

"But what if it *wasn't* the Spirit? What if that's just what *I* want to happen?"

Elder Zamora chuckled, "I don't believe that. I've seen how you follow the Spirit. There's no doubt in my mind the Spirit told you exactly what to say."

Sitting on the edge of the couch, he leaned toward his companion. "I've seen the way you stop when we're walking down the street, listening, waiting for the promptings of the Holy Ghost to tell us which way to turn. I've seen the way your eyes light up in the middle of a discussion when our contacts have concerns and the Spirit tells you how to resolve them. I've seen the way you pray—the way you focus on each investigator—discerning the help they need and ask for it."

Leaning even closer, Elder Zamora's voice became almost a whisper. "Elder Daniels, . . . I saw how you listened to the Spirit today—the way you waited for confirmation before promising that little girl anything."

Elder Daniels lifted his eyes, meeting the gaze of his companion, "Do you really think so?"

"Listen," Elder Zamora replied, "Bishop Soriano asked you to give that blessing for a reason. You've been preparing for this day your entire mission—maybe your entire life. He didn't ask me to do it. He didn't call for his counselor to do it. He asked *you!*"

Grabbing his scriptures, Elder Zamora opened them to the 58th Section of the Doctrine and Covenants.

*"For verily I say unto you, blessed is he that keepeth my commandments, whether in life or in death; and he that is faithful in tribulation, the reward of the same is greater in the kingdom of heaven. Ye cannot behold with your natural eyes, for the present time, the design of your God concerning those things which shall come hereafter, and the glory which shall follow after much tribulation. For after much tribulation come the blessings. Wherefore the day cometh that ye shall be crowned with much glory; the hour is not yet, but is nigh at hand."*

"Comp," he continued, closing the book in his lap, "do you remember the story of Abraham and Isaac?"

"Sure."

"Can you imagine how long that journey must have been, the journey when Abraham took Isaac up to the mountain to be sacrificed? All that way, Abraham must have been thinking, *I can't believe I'm doing this!*

I'll bet the whole way he was hoping he'd hear the voice of the Lord saying, 'All right, Abraham, that's good enough. I've seen your faith. Take Isaac back home to Sarah.' But that didn't happen, did it? Abraham had to sweat it out, showing the Lord he was willing to do *whatever* He commanded of him."

"Of course we know how the story ends," he continued. "Remember, it wasn't until Abraham bound Isaac and placed him on the alter with the knife raised over his head that the Lord said, 'Abraham, Abraham. Lay not thy hand upon the lad.'"

"That's what the Lord expects of you. I know what you were thinking when you took your hands off Desiree's head after the blessing. You wanted to see her open her eyes and sit up in bed. You wanted to see her rise from her bed and walk out of that hospital. Right? When, that didn't happen, you started to lose faith."

Squeezing his companion's shoulder, Elder Zamora continued. "At some point, our faith must be tested. Heavenly Father wants to see if you're going to apply all those things you've learned since you started your mission—all those things you've been teaching other missionaries about faith. This, Elder Daniels, is *your* test! This is the trial of *your* faith!"

Elder Daniels eyes fell to the floor again, "I guess I'm not doing very well, am I?"

"There's a lot of fight left in you. I know you too well for that." Rising to his feet he said, "Now, let's give you that blessing, so we can get to bed. It's going to be another long day tomorrow, . . . and maybe a long night too."

\* \* \* \* \*

*". . . your life will be spared . . . your body will heal quickly . . . you will rise up from this bed and walk . . ."*

Quietly, Elder Daniels slipped out of his sheets and knelt next to his bed. Without glancing at the clock he knew it was a little after three in the morning.

While feeling under his bed for his foam flip-flops, a cockroach scurried across the back of his hand sending chills down his spine. Although his skin crawled at the thought of the disgusting creature, another matter weighed too heavily on his mind to worry about a hit-and-run by a six-legged insect.

Sleep was out of the question. Even with the pair of flip-flops placed under his knees, the sharp pains that ran up his legs told just how much of the night he'd spent in that position pleading his case before the Lord.

"Please, Father, . . ." his tender voice whispered, . . . "please help her get through the night." It was a plea he'd uttered a countless number of times. His mind numb, he no longer knew what else to say.

*". . . your life will be spared . . . your body will heal quickly . . . you will rise up from this bed and walk . . ."*

Closing his eyes tightly, he recalled a time in his mission when he understood very little about faith. He repeated something Elder Flores had taught him. Having memorized the passage from the *Lectures on Faith*, he quietly repeated the words in a whispered tone.

*"Where doubt and uncertainty are, there faith is not, nor can it be. For doubt and faith do not exist in the same person at the same time; so that persons whose minds*

*are under doubts and fears cannot have unshaken confidence; and where unshaken confidence is not, there faith is weak."*

# CHAPTER 22

*Draw near unto me and I will draw near unto you; seek me diligently and ye shall find me; ask, and ye shall receive; knock, and it shall be opened unto you.*
—*D&C 88:63*

Elder Daniels awoke with a start, his heart pounding and his mouth dry. For a moment he had no idea where he was. The dim streetlight entering through the bedroom window made it difficult to make out anything more than shapes. But with each passing second, he became more aware of his surroundings and found himself in the same position in which he'd spent most the night.

The last thing he remembered was kneeling at the foot of his bed listening to his companion snore. The night had passed slowly. It was barely after 5:00 A.M. Even in his groggy state, he remembered being awake when the first jeepneys started running at a little after 4:00 A.M.

The very thought of a jeepney woke him like a shot of adrenaline.

Desiree!

"Comp! Wake up!" he yelled, jumping to his feet.

Awakened by his companion for the second day in a row, Elder Zamora threw his pillow over his head. "Just five more minutes," he begged, hoping his companion would take the first shower.

"Come on! We've got to go!" Elder Daniels shouted, a leg already into his navy-blue pants.

"Go where?"

Elder Daniels hobbled over to his companion's bed, throwing the pillow aside and flipping on the light switch next to his bed. "We've got to get to the hospital and see if Desiree is all right!"

The bright light coming on over his head did nothing to help Elder Zamora's growing irritation. "But the hospital won't even be open yet! The nurse said visiting hours don't start until 7:00 A.M.!"

Pretending not to hear his companion, Elder Daniels continued dressing as quickly as he could. Throwing on the same shirt he'd worn the day before, he reached for a tie, caring very little whether or not it matched anything else he wore.

Realizing his companion wasn't joking, Elder Zamora sat up in bed. "You want to go to the hospital now? What about breakfast? We haven't eaten in a day and a half!"

Elder Daniels slipped on his shoes, not even bothering to lace them up. "Then we'll grab something on the way," he said, weary of his companion's complaints. Stopping for a moment, he looked at Elder Zamora, "I can't stand it any longer," he said. "I have to know that she made it through the night!"

As early as it was, the streets of Lingayen were much busier than Elder Daniels expected. The two Elders had dressed in less than five minutes and were out the door in seven, only to stand in front of their apartment for ten minutes waiting for an empty trike to come along.

"Let's just walk," Elder Daniels suggested impatiently.

"We can't. It's almost seven kilometers away," Elder Zamora replied, thinking more rationally than his companion. "Besides, something has got to come along pretty soon."

Elder Daniels looked at his watch as if every passing minute was pushing a stake deeper into his heart. Nervously, he kicked at the dirt, looking up and down the road for a possible ride.

Elder Zamora laughed. "I've never seen you like this."

Elder Daniels looked at his watch again. "We should have been there by now."

A few moments later, an empty trike pulled off the side of the road.

"Where to?"

"The hospital."

Observing the way Elder Daniels was fidgeting and fussing, he asked, "What happened to him?"

Getting that matter straightened out, Elder Zamora sat back in the seat, enjoying the morning air and the fresh breeze blowing into the open sidecar. For his companion it was a different story.

Cursing the motorcycle for its lack of power and the traffic near the center of town, Elder Daniels sat on the edge of his seat, enjoying none of the ride so far. In front of the hospital, he shoved ten pesos into the driver's hand and jumped out of the trike before the wheels stopped turning.

"Don't you want your change?" the driver asked, shrugging his shoulders and driving away when the tall American didn't even turn around.

The armed guard was nowhere to be found. Elder Daniels pushed the front door open and stepped inside, his companion doing everything in his power just trying to keep up. Unlike the morning before, the place seemed dead.

*No!* Elder Daniels thought, pushing the doubt away. *Not dead!*

In five long strides he was at the end of the hallway standing face to face with the closed door to Desiree's room. For a moment he stopped, taking in a deep breath to calm himself. "Please Father," he whispered, "Please let her be alive."

Not even sure if his companion was behind him, Elder Daniels knocked once on the door, turning the knob and pushing it open a few inches without even giving anyone a chance to answer it. What he saw through that small opening made his heart fall to the floor.

The only person in the room was a small nurse, very round and very short. With her back to the door, she didn't even hear the knock or the door swing on its hinges.

Tearing off the hospital sheets, she threw them on a pile on the floor next to the bed. On her cart was a bucket of water from which she took a rag and started wiping down the IV machine. That was when she noticed the two figures standing in the doorway.

"May I help you?"

"W-w-where . . ." Elder Daniels tried to speak but the words didn't come out.

Pushing past his companion, Elder Zamora stepped toward the nurse, extending his hand and introducing himself. "Good morning, I'm Elder Zamora and this is Elder Daniels. We're friends of the Sorianos. Can you tell us where we might find the little girl?"

"She's not here."

"Where is she?" Elder Daniels asked breathlessly. "Dagupan? . . . Manila? . . ."

Nonchalantly, the nurse continued wiping down the machine, not even looking up when she said, "She's gone home."

"Home?" Elder Daniels shouted.

"Oh no, it's too late," he moaned, picturing her with the other spirits in heaven. "She didn't make it!"

Dropping the rag back in the bucket, the nurse rolled her eyes. "She woke up a little after midnight and asked if she could go home." Reaching down to gather the sheets on the floor, she continued, "The doctor ran every test he could think of and couldn't find anything wrong with her. No bleeding. No broken bones. No nothing!"

Looking back at the missionaries, she shrugged her shoulders. "There was no reason to keep her any longer so he discharged her and sent her home."

# CHAPTER 23

*I have fought a good fight. I have finished my course. I have kept the faith.*
— *2 Timothy 4:7*

Elder Daniels stared out the airplane window seeing nothing but the tops of the flat, cirrus clouds below. Their rolling-white texture gave the illusion that the airplane was skimming their surface, when eight-thousand feet separated the large 747 jetliner from the white expanse below.

Every few minutes he caught a glimpse of the ocean even further below. It's azure-blue surface reflecting patches of sunlight

"May I take your tray, sir?"

Elder Daniels head snapped toward the aisle. "What?"

"May I take your tray?" The flight attendant asked again.

"Oh, . . . sure." Handing the young Japanese woman his food tray, he smiled politely trying to hide his guilt in not even touching his meal. There was nothing wrong with the food, he'd just lost his appetite.

Around the plane, he noticed people doing one of two things. First, there were vacationers, intently watching the movie screen on the wall of the cabin section in front of them. Elder Daniels had noticed them on more than one occasion when a loud roar of laughter erupted from the seemingly quiet cabin. With headphones crammed in their ears and eyes glued to the screen, they seemed to forget the second group of people—the sleeping passengers—a group that consisted largely of missionaries returning home.

Some of the missionaries had small pillows behind their heads and blankets pulled up over their shoulders. Others looked like they were bobbing for apples. Elder Daniels chuckled, remembering how he'd looked forward to a long nap for the last two years.

For twenty-four months he'd longed for the chance to drift away to sleep, not having to worry about the next discussion or finding people to teach, or how they were going to meet their baptismal goal.

It made no sense to him why he wasn't asleep like the other missionaries—he'd certainly worked every bit as hard as them in the mission field. Yet for some reason, sleep seemed as distant as the ocean floor below.

*How much could have changed in two years?*

Turning back toward the window, he pondered that question. He remembered the first pair of shoes he'd worn in the MTC—a pair of wing-tips. They'd reminded him of his father. Classy. Well dressed. Professional. He'd bought them for that very reason.

He'd been disappointed when he had to leave them behind in his first area. Two months of walking through flooded streets made the leather shrink to the point they no longer fit. Besides, he recalled, after that first couple of weeks of rain, they never kept a shine like his father's pair. He could only hope the homeless man he'd given them to had made better use out of them than he. After that, he'd always bought his shoes a size larger than he needed.

Looking down at the pair on his feet, he wondered what his mother would say when she saw them. With nothing more than glue holding the heel to his right shoe and a piece of hard plastic inserted under the insole of his left to keep rocks and debris from coming in the hole, he cringed at the thought of his mother's lecture. Sure, he could have purchased another pair, but that would have been shameful. Every scrape, every nick, every crease in this pair of shoes had a memory to go with it. If possible, he would have saved every pair of shoes he'd worn on his mission. Reminders like that were hard to come by.

Fairing no better were his pants—the faded blue material looking more like the upholstery of the old 1997 Honda Civic he'd driven in high school than a pair of dress slacks. They too carried the reminder of days long gone.

In his left pant leg was a mended tear as long as the dog's tooth that had torn it. He was lucky not to have a similar scar on his leg. His right pant leg bore the mark of another accident—the grease from his bike chain that no amount of soap or scrubbing could remove. Swerving quickly to miss a trike that darted into his lane, he'd ended up in a shallow ditch with a pile of twisted metal. That one had left a sore bruise on his knee, but nothing as painful as the unkind words of the trike driver who sped off saying, "Go back to America, GI."

Without even looking, he knew the origin of every stain that adorned his once spotless short-sleeve shirt. It wasn't that he was a messy eater—that's just the sort of thing that happened while sitting on a nipa hut floor trying to get soup from bowl to mouth.

His tie had fared no better. The one he'd chosen to wear on this momentous occasion was not the nicest in his collection, but it was his favorite. He'd worn it more often than any other. In fact a member in one area had asked if he had any others. It was special—given him as a remembrance by Elder Flores.

To anyone else the tie wouldn't appear to be valuable—at least not by monetary standards. To some, it wasn't even attractive. A paisley design with shades of blue and green, it had more snags from jeepney rails and bamboo doors than he'd ever got fishing with his Dad.

To Elder Daniels none of it mattered. That tie was one of his most valued possessions. To him it represented a brotherhood—a bond between companions that could never be replaced.

It wasn't only his clothing that had changed in those two years. Elder Daniels had changed. The emotional and spiritual growth had come about slowly but he'd changed to a much greater degree than he could ever have imagined.

When the beverage cart passed by for a second time, Elder Daniels was thinking about that change.

\* \* \* \* \*

"Elder Daniels," President Hart said, "I want you to train a new missionary your last two months in the mission field."

"Okay, President," he said, realizing that meant he would no longer be an Assistant to the Mission President. "Where do you want me to serve?"

"In Mangaldan."

"Mangaldan, President? Aren't there sisters in Mangaldan?"

"There were sisters there. I had to pull them out last week because of some problems with the branch leadership."

"Anything I should know about?"

Pausing for a moment, President Hart chose his words carefully. "Let's just say the branch president has had some issues with American missionaries assigned to the area."

Elder Daniels listened carefully. "President, you're saying the branch president doesn't want Americans there so you're sending me, an American missionary, in?"

With a bit of a smile, President Hart shook his head. "No, I'm not sending an American missionary to Mangaldan. I'm sending *two* Americans missionaries to Mangaldan. I want you to train Elder Johnson, an Elder from Smithfield, Utah. If that branch president can't work with the two of you, he no longer needs to be the branch president."

Elder Daniels smiled. *And I used to be frightened of this man.*

"Elder Johnson is a special missionary," President Hart continued, "He's very shy and withdrawn. I guess you could say he doesn't have a lot of self-esteem. I want him to have a good experience in his first area. I want him to learn as much as he can from you."

"Rest assured, President," Elder Daniels promised, "I'll do my best."

"I know you will, son. You always do."

\* \* \* \* \*

Stuffing a pillow in the small of his back, Elder Daniels shifted to a new position. His body was tired of sitting in the same place. What a learning experience that area had been. Not only for Elder Johnson who was in his first area, but also for Elder Daniels who was in his last.

\* \* \* \* \*

"Come on, let's try again." Elder Daniels coaxed, trying to get his companion through the practice discussion.

With discouragement building in his voice, Elder Johnson closed his eyes, trying to visualize the words as they were written in his discussion pamphlet. "Ang karamihan sa mga tao ay nan-nani-nan . . ."

"Naniniwala."

Nodding his head, Elder Johnson went on. "Nan-naniniwala sa Dios, k-kahit na t-t-tini . . . Oh forget it!" he cried out in desperation," I'll never learn the discussions in Tagalog!"

Elder Daniels patted him on the back. "You're doing fine." In every sense of the word, he empathized with Elder Johnson, and had from the moment he met him.

It took every bit of courage Elder Johnson had to open his mouth in a discussion. So many times he'd stumbled over the words, stuttering and mispronouncing even the simplest phrases that at times their investigators turned away, so embarrassed for him it hurt.

Night after night he'd cried himself to sleep, sobbing until the tears pooled on the pillow surface. Twice he'd screamed out in the middle of the night, waking Elder Daniels and weeping in his arms like a small child. Every aspect of missionary life scared Elder Johnson to death.

Elder Daniels put a hand on his companion's shoulder. "Hey, you're doing great. You're a much better teacher than I was three weeks in the mission field."

"Did you ever think of going home?"

"Yeah." he answered, "I was very close to going home."

Elder Johnson's head snapped up, trying to figure out if his companion was serious. "You did? Seriously . . .? What kept you here?"

Well, let me tell you a story about that, . . ."

After relaying his experience with his letter and Elder Jones, Elder Daniels admitted. "I guess I realized that God wouldn't have given me the kind of challenges I was facing if He didn't think I could make it through them."

"Do you really believe that?"

"It doesn't matter what *I* believe, Elder Johnson. It matters what *you* believe."

\* \* \* \* \*

"Let's go! We don't want to be late."

"Give me one more minute," Ann Daniels pleaded as she darted back into the bedroom. "I can't find my other earring!"

Rolling his eyes, her husband looked to his eleven-year-old daughter who was sitting on the couch looking bored.

"Allison, when you grow up and your son is on a mission," he said, "use those two years to decide what you're going to wear to pick him up."

"I found it!" came a relieved voice from the other room.

"Do you think I'll make a good missionary?"

Steven Daniels knelt down by his little girl, "Of course you will, honey. You'll make an excellent missionary. Do you want to serve a mission?"

"Oh, yes!" she answered, "Maybe even two missions!"

With a chuckle, her father bent over, tenderly kissing her forehead. "Okay, dear. Just don't go too soon. I don't think your mother could handle sending another one out for a while."

"Mom! Come on let's go!" Joshua yelled. "Aaron's going to get there before we do!"

"I'm coming!"

"So is Christmas!"

"Okay, okay, I'm ready," Sister Daniels sighed, coming in the room in time to catch her son's last remark. "If I could only get you guys this excited for church!"

"Do we have the banner and balloons?"

"Yes mom," Allison answered wearily. "Josh already put them in the car."

"How about the flight information? And the camera! We can't forget the camera!"

With his eyes closed, Brother Daniels nodded slowly. "We're all ready, dear. We've got the banner, balloons, gate information, camera, film in the camera, and everything else we need." Pushing her firmly toward the door, he added, "Let's just get in the car and pray we don't forget any kids."

With no other choice but to head for the car, Sister Daniels headed out the door, her children already piling in the car and her husband shutting the door behind them. Halfway down the walk, she abruptly stopped.

"What now?"

"My phone's ringing!" she replied.

"Let it go to voicemail. We're going to be late!"

"It might be important," she refuted, searching through her purse. "Oh! I hope his flight isn't late! What if he missed the plane in Seattle? Oh, Steven...what if there's been an accident?

Putting the phone to her ear, her voice cracked as she said, "Hello...this is Sister Daniels...who's this?" Pulling the phone closer to her ear, she relaxed when she realized it wasn't the airline on the other end.

"Oh, . . ." she said sounding relieved. Yes! We're going to the airport to pick him up right now, . . . we'd love to have you join us! . . . That's right, Delta 1422, arriving at Gate 11 at 12:37, . . . Great! I'm so glad you called. We'll see you there!"

Hanging up her phone, she opened the car door. Barely inside before her

241

husband started down the driveway. "You'll never believe who that was!"

\* \* \* \* \*

Elder Daniels opened his missionary journal and flipped through the pages nostalgically. Just as Elder Neil had said earlier in his mission, the latter-half of his mission had flown by. He'd spent only four months as a zone leader in Lingayen before President Hart called him as an Assistant to the Mission President and he'd thoroughly enjoyed every moment.

From the moment he set food in Baguio City, he loved his new assignment. Called the "Vacation Capital of the Philippines," Bauio City's cool climate reminded him of home. At nearly the same altitude as Orem, Utah, the days and nights had felt much like early-Fall back home. He'd never imagined wearing a jacket or sweater in the Philippines, but temperatures became quite cool in the evenings—at least to someone acclimated to the provincial lowlands.

Being called as an Assistant to the Mission President had changed his entire focus as a missionary. Rather than proselyting 10-12 hours each day, or working with companionships within a zone, he and his companion had been responsible for all 166 missionaries assigned to 12 zones in the Philippines Baguio Mission. The position required a great deal of travel and gave them opportunities to teach, even though they weren't teaching Church investigators.

His fondest memories of the six months he spent as an Assistant to the Mission President were teaching his fellow missionaries at zone conferences. He and his companion had held workshops while President Hart had conducted interviews. Their lessons varied according to the promptings they received from the Lord.

One of his favorite workshops had been about drawing on the Powers of Heaven and how that power was governed by faith. As he'd been taught by Elder Neil, he and his companion instructed the missionaries how to set and achieve goals they'd previously thought impossible.

They taught about prayerfully selecting righteous desires and setting specific dates by which they wanted to accomplish them. They taught about listing their resolves—things they would do on their end to achieve their goal. They explained how to determine what help they would need from the Lord and how to plead their case before Him. They described how to qualify for the Lord's assistance by committing themselves to living a 'higher law' of obedience. And they testified through personal experiences how they'd seen the Powers of Heaven at work in their own success as missionaries and zone leaders.

He'd loved every minute of serving as an Assistant to the Mission President. It had seemed odd to him that in his final interview with President Hart he'd been given a specific warning.

"Elder Daniels," President Hart said as he put an arm around his shoulder. "I want you to understand and remember something. Satan works harder on those individuals who have served as Assistants than any other returned missionary."

\* \* \* \* \*

As the airplane began to lose altitude, Elder Daniels woke with a start. *The plane's going down! We're going to crash!*

Imagining the aircraft in a steep descent, he gripped the armrest in terror and quickly assessed his surroundings. When he saw other passengers calmly putting away their magazines and laptops, he realized the airplane wasn't on fire or falling from the sky.

*"The captain has turned on the Fasten Seat Belt sign and asked us to prepare for landing. Please stow all food and beverage trays and bring your seats to their upright position…"*

When his heart rate finally subsided, he relaxed and began to realize the significance of what was about to happen.

*I can't believe it. I'm finally going home.*

For the next twenty minutes he stared out the cabin window and felt completely at peace. As he stared out the window, he began to reacquaint himself with the landmarks he'd resisted thinking about for two years.

He gazed upon the Wasatch Mountains, naming every peak and rise. He admired The Great Salt Lake with its massive body and white salty shores. He imagined the Salt Lake Valley blanketed with snow. It felt strange that he could now think freely about these things so freely.

Downtown Salt Lake City—what a glorious sight! Clean and refreshing, it was so different from the crowded and dirty streets of Manila. He could see the parks, the golf courses and the baseball fields—all a deep shade of emerald green. He saw the streets, perfectly organized and named: First South, Second South, Third South, and so on. He saw the city buildings, large and majestic, yet almost insignificant against the towering backdrop of mountains behind them. He saw the State Capitol with the United States flag flying from its precipice.

*This is the place!*

Most distinctive of all was the Salt Lake Temple—The House of the Lord—nestled away in the heart of the city. Although not as tall as of the surrounding structures, it was most-assuredly the most awe-inspiring. Its stunning granite walls, nine-feet thick at the base and six-feet thick at the top, would stand until the end of time—through the millennium. It was a symbol of eternity.

Even from a distance he admired its architectural beauty. Every line, every shape, every fixture drew the eyes heavenward. Six magnificent spires, with the stature of the Angel Moroni atop the tallest, sounding his trumpet to every nation.

Elder Daniels shook his head, realizing for the first time how much he'd missed this place. He hadn't even seen his family, but he already felt like he was home.

\* \* \* \* \*

"Let's get closer!" Allison shouted. "I want to see him coming down the ramp!"

Sensing his youngest daughter's excitement, Brother Daniels edged her forward. "Well, move up front so you can see. And tell us when he's coming!"

Darting through the growing crowd of people in the baggage claim area of the Salt Lake City Airport, Allison moved as far forward as she could. She was determined to be the first to see her older brother come down the escalator.

Would she recognize him? After all, she'd only been nine years old when he left. The better question was, would he recognize her?

"Is the camera ready?"

"Yes mother." Joshua assured her impatiently. "I'm just waiting for Allison's signal."

"Oh, what if he can't see us?" she asked, worrying about every possibility.

"Is that better?" her husband asked, holding the banner as high as he could in his outstretched arms.

"Yes."

Ann Daniels was a wreck. She admitted it. But for two long years she'd waited for this day. It had to be perfect.

The very first passenger came into sight just as a voice came over the loudspeaker. "For those passengers on Delta Flight 1422 from Seattle, your luggage will be on carousel 6."

Allison Daniels hopped on one foot as she waited, wringing her hands together behind her back. It was a nervous habit she'd picked up from her mother who was doing the same thing almost twenty yards away.

The first few people to come off the plane were business class passengers. With dark suits and ties, the men carried briefcases and laptop computers while the women wore business suits and carried small handbags.

"I don't see him yet!" Allison yelled across the terminal, embarrassing her oldest brother in the process.

To their credit, most of the people walked at a descent pace, but for some it was harder than others. An elderly woman, holding onto her husband's arm for support, kept other passengers riding the escalator in check behind her. Behind them, two restless boys hit each other in the arms to a chorus of, "Stop it! You stop, it! No you stop it!"

"Boys! Please!" their mother begged. "You can wrestle with each other when you get to Grandma's."

A young mother carrying an infant in one arm and two pieces of luggage on her shoulder, tugged at her two-year-old son who dropped a water bottle he'd carried from the plane.

"Just leave it," she pleaded, knowing that others behind her had already grown impatient.

Just then, a man in a suit bent down and retrieved the water bottle. "Here you go, little buddy," he said, handing it to the little boy. "Drink lots of water. Plane rides make me thirsty."

His eyes full of tears, the two-year-old broke out in a smile. When the man in the suit stood up, Allison saw the black nametag and locked eyes with her brother.

Before he could brace himself, she nearly bowled him over as she jumped into his arms.

"Aaron. You're home!"

"My goodness," he said as he tried to catch his breath and pick her up at the same time. "Look at you! All grown up and beautiful as can be!"

"Oh stop it," she said, not at all as embarrassed as she pretended to be.

"Come on," she said, "Mom's going crazy. They're right over here."

It didn't take but a moment to find the rest of the family camped out under a sign that read, *'Welcome Home Elder Daniels.'* All he had to do was look for the biggest smiles in the airport.

Throwing his carry-on strap over his shoulder, Elder Daniels walked up to his mother, throwing his arms around her and feeling the tears flow down his cheeks.

"Hello, Mother," he said, his voice deeper than she remembered.

For a moment, those two words echoed in her mind, washing away every fear and worry she'd built up over twenty-four months of separation. She had dreamed of this day from the moment they pulled away from the MTC. Waiting. Praying. Dreaming. Somehow she felt closer to him than ever before.

When she finally released him, she stepped aside, letting his brother and middle sister do the same. As others passed by, a few of them stopped, appreciating the significance of this moment. Like the man on the plane two years before, many of them smiled, remembering their own missionary homecomings and that of sons and daughters who had walked away and returned within these very walls.

Steven Daniels waited patiently for his turn. He'd insisted that he go last. It was one of the proudest moments of his life.

Without a word, he stepped forward, receiving a firm and resolute 'missionary handshake.' His vision blurring through his tears, he pulled his son into his arms and wrapped them around him. There was no patting him on the shoulder. No patronizing slap on the back—only the warm embrace of a proud and loving father.

"Hello Father."

Not at all ready to let go, Steven Daniels just held him in that powerful hug. "Welcome home son!"

Feeling a hand on his shoulder he turned back around to face his mother. "I know this isn't easy for you to hear, but Alicia isn't coming."

"I know mom," he replied, cutting her off in mid-sentence. "I didn't expect her to be here."

Her eyes moving past him, she pointed over his shoulder. "But there is someone here you might want to see."

"Who?" he asked, trying to figure out what she was talking about. Turning back around he watched his father step aside, revealing a vision of beauty that nearly took his breath away.

"Welcome home, Elder Daniels."

"Sister Adams?"

"It's Stacey."

"How did you know I was coming home today?"

"I met your parents at Stake Conference a couple months ago. They told me. I hope you don't mind me being here."

"Mind? Heaven's no!" he replied, feeling his knees go weak. "Can I introduce you to the rest of my family?"

"I'd like that," she said with a smile. "I'd like that a lot!

# ABOUT THE AUTHOR

Jason A. Densley is a native of Idaho Falls, Idaho. He is a commissioned officer in the United States Air Force with over twenty-years of military service. He holds a B.S. degree in Psychology from the University of Utah, a Master of Law degree from California Southern University and a Master of Military Operational Arts and Sciences from the Air University. Jason served as a full-time missionary for the Church of Jesus Christ of Latter-Day Saints in the Philippines Baguio Mission from 1990 to 1992. He has also served as a ward mission leader, stake missionary, gospel doctrine teacher and seminary teacher. Jason is an often-requested speaker at youth conferences, firesides and training seminars. He is married to the former Melinda McAllister from Dothan, Alabama, and has four children.